CENTRAL ISSUES IN CONTEMPORARY ECONOMIC THEORY AND POLICY

General Editor: **Gustavo Piga**, *Managing Editor, Rivista di Politica Economica, Rome, Italy*

Published titles include:

Mario Baldassarri, Luigi Paganetto and Edmund S. Phelps (*editors*)
INTERNATIONAL ECONOMIC INTERDEPENDENCE, PATTERNS OF TRADE BALANCES AND
ECONOMIC POLICY COORDINATION

Mario Baldassarri (*editor*)
KEYNES AND THE ECONOMIC POLICIES OF THE 1980s

Mario Baldassarri (*editor*)
OLIGOPOLY AND DYNAMIC COMPETITION

Mario Baldassarri (*editor*)
THE ITALIAN ECONOMY
Heaven or Hell?

Mario Baldassarri and Paolo Annunziato (*editors*)
IS THE ECONOMIC CYCLE STILL ALIVE?
Theory, Evidence and Policies

Mario Baldassarri, John McCallum and Robert A. Mundell (*editors*)
DEBT, DEFICIT AND ECONOMIC PERFORMANCE

Mario Baldassarri, John McCallum and Robert A. Mundell (*editors*)
GLOBAL DISEQUILIBRIUM IN THE WORLD ECONOMY

Mario Baldassarri and Robert A. Mundell (*editors*)
BUILDING THE NEW EUROPE VOLS I & II

Mario Baldassarri (*editor*)
PRIVATIZATION PROCESSES IN EASTERN EUROPE
Theoretical Foundation and Empirical Results (Vols I & II)

Mario Baldassarri (*editor*)
HOW TO REDUCE UNEMPLOYMENT IN EUROPE

Mario Baldassarri (*editor*)
THE NEW WELFARE
Unemployment and Social Security in Europe

Mario Baldassarri, Michele Bagella and Luigi Paganetto (*editors*)
FINANCIAL MARKETS
Imperfect Information and Risk Management

Mario Baldassarri and Bruno Chiarini (*editors*)
STUDIES IN LABOUR MARKETS AND INDUSTRIAL RELATIONS

Mario Baldassarri and Pierluigi Ciocca (*editors*)
ROOTS OF THE ITALIAN SCHOOL OF ECONOMICS AND FINANCE
From Ferrara (1857) to Einaudi (1944) (three volumes)

Mario Baldassarri, Massimo Di Matteo and Robert A. Mundell (*editors*)
INTERNATIONAL PROBLEMS OF ECONOMIC INTERDEPENDENCE

Mario Baldassarri, Cesara Imbriani and Dominick Salvatore (*editors*)
THE INTERNATIONAL SYSTEM BETWEEN NEW INTEGRATION AND NEO-PROTECTIONISM

Mario Baldassarri and Luca Lambertini (*editors*)
ANTITRUST, REGULATION AND COMPETITION

Mario Baldassarri, Alfredo Macchiati and Diego Piacentino (*editors*)
THE PRIVATIZATION OF PUBLIC UTILITIES
The Case of Italy (Vols I & II)

Mario Baldassarri, Luigi Paganetto and Edmund S. Phelps (*editors*)
EQUITY, EFFICIENCY AND GROWTH
The Future of the Welfare State

Mario Baldassarri, Luigi Paganetto and Edmund S. Phelps (*editors*)
THE 1990s SLUMP
Causes and Cures

Mario Baldassarri, Luigi Paganetto and Edmund S. Phelps (*editors*)
WORLD SAVING, PROSPERITY AND GROWTH

Mario Baldassarri, Luigi Paganetto and Edmund S. Phelps (*editors*)
INTERNATIONAL DIFFERENCES IN GROWTH RATES
Market Globalization and Economic Areas (Vols I & II)

Mario Baldassarri and Paolo Roberti (*editors*)
FISCAL PROBLEMS IN THE SINGLE-MARKET EUROPE

Mario Baldassarri and Franco Modigliani (*editors*)
THE ITALIAN ECONOMY
What Next?

Mario Baldassarri (*editor*)
MAFFEO PANTALEONI
At the Origin of the Italian School of Economics and Finance

Mario Baldassarri, Luigi Paganetto and Edmund S. Phelps (*editors*)
INSTITUTIONS AND ECONOMIC ORGANIZATION IN THE ADVANCED ECONOMIES
The Governance Perspective (Vols I & II)

Geoffrey Brennan (*editor*)
COERCIVE POWER AND ITS ALLOCATION IN THE EMERGENT EUROPE

Mario Baldassarri (*editor*)
INDUSTRIAL POLICY IN ITALY
Phases, links, perspectives to the 90s

Stefano Manzocchi (*editor*)
THE ECONOMICS OF ENLARGEMENT

Roberto Cellini and Guido Cozzi (*editors*)
INTELLECTUAL PROPERTY, COMPETITION AND GROWTH

Debora Di Gioacchino, Sergio Ginebri and Laura Sabani (*editors*)
THE ROLE OF ORGANIZED INTEREST GROUPS IN POLICY MAKING

Riccardo Leoni and Giuseppe Usai (*editors*)
ORGANIZATIONS TODAY

Marco Malgarini and Gustavo Piga (*editors*)
CAPITAL ACCUMULATION, PRODUCTIVITY AND GROWTH
Monitoring Italy 2005

Gustavo Piga and Khi V. Thai (*editors*)
THE ECONOMICS OF PUBLIC PROCUREMENT

Central Issues in Contemporary Economic Theory and Policy
Series Standing Order ISBN 0–333–71464–4
(*outside North America only*)

You can receive future titles in this series as they are published by placing a standing order. Please contact your bookseller or, in case of difficulty, write to us at the address below with your name and address, the title of the series and the ISBN quoted above.

Customer Services Department, Macmillan Distribution Ltd, Houndmills, Basingstoke, Hampshire RG21 6XS, England

The Economics of Public Procurement

Edited by Gustavo Piga and Khi V. Thai

First published 2007 by
PALGRAVE MACMILLAN
Houndmills, Basingstoke, Hampshire RG21 6XS and
175 Fifth Avenue, New York, N. Y. 10010
Companies and representatives throughout the world

PALGRAVE MACMILLAN is the global academic imprint of the Palgrave Macmillan division of St. Martin's Press, LLC and of Palgrave Macmillan Ltd. Macmillan® is a registered trademark in the United States, United Kingdom and other countries. Palgrave is a registered trademark in the European Union and other countries.

ISBN-13: 978–0–230–52086–8   hardback
ISBN-10: 0–230–52086–3   hardback

This book is printed on paper suitable for recycling and made from fully managed and sustained forest sources.

A catalogue record for this book is available from the British Library.

A catalogue record for this book is available from the Library of Congress.

10   9   8   7   6   5   4   3   2   1
16   15   14   13   12   11   10   09   08   07

Printed and bound in Great Britain by
Antony Rowe Ltd, Chippenham and Eastbourne

Contents

THE ECONOMICS OF PUBLIC PROCUREMENT

Edited by
Gustavo Piga and **Khi V. Thai**

Contents

The Economics of Public Procurement

Gustavo Piga - **Khi V. Thai**
Università di Roma "Tor Vergata"   Florida Atlantic University

Driven by demand for further control over public spending and more efficient acquisition processes, procurement has become a key public function. Significant technological changes, international trade and global competition have forced governments and public institutions to extend policy interests beyond cost minimization, and to pursue new challenges including innovation, competition, transparency and reforms. Further, policy makers have become aware of the role of public procurement for many other socio-economic purposes. Crossing both economics and business, public procurement has raised the interest of practitioners directly involved in the management of purchases and with academic researchers to answer key questions, explore new issues, and to discuss an extensive range of topics.

This volume, which reflects this vast increase in economists' interest for procurement, collects the revised versions of some of the papers (all unpublished) presented at the Second International Procurement Conference held in the Villa Mondragone of the University of Rome Tor Vergata, Frascati (Rome), organized by the Department of Economia e Istituzioni of the University in collaboration with the Public Procurement Center at Florida Atlantic University.

The volume is organized in five sections: «Managing Risk in Procurement», «Efficiency in Procurement», «Contracting in Procurement», «Transparency in Procurement» and «Procurement Design». In what follows we give the reader a brief overview of the papers' content.

* * *

1

While great emphasis in procurement is given to competition during tenders, it should not be forgotten that competition, compared to alternative mechanisms of allocation that soften it, modifies strategic behavior by bidders in directions that are not always favorable to the procurer.

This is evident in the case in which contractors face the risk to go bankrupt before the completion of the work and do not face unlimited liability thanks to the right to file for bankruptcy. The option to do so makes the bidding more aggressive (or the incentive to provide low quality if it there is private information on it by the bidder) as it reduces the losses if firm's costs are high. It is also a very relevant concern, as Engel and Wambach show, for those firms (typically small ones) that have larger cost of preparing the bid and are then pushed to implement more risky (aggressive) strategies in terms of price. We suspect that the possibility, allowed in some countries like the US but not in Europe, to provide small firms with a bonus or prize during the tender not only fosters more competition but also — by reducing the cost of bidding conditional on winning the contract — diminishes the probability of default.

The issue of bankruptcy is not a rarity in procurement: more than 80,000 contractors went bankrupt in the U.S. in the period between 1990 and 1997, leaving unfinished business with liabilities exceeding US $ 21 billion.

Engel and Wambach in this volume show that means to weaken competition (multi-sourcing, rationing, lotteries, and others) might lead to better results by reducing default probabilities than the standard competitive auctions that are becoming popular worldwide and have recently been allowed even in an open format with the new Directive in the European Union. Insofar as these same alternative methods reduce the winners' curse present in some of these same competitive formats, some of them show the very desirable property of reducing risk while reducing outlays, a feature that should concern vastly procurers worldwide. For example, Engel and Wambach argue that in some setting the reverse auction in open format, recently introduced in the EU, might have less desirable properties than the traditional sealed bid tender as it might lead to higher risk of default.

However alternative methods to reduce the moral hazard in the tender due to limited liability are not always easy to implement. For example, multi-sourcing, as Engel and Wambach underline, may not fully be feasible if there are capacity constraints or if there are switching costs from one firm to the other for the procurement agency.

Other methods have definitely undesirable properties. Albano, Bianchi and Spagnolo in this volume concentrate on a popular type, «Bid Average Methods». These are formulas to evaluate price offers that generally are meant to reduce the weight given to low (and therefore economically convenient) prices on the ground that they might turn out to increase the risk of completing the contract by the resulting winner. By focusing on some specific examples utilized worldwide, they show that firms respond to such rules in ways that are many times unfavourable for the procurer.

Albano, Bianchi and Spagnolo seem to have a point when they argue that «it appears contradictory to use a competitive awarding procedure that hinges on price, coupled with an awarding rule that is meant to limit price competition». They suggest alternative methods (like beauty contests and negotiations) to soften competition if this is truly a concern (as Engel and Wambach show that it might be the case). They also suggest alternative instruments to deal with the risk of bad contractual performance that do not require giving up standard competitive auctions: surety bonds, in particular, that have yet to find a role in the European Union.

When focusing on Bid Average Methods, they prove that some of them: either 1) provide an incentive for firms to find a «focal point», possibly collusive, or 2) make coordination among bidders more feasible and even easier to implement or finally 3) make the outcome for the procurer extremely uncertain and prone to inefficiencies.

But the issue of collusion in tenders and more generally of efficiency in procurement is obviously not limited to average-bid methods; once issues of risk are taken care of, obviously the goal of the procurer is to make sure that best money for value is obtained. Some features of competition, like the industrial structure in the relevant market, cannot be influenced by the procurer in the short-run and must be considered as given; others might. In particular, auction design can go a long way in affecting the bid that each given firm will want or will be able to post in the tender. Both papers by Lunander and Nilsson and by Lundberg are concerned with the issue of tender format and competition. They do so taking advantage of experimental design, the first, and a large amount of tender data, the other.

Lunander and Nilsson tackle the optimal design of tenders for goods that exhibit synergies and economies of scale in production. This is an issue that is proving to be always more and more relevant as the institutional set-up of procurement agencies is increasingly moving — also due to the development of ICT and web-based purchasing portals — toward centralization, which increases both the size of tenders and the tendering of similar objects. A type of tender increasingly used by procurers is the combinatorial one, that allows not only to make offers on single lots, but also offers on one lot conditional on the award of other lots. This provides firms with the added possibility of taking advantage with certainty of cost synergies and reflecting these in the tender bids. Little is known about the collusive impact of such combinatorial tenders. In particular, do bidders have more difficulties to collude under a combinatorial auction than under standard simultaneous sealed bid auctions? This is the question that Lunander and Nilsson try answering to. Their results, while in need of being strengthened by further types of experimental designs, show encouraging responses as to the features of combinatorial design. Indeed, bidders seem to be less able or inclined to reach collusive agreements in such settings, either because they represent a new way to exploit cost synergies instead of an illegal cartel or because designing a collusive strategy in a combinatorial bid might be too complicated. Furthermore the experiment confirms as expected the efficiency advantages for a procurer of a combinatorial tender when in the presence of economies of scale.

Lundberg's paper is also interested with the impact on auction results of different formats. She takes into consideration single-unit and simultaneous (non combinatorial) sealed bid auctions of interior cleaning services in Sweden. Her unique dataset reminds us first of all of the urgent need for further expansion of data availability to the scientific community so as to improve our understanding of procurement outcomes (an issue which many procurement agencies do not seem to view favourably). It is also of particular interest since in the period considered (1991-1999) many Swedish contracting authorities would not communicate ex-ante *whether the award would be based only on price or on price and qualitative criteria. This system, now not allowed anymore by the European Union rules, introduces large doses of discretion in the hands of the procurer and can lead to inefficiencies of various type particularly if one takes into account that this market is* (ex-post) *dominated by large firms or in-house production units that won 75% of all contracts. Municipality characteristics by governing party and density are shown, together with the variable unemployment, to affect the value of the winning bid.*

While one sometimes tends to forget, efficient procurement is not limited to the type of auction format. It also concerns contractual aspects like sub-contracting or more «primitive» choices as to whether in the first place negotiate directly or use an auction. Von Grawer-May and Wambach in this book tackle the issue of sub-contracting, a pervasive phenomenon in procurement valued in 2001 at 635 billion in the EU. They do so mostly taking the perspective of the firm that, participating to a tender, has to decide how, when and for how much to sub-contract. The authors finally conclude with some policy-advice for public procurers (that may decide to have a say in the tender notice on how sub-contracting is implemented by potential winners), taking the correct strategic stance of first understanding how bidders react to various types of sub-contracting schemes and then providing advice for policy-makers. As for the timing, firms may decide to sub-contract before (conditional on winning) or after submitting the offer to the procurement agency. Later sub-contracting leads to lower prices in the procurement main auction as sub-contractors are more aggressive in competing for a contract when they know the contractor has won the tender. Also, technical specifications are better known and offers can be made more precisely. However, sub-contracting earlier (before the tender) gives the firm precise knowledge of the sub-contractor's costs. How this trade-off is solved, the authors argue, depends on the technological efficiency of the firm compared to its auction rivals. Strategic behaviour of sub-contractors should also be kept in mind when deciding when to sub-contract. Sometimes it can be shown that the best auction format is a two-step procedure where the firm short-lists a few potential candidates and after winning the contract implements an auction only among short-listed subcontractors. Firms can use different strategies to make bidders even more aggressive in the first selection stage, possibly by rewarding them in the second and final selection stage after the contract has been won. In such a setting, Authorities have to keep in mind that by requiring ex-ante that firms have already signed sub-contracts this might make firms bid less aggressively during the contract-award phase at the expense of efficient procurement.

Guccio, Pignataro and Rizzo are concerned with the greater appeal that competitive procedures might have with respect to negotiations in a critical sector like the health one. For one, the use of sealed bids makes it difficult to establish any relationship between the purchaser and the seller in a sector that requires certainty about the quality of the product and reputation concerns should be given great weight. Second, the particular characteristics of the goods purchased and their high-tech nature might make negotiations more effective than auctions in obtaining low prices. The empirical analysis on Italian health purchases however shows that auctions perform better than negotiations in almost all product categories. Authors attribute this to the competition effect. In the purchases of technical equipment for health where the goods characteristics are more complex, however, a negotiation seems to bring better economic results.

The issue of negotiation vs. competitive auction cannot be left exclusively within the realm of efficiency considerations. It must also take into consideration issues of transparency and ethically-compatible behaviour, especially in the public sector where the money that is spent does not belong to the spender but is entrusted to her by the taxpayer. Ethical considerations would seem to push for formal rules that limit the discretion of the contracting authority and reduce therefore the space for direct negotiation, a typical instrument used in the case of private firms' purchasing. However, formal procedures have a drawback in that, as discussed above, they seem to fail to fully capture the possible complexities of providing the re-

quired goods and services or infrastructure, both at the tendering stage and in the contractual phase. Formal procedures also are generally less capable of fully internalizing the value of acquired reputation among bidding firms. So the question becomes: Is there a way to reconcile a guarantee of transparency in procurement with the equally important issue of building a virtuous reputation-based system? Picci in this volume answers affirmatively to this question. He posits that Internet-based reputation systems like eBay are transferable to the public sector acquisition process, even for public works.

Internet is a powerful tool to spread traditional «word of mouth» to unprecedented levels. On eBay, for example, people are wary of conducting business with agents who performed badly in the past. Picci imagines a publicly accessible database where information on a public projects is continuously updated over the life of the project. The availability of an information system of this type would allow the computation of a vast array of useful indexes and measures helpful in addressing the weak governance of public works that plagues so many countries. This accessibility would give rise to so-called «voice-activities» of the relevant stake-holders, including consumers-taxpayers, that would be able to rank various administrations and push them to perform better in terms of the quality of the contract execution. Picci is aware that such voice-activities might be controlled by constituencies that have a non-benevolent goal in mind and suggests alternative ways on how to deal with those problems.

Coppier and Piga reinforce Picci's argument by showing that traditional measures of transparency are little capable of eradicating corruption. They show an only apparently puzzling figure arising from the data: there where transparency is high the country is more corrupt, according to institutional measures of corruption. Coppier and Piga show, with the help of a theoretical model, that this result may be the outcome of a benevolent planner that tries to reduce corruption via transparent policies. Such an effort might be nevertheless frustrated by the fact that making procurement transparent is a costly enterprise. The authors conclude that more structural measures must be devised to eradicate corruption in public procurement, possibly following the lines of what suggested above by Picci.

But the dimensions of optimal procurement are vast and diverse, as the papers by D'Amato and Doni show. D'Amato tackles the issue of how much cooperation across regulators and procurement agencies is necessary in a setting where environmental concerns are relevant in the decision-making process and there are informational asymmetries in favour of the regulated firm. When the environmental agency does not cooperate with the procurement agency this results in a downward distortion in environmental quality. Doni instead shows that the issue of what information to release regarding the quality evaluation of a given offer, and to whom this information is released, can vastly condition the welfare of the procurer and of society, albeit not always in the same way. The issue is particularly relevant, the author argues, as the new EU Directive specifically provides opportunities to award a contract first by evaluating quality and then by accepting an economic offer. Under specific circumstances Doni shows that a policy of private revelation to each single firm of the procurer's evaluation leads to better outcomes for society than secrecy or public revelation. The latter however might maximize the procurer's utility.

I - MANAGING RISK
IN PROCUREMENT

Public Procurement Under Limited Liability

Andreas R. Engel - **Achim Wambach**

TWS Partners, Munich   University of Cologne

Public procurement faces the risk that the contractor goes bankrupt before the completion of the work. The possibility to declare bankruptcy makes the contractors behave more aggressively. This leads to abnormally low tenders and to the break-down of revenue equivalence. Upon this result we investigate frequently used public procurement methods that were designed to avoid the bankruptcy of the winning contractor. We show that the average-bid-method or methods that exclude the lowest offer fare quite badly. We also show that — in contrast to standard auction theory — multi-sourcing, rationing and other means to soften competition may fare better than a standard auction. [JEL-Classification: D44, D45, D82, G33, H57]

1. - Introduction

Procurement auctions are an important mechanism in the public and private sector to buy goods and services. But many projects — especially in the construction industry — are delayed or more expensive because of the bankruptcy of contractors. For example, more than 80,000 contractors went bankrupt in the United States in the period between 1990 and 1997, leaving unfinished construction projects with liabilities exceeding US$ 21

The Authors would like to thank Esther Hauk, seminar participants at the CESifo area conference on Industrial Organization in Munich, at the theory seminar in Berlin and the seminars at the RSSS and the ANU in Canberra for helpful comments and suggestions. Engel gratefully acknowledges financial support from the German Academic Exchange Service (DAAD) under grant D/04/30600.

11

billion.[1] The direct costs of bankruptcy (e.g., lawyers) make up 7-20% of the liquidation proceeds and the indirect costs (e.g., delays) are estimated to be even higher.[2] Bankruptcy arises if the payment and therefore also the winning bid lies below the realization of the cost of the project. The reason why firms bid low enough such that they risk bankruptcy can simply be an overoptimistic or wrong calculation or, as we show, the right to file for bankruptcy (due to limited liability).[3] The intuition is as follows: as the firm can declare bankruptcy to avoid losses if the project is going bad and makes profits otherwise, it pays to bid more aggressively. Thus, a very low bid might not be good news for the agency as it implies a higher risk of bankruptcy. This problem is also mentioned in a report of the European Commission's Enterprise section (1999) which accentuates that *«clients often underestimate ... the risks of abnormally low tenders (ALTs), especially the possibilities of bankruptcy and failure of enterprises...»*.

In this paper we define ALTs as bids which are lower as they would have been under unlimited liability and lead to a positive probability of bankruptcy of the winning firm. Although contract non-fulfillment seems to be an important factor in practice, most theoretical models ignore the fact that firms have limited liability and face the risk of bankruptcy before the completion of the project. We therefore take explicit consideration of the possibility of bankruptcy and analyze the bidding behavior in different procurement mechanisms in an environment with cost uncertainty. By comparing standard

---

[1] Dun and Bradstreet Business Failure record, cited from CALVERAS A. *et* AL. (2004).

[2] For details see WHITE M.J. (1989). The recovery rate in the high-income OECD states is 72% (WORLDBANK, 2004).

[3] A third reason is anticipation of renegotiation. If it is very costly to replace the winning firm, the procuring agency can renegotiate the contract at additional cost (cost overrun). Anticipating renegotiation, firms in turn will bid more aggressively. The magnitude of cost overruns varies, from an average of 22% for the largest Spanish public works projects (GANUZA J., 1997) to more than 220% in a sample of US-defence contracts (PECK M. - SCHERER F.M., 1962). Cost overruns are analyzed in LEWIS T. (1986); ARYAN L. - LEITE A. (1990); GANUZA J. (2003) and BAJARI P. - TADELIS S. (2001).

auction formats and common modifications of standard auctions, we show that means to weaken competition might lead to better results than the standard auctions. We also show that frequently used ways of dealing explicitly with the problem of ALTs lead to undesirable results if they are such that it pays not to be among the lowest bidders. Extending the analysis we investigate reserve prices and entry fees.

In the model we use, firms (bidders) have *ex-ante* uncertainty about their cost. The reason for this can be the uncertainty about the cost of the project in general, errors in the calculation or financial need, either caused by preceding projects or by projects still in process.[4] After the auction, the winning bidder sees the realization of the cost which can be high or low. If the payment is higher than the realized cost, the winning bidder makes a profit; if not, he declares bankruptcy. In our framework, bidders have no budget as our focus is on the effect that different efficiency levels have on the bidding behavior under limited liability.[5] The option to declare bankruptcy makes the bidding more aggressive as it reduces the losses if costs are high.[6] Hence, prices turn out to be lower than under unlimited liability. As bidders' losses are limited but their profits are not, the utility function becomes convex and this makes bidders behave like risk-lovers. By comparing the standard auctions, we obtain that the allocations in a first-price sealed-bid (FPSB) and a second-price sealed-bid (SPSB) auction are still efficient. Furthermore, we show that — for the case of a sufficiently large number of bidders — the expected payment in both auction formats is the same but as the distributions of the

---

[4] ARDITI D. *et* AL. (2000) investigate the factors associated with company failures in the US-construction industry. Human issues like lack of knowledge explains 7.5% of company failures, budgetary issues like heavy operating losses and insufficient profit explain 60.2% of the failures.

[5] Hence, one could say that we investigate the bidding behavior of contractors that are close to ruin. If bidders differ also in budgets, a second effect would arise, namely that the bidding behavior differs also with respect to the size of the budget. See ZHENG C.Z. (2001) or BOARD S. (2005) for this additional wealth effect.

[6] One could argue that if bidders have private information about the quality then only the lowest quality is offered. This would be in line with MANELLI A. - VINCENT D. (1995) who show that take-it-or-leave-it offers fare better than auctions in respect to quality. The effect that auctions favor the lowest bid (and the corresponding low quality) is reinforced by limited liability.

payments differ, the probability of non-fulfillment differs too. Thus, the revenue-equivalence theorem breaks down in spite of identical expected payments. Going beyond the standard auctions, we show that multi-sourcing, rationing, lotteries, and other means to soften competition lead to better results for the procurement agency. Furthermore, we investigate how entry fees and reserve prices affect the bidding behavior and resulting outcome.

However, explicit ways of dealing with ALTs like average-bid methods and other mechanisms where it pays off for bidders *not* to be the lowest bidder lead to undesirable results. For instance, the Public Works Directive of the European Union lays the rules on how European governments have to procure. While governments are generally obliged to buy from the lowest tender[7] explicit consideration of the problem of ALTs is also ‘given: "*§4: If, for a given contract, tenders appear to be abnormally low in relation to the works, the contracting authority shall, before it may reject those tenders, request ... details of the constituent elements of the tender which it considers relevant and shall verify those constituent elements taking account of the explanations received.*" As a result, in order to deal with the problem of ALTs and the non-fulfillment of contracts some countries have explicitly defined what will be taken as an ALT and should be rejected. Bids are called abnormally low if they are a certain percentage below the average bid[8] or sometimes abnormally below the second lowest bid. But if such rules lead to different treatments of submitted bids, bidders will anticipate the exclusion and will bid higher which in turn changes what should be considered an ALT. Other countries have adapted their procurement design, especially their allocation rules. As an example, Taiwan is reported to have used a design where the bid closest to the average bid wins the contest. As everyone wants to be average, no one will place a low bid.[9]

---

[7] Article 30 PWD (Public Works Directive 93/37/EEC (1993)) of the European Union says «*1. The criteria on which the contracting authorities shall base the award of contracts shall be: (a) ... the lowest price only;...*».

[8] About 10-20% in Belgium, France, Italy, Portugal, Romania, Spain, and Greece.

[9] A different way of avoiding *ruinous competition* was used in the Netherlands where a pre-procurement with all firms and with the disclosure of all bids took place, allowing firms to withdraw their bid if it was obviously a too optimistic calculation (Lupp W., 1993).

We show in our analysis below that several of these reported ways of tackling the problem of ALTs and bankruptcy lead to undesired consequences as these rules will not only affect the allocation but will also have strategic effects on the bidding behavior.

Related Literature

There are just a few papers which analytically discuss the relation between limited liability and auctions. Zheng (2001) shows in the context of a common-value selling auction that if bidders are budget constrained, the value of the object auctioned is uncertain, and the payment can be postponed, it may be the case that the most budget constrained bidder is the bidder most likely to win the auction. The reason is that if a bidder declares bankruptcy, he will loose his entire budget. As these costs of bankruptcy are smaller the smaller the budget, the bidder with the lowest budget might well be the bidder with the highest interest in winning the object and therefore the bidder with the most aggressive bid.

The article closest to this paper is that of Parlane (2003). In her article, individual cost uncertainty is modelled as a general distribution with a continuous distribution density on a bounded support. She shows that the expected procurement price is higher in an FPSB-auction than in any other efficient mechanism where only the winner pays. The intuition for this result is straightforward: as the possibility of bankruptcy leads to a convex utility function, bidders behave as if they were risk-loving. Only in an FPSB-auction the winning price-conditional on winning-is certain. Any other mechanism leads to uncertainty in the winning price which makes bidders bid more aggressively.

Board (2005) uses a mechanism design approach in a similar framework as Parlane (2003), although he considers a selling rather than a procurement auction. He argues that limited liability makes the bidding more aggressive by cutting off the downside loss. Board shows that the expected selling price is higher under limited liability than under unlimited liability. He also shows that the FPSB-auction leads to the lowest expected selling price of all standard winner-pays auctions and he outlines conditions under which the FPSB-auction will lead to the lowest probability of non-fulfillment. Furthermore, he investigates wealth effects and shows that the bids decrease in wealth, an effect which was first shown by Waehrer (1995). To our knowledge, we are the first to discuss the effects of different procurement mechanisms beyond the standard auctions in a framework with limited liability.

In an experimental paper, Roelofs (2002) investigates a common-value auction with default. In his framework, default gives the winner an opportunity to avoid the winner's curse, i.e. limited liability works as an insurance against the winner's curse. The experiment shows that the possibility of default leads indeed to more aggressive bidding.

Calveras et al. (2004) analyze the use of surety bonds and letters of credits and discuss to what extend these instruments can help to eliminate the problem of ALTs. They show that, if a surety company is specialized in screening applicants, surety bonds can indeed be useful instruments to mitigate the problem of ALTs.

In a different context without limited liability, Bulow and Klemperer (2002) show that rationing and/or multi-sourcing can be revenue enhancing in a selling auction. Their result was derived in a framework with common values and asymmetric bidders. As multiple shares reduce the impact of the winner's curse, it leads to less cautious bidding and hence to a higher revenue than a single source. Limited liability gives an alternative explanation why these mechanisms might be preferred to a standard auction.

A non-technical and more detailed overview about how to manage risk bids can be found in Engel et al. (2006). The paper is structured as follows: in section 2 the model is described and the results for the SPSB - and FPSB - auction are derived. In section 3 we discuss reported ways of dealing with ALTs including reserve prices and entry fees. Section 4 concludes.

2. - A Simple Model of Limited Liability

A risk-neutral procurement agency has one tender contract to offer. There are n potential risk-neutral bidders (indexed by i) with costs of either c_i or $c_i + \Delta$ (with a probability of ρ and of $(1 - \rho)$ respectively (with $0 < \rho < 1$)). The cost term $c = c_i$ is distributed on the support $[\underline{c}, \overline{c}]$ and is identical for all bidders. We denote $F(c)$ as the distribution and $f(c) = F'(c)$ as the density of the cost term.[10]

The order of events is as follows: *(1)* The agency announces the auction rules and defines the specifications of the project. While bidders know their individual cost term c at this stage, they do not know if they have to incur the additional cost of Δ later on. *(2)* Bidders bid in the auction. A winner is declared according to the auction rules who receives a payment p. Losing bidders have a payoff of zero. If the bidder with the lowest cost term wins, we call this allocation efficient. *(3)* The winner observes his realized cost and either makes a profit if the payment is higher than the realized cost, or he decides to declare bankruptcy otherwise.[11] To avoid multiplicity of equilibria later on, we assume that, if a bidder goes bankrupt, he has to bear small costs of bankruptcy ε.[12] Thus, if a bidder with cost term c wins the contract at payment p (or the price from the agency's point of view), his expected payoff is given by

(1)
$$\pi = \begin{cases} (p - c) - (1 - \rho)\Delta & \text{if} \quad p \geq c + \Delta \\ \rho(p - c) - (1 - \rho)\varepsilon & \text{if} \quad c \leq p < c + \Delta \\ -\varepsilon & \text{if} \quad p < c \end{cases}$$

The expected utility of the procuring agency is given by

(2)
$$u(p, \phi) = (1 - \phi)(v - p) - \phi B$$

---

[10] The realization of the cost is bounded on the support $[\underline{c}, \overline{c} + \Delta]$. It is assumed that Δ is smaller than the ≠ in cost levels ($0 < \Delta < (\underline{c} - \overline{c})$).

[11] It is important that the agency has to stick to the rules set in *(1)* and there is neither renegotiation nor resale.

[12] This costs can also be interpreted as the loss of a budget of size ε.

17

where υ is the valuation for a project successfully implemented and B are the costs the agency has to bear in case of non-fulfillment.[13] ϕ is the probability that the winning bidder goes bankrupt. As we show next, this probability depends on the procurement mechanism used.

Second-Price Sealed-Bid Auction

In an SBSB-auction, the contract is awarded to the bidder with the lowest bid and the payment is the second lowest bid.

Proposition 1. In an SPSB-auction, in the limes of $\varepsilon \to 0$, it is a weakly dominant strategy for each bidder to bid his cost term[14]

$$(3) \qquad \beta_{SPSB}(c) = c$$

Thus, in an SPSB-auction, the bidder with the lowest cost term wins the contract, i.e. the sourcing is efficient. In the SPSB-auction the winner receives the second lowest bid as the payment which is the expectation of the second lowest order statistic. This is given in the following equation, with $f_i(c)$ as the density of the ith lowest order statistic and $c^{(i,n)}$ as the ith (lowest) order statistic out of n draws:

$$(4) \qquad E\left[p_{SPSB}(c)\right] = E\left[c^{(2,n)}\right] = \int_{\underline{c}}^{\bar{c}} c f_2(c)dc$$

$$= \int_{\underline{c}}^{\bar{c}} nc(n-1)F(c)\bigl(1-F(c)\bigr)^{(n-2)} f(c)dc$$

From the contracting agency's point of view, the probability that the contract will not be finished is equal to $(1 - \rho)$ times the

---

[13] We use a very simple form of the agency's bankruptcy costs, namely additional costs like delays, other accountable costs or costs of re-auctioning. One could ask what happened to the money paid (e.g., halffinished project left with some value to the agency) but this is not part of our analysis. For an analysis of different recovery rates of half-finished projects see BOARD S. (2005).

[14] The proof can be found in the appendix.

probability that the second lowest cost term (payment) is less than Δ away from the lowest cost term. Formally, the latter term is the probability that $c^{(2,n)} - c^{(2,n)} < \Delta$:

$$(5) \qquad \text{Prob}\left[c^{(2,n)} - c^{(1,n)} < \Delta\right] = \int_{\underline{c}}^{\bar{c}} f_1(c)\int_c^{c+\Delta} f_2(z\,|\,z \geq c)dzdc$$

$$= \int_{\underline{c}}^{\bar{c}} \int_c^{c+\Delta} n(n-1)f(c)f(z)\left[1 - F(z)\right]^{(n-2)}dzdc$$

with $f_2(z\,|\,z \geq c)$ being the density of the second lowest order statistic, conditional on c being the lowest order statistic.[15] Thus, the probability of non-fulfillment is given by

$$(6) \qquad \phi_{SPSB} = (1-\rho)\int_{\underline{c}}^{\bar{c}} \int_c^{c+\Delta} n(n-1)f(c)f(z)\left[1 - F(z)\right]^{(n-2)}dzdc$$

The expected utility for the agency is

$$(7) \qquad E[u(p,\phi)] = (1 - \phi_{SPSB})(\upsilon - E[p_{SPSB}]) - \phi_{SPSB}B$$

First-Price Sealed-Bid Auction

In an FPSB-auction, the bidder with the lowest bid wins the contract and receives his respective bid as the payment. Here multiplicity of equilibria is not a problem, therefore we set $\varepsilon = 0$. Furthermore, we distinguish between two cases: n small and n large. This can be relevant for the agency as with many bidders (n large) the equilibrium is such that the competition is tough and all bidders will bid aggressively (below $c + \Delta$). With only a few bidders (n small), the incentives are such that more efficient bidders do not have to bid aggressively as this would lead to a lower expected payoff.

---

[15] For the uniform distribution equation *(5)* is $(1-[1-F(\underline{c}+\Delta)]^n)$ which is smaller than 1.

Proposition 2. In an FPSB-auction, for

$$n \geq max\left\{\hat{n}; 1 + \frac{1}{\Delta p f(c)}\right\},$$

an equilibrium exists where a bidder with cost term c will bid the expectation of the lowest cost term of the $(n-1)$ competing bidders, conditional on his cost term being the lowest[16]

(8) $$\beta_{FPSB}(c) = E\left[c^{(1,n-1)}\Big|c^{(1,n-1)} \geq c\right]$$

with $\hat{n}$ being the smallest n that satisfies

$$\int_c^{\bar{c}} \frac{(1 - F(z))^{(n-1)}}{(1 - F(c))^{(n-1)}} dz < \Delta.$$

The interpretation of the n large case is the following: the competition in the auction (a large number of bidders or a high ρ) must be sufficiently large in order to force all bidders to bid below the threshold of $c + \Delta$. Raising the bid above the threshold would lower the expected payoff of the bidder because the gain in payment is smaller than the loss in the probability of winning.

In the FPSB-auction for n large, the expected price for the procurement agency is

(9) $$E_{[pSPSB]} = \int_{\underline{c}}^{\bar{c}} nc(n-1)F(c)(1 - F(c))^{(n-2)} f(c)dc.$$

Thus, under the condition that the winning bidder does not go bankrupt, the expected price in the FPSB-auction for n large is the same as in the SPSB-auction.

---

[16] The proof can be found in the appendix. Note that the bidding strategy, the expected price, and the probabilities of bankruptcy would be the same in a Dutch auction.

As $ß_{FPSB}$ is increasing and continuous in equilibrium the bidder with the lowest cost term submits the lowest bid and wins the auction. Thus, also an FPSB-auction for n large is efficient. Under the condition of n large, each bidder bids more than c but less than $c + \Delta$. From the point of view of the contracting agency, the probability of not being served is therefore given by the probability that the cost realization is $c + \Delta$ which is

(10) $$\phi_{FPSB} = 1 - \rho.$$

Thus, the probability of non-fulfillment in an FPSB-auction which — in contrast to the SPSB-auction — does not depend on the distribution of the payment is higher than the probability of non-fulfillment in an SPSB-auction.[17]

The expected utility of the procurement agency in the FPSB-auction is

(11) $$E[u(p,\phi)] = \rho(\upsilon - E[p_{FPSB}]) - (1 - \rho)B.$$

Therefore, we can give a new reason why revenue equivalence breaks down: given that the expected price is the same and that the distributions of the payments differ, the probability of non-fulfillment and the utility of the agency differs in the two formats.[18] Combining the previous results, the expected utility for the procurement agency is higher in the SPSB-auction.

---

[17] PARLANE S. (2003) derives the result that the expected payment in the FPSB-auction is higher than in the SPSB-auction. Upon this result, she speculates that the probability of non-fulfillment is smaller in the FPSB-auction. However, this is not true in general as in our framework the probabilities are reversed. BOARD S. (2005) shows that if the general cost distribution function is convex, the probability of non-fulfillment is higher in the SPSB-auction. However, in our framework the realization of the cost distribution $H(\cdot)$ is concave in the relevant region, so the probability of non-fulfillment is lower in the SPSB auction. Conditional on winning with cost term c the probability of non-fulfillment in the FPSB-auction is $H(p_{FPSB})$ while it is $\int H(p_{SPSB})f(p_{SPSB})dp_{SPSB}$ in the SPSB-auction. Due to Jensen's Inequality if $H(\cdot)$ is concave, the probability of non-fulfillment is smaller in the SPSB-auction.

[18] As the expected payment is the same in both auction formats and the probabilities of bankruptcy differ, payoff equivalence for the bidders is no longer valid. A standard result in the auction literature is that risk-loving behavior leads to different expected payments in different auction formats. In our case, we have found a different channel why payoff equivalence breaks down, although expected payments are identical. Here the payoff equivalence theorem is no longer valid because of the differences in the payment distributions.

If the number of bidders is small (n small), this is no longer the case. If n is small, the more efficient bidders can abstain from the aggressive bidding. We show that the equilibrium bidding function will be monotone increasing and that bidders with cost terms below a critical c^* will bid above the threshold $c + \Delta$ and bidders with cost terms higher than c^* will bid below the threshold. The intuition behind this result is the following: while bidders with high cost terms still have an incentive to bid below $c + \Delta$ to win more often, bidders with low cost terms can abstain from bidding aggressively: shading the bid below $c + \Delta$ would raise the probability of winning slightly but it would reduce the profit if he wins substantially. Therefore, bidders with low cost terms will bid above $c + \Delta$.[19]

Proposition 3. In an FPSB-auction, for $n<\hat{n}$, an equilibrium with the following properties exists: there exists a c^* with $\underline{c}<c^*<\overline{c}$, the bidding function is monotone increasing, and bidders with costs $c \leq c^*$ will bid above $c + \Delta$ and bidders with costs $c > c^*$ will bid below $c + \Delta$.

For $c \leq c^*$:

(12)
$$\beta(c) = c + \Delta + \int_c^{\overline{c}} \frac{1-G(z)}{1-G(c)}dz - \int_{c^*}^{\overline{c}} \frac{1-G(z)}{1-G(c^*)}dz$$

For $c > c^*$:

(13)
$$\beta(c) = c + \int_c^{\overline{c}} \frac{1-G(z)}{1-G(c)}dz$$

Compared to the case when n is large, the FPSB-auction for n small leads to a higher expected price and to a lower probability of non-fulfillment. This result is driven by the fact that there is less competition not only due to a smaller number of contractors but

[19] The proof of proposition 3 can be found in the appendix. One could argue that bidders to the left of c^* are still risk-neutral and bidders to the right become risk-loving. The result that bidders with low cost terms may not run into bankruptcy, while bidders with high cost terms may do so, was also shown by PARLANE S. (2003).

also due to less aggressive bidding by the more efficient bidders. As a general result, prices in the FPSB-auction are at least the same (as we have shown for n large) or higher as in the SPSB-auction.[20]

3. - Alternative Procurement Mechanisms

In this section we analyze different procurement mechanisms. As mentioned in the introduction, governments have used different ways of dealing with ALTs. First, we investigate some of the mechanisms already proposed in the literature and then we turn to different ways of allocating contracts. Our aim is to find an understanding of the interaction of the different parameters and to give some implications for the choice of the right mechanism. Since all alternative methods allocate the contract at prices higher than a standard auction, the probability of non-fulfillment is lower per se. But the decision which of these mechanisms to use is faced by a trade-off between low prices (if bankruptcy costs are low) and a low probability of non-fulfillment (if bankruptcy costs are high). We shed some light on the question which mechanism addresses this trade-off best.[21]

Average-Bid Method

In Taiwan an auction format was used where the winner was the bidder with the bid closest to the average. In Italy, a similar auction was employed where the bidder was the winner whose bid was closest to but less than the average bid.[22] Similar to that rule is a method in Peru where all bids 10% above and below the average are eliminated. The contract goes to the bidder whose bid is closest (from below) to the new average.[23] Note that these

---

[20] For this result in a more general framework see Board S. (2005).
[21] For a broader overview of mechanisms including supporting weaker bidders and surety bonds see Engel A. *et* al. (2006).
[22] See Ioannou P. - Leu S. (1993).
[23] See Henriod E. - Lantran J.-M. (2000).

allocation rules are no longer standard auctions as the bidder with the lowest bid does not win. To illustrate the effects of mechanisms that allocate the contract such that it pays not to be among the lowest bidders, we consider a sealed-bid auction where the bid closest to the average bid wins. If there is more than one winning bid, there will be a lottery among the winners. Then, it holds:

Lemma 1 For any price $P > \bar{c}$, it is an equilibrium if every bidder bids P.

PROOF. The proof is straightforward. Suppose everyone bids P, then everyone makes the average bid. Thus, everyone has the same chance of winning the contract and will make a positive expected profit if one wins. Offering any other bid implies moving away from the average. Thus, the deviating bidder will lose the contest for sure. Therefore, bidding $b(c) = P \ \forall c$ is an equilibrium.

As everyone tries to be just average this will take the competition out of the contest. Thus, although the average-bid method was intended to exclude all ALTs, the change in the bidding behavior leads to very high prices.[24] The logic behind the result for average bidding extends to other mechanisms as well. We were told that in some regions of Switzerland, an auction design was used where the winning bid was not the lowest bid but the second lowest bid. Although this design was probably chosen to avoid the abnormally low(est) bid the result stated above also holds here. The rule has strategic effects on the bidding behavior and as everyone tries to become second and not first, prices might turn out to be very high again.[25]

---

[24] IOANNOU P. - LEU S. (1993) argue that the average-bid method may be preferred over low-bid methods FPSB-auction as it does not give priority to risky bids and awards the contract to average prices. However, they do not derive a Nash-Equilibrium for their bidding strategy.

[25] An issue which complicates this analysis is the possibility of shill or fake bidding. In some cases, the agency does not control who offers a bid and how many bids someone offers. If the rule is such that the average bid wins, it may pay off for a bidder to offer one extremely high bid to raise the average and a second bid close to the expected average.

Truncated English Auction (Rationing)

Rationing is a common method in an environment with excess demand where bidders get only a proportion of their requested demand.[26]

Consider the following truncated English auction. Do an English auction until m bidders are left (with $m \leq n$). Consider $m = 2$ as the extreme case. This implies that the winner is one of the two bidders with the lowest cost terms. As the auction stops at $c^{(3,n)}$ the price is $p_{TE} = E[c^{(3,n)}]$ which is higher than in the standard English auction. A rather simple method to choose between the m remaining bidders is a lottery where everyone obtains the contract with probability $1/m$.[27] The probability of non-fulfillment is then given by

$$(14) \qquad \phi_{TE} = \left(\frac{1}{2} Prob\left[c^{(3,n)} - c^{(1,n)} < \Delta \right] + \frac{1}{2} Prob\left[c^{(3,n)} - c^{(2,n)} < \Delta \right] \right)(1 - \rho)$$

which is lower than in an English (or SPSB-) auction.[28]

Lotteries

The use of lotteries where the agency sets a price and awards the contract randomly was quite common in the 1980s, especially in the US where the allocation of spectrum licences was done via lotteries until 1994.[29] Consider the following: the government sources at the payment $p_L = \bar{c} + \Delta$ and holds a lottery between all bidders. This will lead to zero bankruptcy at a very high price.

---

[26] For instance, in equity IPOs and Central Bank Tenders. See Gresik T. (2001) or Gilbert - Klemperer P. (2000).

[27] For an analysis of $1/m$ auctions in a framework with common values see Harstad R. - Bordley R. (1996).

[28] The same can be done with a screening process instead of the lottery. As further price competition in the second round would increase the probability of non-fulfillment, the agency should check the offers of the prequalified bidders in more detail (e.g., through screening or due diligence) and award the contract to the most qualified bidder. In this case the agency has to invest screening costs only for a small number of bidders and learns more about the pre-qualified bidders.

[29] Milgrom P. (2004), pages 3, 79.

Note that this lottery is the same as the truncated English auction with $m = n$. The allocation of a lottery is very inefficient but depending on how high the costs of bankruptcy are, the truncated English auction or even a lottery might fare better than any standard auction.

Multi-Sourcing

Risk diversification means that an agency "should not put all eggs into one basket". Using the same principle, the agency can reduce the risk of non-fulfillment by sourcing the contract to more than one firm. Multi-sourcing (also called share auctions or split award contracts) is used when a contract is split up in m parts and m contractors win a certain share of the contract. As an example, many automobile manufacturers use more than one supplier for their components.[30] The advantage of multi-sourcing is the flexibility to switch between projects, i.e. a solvent firm can finish the lot of a bankrupt firm.[31]

Assume that the agency uses an SPSB-auction and that the agency can split the contract, i.e. she can allocate the contract to two or more contractors. If the agency procures two equal shares, the contract goes to the two contractors with the lowest bids and the payment is the third lowest bid. In this scenario, bidding the cost term c is again a dominant strategy.[32] Therefore, the expected price will be $p_{M,50/50} = E[c^{(3,n)}]$. Since we assume that one firm can finish the part of the other, the probability of non-fulfillment is the probability that both contractors go bankrupt: $\phi_M = (1 - \rho)^2 Prob[c^{(3,n)} - c^{(1,n)} < \Delta]$ which is lower than in the single-source SPSB-auction.

The advantage of multi-sourcing is, that if one firm goes

[30] See PERRY M. - SAKOVICS J. (2003); for defence contracts of the U.S. government and PC-CPU's see ANTON J. - YAO D. (1989).

[31] In a common-value environment, BULOW J. - KLEMPERER P. (2002) show that multi sourcing can increase revenues in selling auctions. If bidders are asymmetric, the second source gives the disadvantaged bidders a higher incentive to participate (especially in a sealed-bid auction). We show that a second source might also mitigate the problem of ALTs.

[32] For this and more results on the competition in multi-share auctions see WAMBACH A. (2002).

bankrupt, the other one(s) can finish the project and so on. As the agency can switch contractors in the case of bankruptcy, this (theoretically) leads to zero probability of non-fulfillment (for $n \rightarrow \infty$), as all contractors have to go bankrupt for the project to fail. But, notice that this scheme does not always work, because the contractors can be capacity constraint or can have costs of switching. In many cases the agency has to use multiple sources, because no firm has the capacity to finish the whole project. Therefore, the shares can not be as extreme as above. Also, if the agency suffers costs of switching between contractors, the advantage of multi-sourcing is reduced. Another problem with multi-sourcing arises, if the default risk of the contractors is correlated. Then the flexibility to switch between contractors is no longer of use, because if the probability of default of one firm is high then the probability of the other contractors is high as well.[33]

Multi-sourcing may be the best choice for the procuring agency for two reasons. First, as in the case of lotteries and rationing, multi-sourcing increases the expected payment as bidders bid less aggressively and an increase in payment reduces the probability of non-fulfillment.[34] Second, multi-sourcing may allow the procurement agency to switch to a solvent firm in case one of the contractors goes bankrupt. Thus, if the agency can use multi-sourcing (contractors are not capacity constrained) and if the costs of switching between contractors are small, multi-sourcing leads (at least) to the same price or even to a lower price and a lower probability of non-fulfillment than other means to weaken competition. The disadvantage is that the price is in general higher than with singlesourcing.

Comparison Between the Procurement Methods

For the purpose of illustration, we compare three different mechanisms for the uniform distribution from the agency's point

---

[33] For the limits of multi-sourcing see ENGEL A. *et* AL. (2006).
[34] A discussion of unequal share sizes (e.g., 70/30) and the resulting lower expected prices, see ENGEL A. *et* AL. (2006).

of view. As mentioned above, the lottery between n bidders (rationing between n bidders) and the average-bid method lead to zero probability of non-fulfillment but as the latter can lead to higher prices we only investigate the lottery ($p_R = \bar{c} + \Delta$). The utility of the agency in this case is $u_R = \upsilon - (\bar{c} + \Delta)$.

The second mechanism is the multi-source SPSB-auction with two equal shares which leads to a price of

$$E[p_M] = \frac{3\bar{c} + n\underline{c} - 2\underline{c}}{n+1}$$

and $u_M = (\upsilon - E[p_M])(1 - \phi_M) - B\phi_M$.

The third mechanism is the single-source SPSB-auction with a price of

$$E[p_{SPSB}] = \frac{2\bar{c} + n\underline{c} - 2\underline{c}}{n+1}$$

and $u_{SPSB} = (\upsilon - E[p_{SPSB}])(1 - \phi_{SPSB}) - B\phi_{SPSB}$.

Agencies with high costs of bankruptcy (υ and B large) prefer a mechanism that induces less bankruptcy, i.e. a mechanism that weakens competition. This may be the goal of a welfare-maximizing agency (e.g., the government). On the other hand, agencies with low costs of bankruptcy can use the competition in the auction to lower the price. This is more likely to be the goal of a revenue-maximizer (e.g., firms in the private sector). Thus, the trade-off for the agency is to pay informational rents on the one hand (high price but a low probability of non-fulfillment) and opportunity cost on the other hand (high probability of non-fulfillment but a low price).

In graph 1 the different mechanisms are compared. The lottery (light grey) is only preferred if the uncertainty and/or υ is very high. The competition of a single-source SPSB-auction (black) is desired if the agency has a low valuation and/or the magnitude of the uncertainty is very low. In the other cases, multi-sourcing is the preferred mechanism.[35] But note that switching projects in

---

[35] Multi-sourcing fares even better compared to the SPSB-auction if the agency uses unequal shares. See ENGEL A. *et al.* (2006) for a discussion of this result.

GRAPH 1

COMPARISON OF THE THE SPSB, MULTI-SOURCING, AND THE
LOTTERY FOR $n = 8$, $\rho = 0.5$, $c \in [0, 1]$, AND B = 0.5

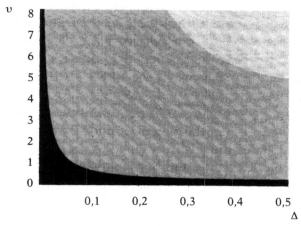

the case that one winner goes bankruptcy is costless in our multi-sourcing framework. If switching is costly, the preference for multi-sourcing would be weaker.

Reserve Price and Entry Fees

Here we investigate additional instruments apart from differences in the allocation or payment rules, namely reserve prices and entry fees. Both are used to pre-qualify bidders, for instance in most European UMTS spectrum license auctions.[36] Using a reserve price r or an entry fee k in a standard procurement auction can lower the expected price for the agency by excluding bidders with high cost terms. However, there is also an efficiency loss due to the possibility of not awarding a contract. The standard result in the literature with unlimited liability is that if the agency sets the reserve price (or the entry fee) optimally, the effect of a lower expected price outweighs the efficiency loss. Also, the introduction of an optimal reserve price or an optimal entry fee

---

[36] Entry fees can also be interpreted as costs of preparation for the bidding process.

leads to the same outcome because the allocation is identical and the payoff for the marginal bidder is the same.[37]

In a framework with limited liability, this equivalence no longer holds as the bidding strategy will be affected in different ways: entry fees are paid in advance, so they affect the bidding behavior in other ways than a reserve price. To distinguish the different cases, we have to assume that bidders have a certain budget ε. The bidding strategy in the SPSB auction with limited liability and a reserve price r is straightforward.[38] If $\varepsilon \geq \Delta$, the participants bid as if under unlimited liability as the budget is always sufficient to cover the potential additional costs. I.e. they bid the expectation of the cost $(c + (1 - \rho) \Delta)$ because this strategy will leave each bidder indifferent between winning or not. Bidders with expected costs above the reserve price will not enter the auction. In this scenario, no participating bidder will go bankrupt. The analysis for the entry fee is different. Assume that the agency requests an entry fee k ($\varepsilon - k < \Delta \leq \varepsilon$) which bidders have to pay in advance. For simplicity, let's assume the extreme case $k = \varepsilon$. Then, the participating bidders have not enough assets to cover a high-cost realization and the dominant strategy is to bid the cost term c as the entry fee affects the decision to enter the auction but not the bidding strategy, i.e. the entry fee is sunk. Hence, the entry fee leads to a negative wealth effect (turns solvent bidders into potentially insolvent bidders) and makes bidders bid more aggressively. Which in turn leads to a positive probability of bankruptcy for each bidder.[39] Therefore, if bidders have some but not unlimited wealth, the reserve price fares better than the entry fee as it does not turn solvent bidders into potentially insolvent bidders. But as we show next, there is no general ranking possible.

Assume the case that $\varepsilon < \Delta$ and the agency sets a reserve price r. Then, as the weakly dominant strategy has to leave the bidder indifferent between winning and losing at this payment, the bid will be:

---

[37] See MATTHEWS S. (1995) or KRISHNA V. (2002), page 27.

[38] We only analyze the SPSB-auction as it is technically less demanding and it enables us to show the effects of reserve prices and entry fees.

[39] This wealth effect was also shown by BOARD S. (2005).

$$c + \frac{1-\rho}{\rho}\varepsilon.$$

All bidders with cost terms such that

$$c + \frac{1-\rho}{\rho}\varepsilon > r$$

will never participate. The analysis for the entry fee is the same as above, i.e. the bid will be c as k is sunk. As the bidding functions are different, the payments and the resulting probability of bankruptcy will differ. As a simple example, assume the following extreme case: reserve price or entry fee are chosen such that only one bidder enters the auction. Then, the reserve price or the maximal willingness to pay (in case of an entry fee) will determine the payment. As the maximal willingness to pay of the agency ($\bar{c}+\Delta$) is by definition higher than the reserve price, the payment is higher with an entry fee. Therefore, the expected probability of bankruptcy with an entry fee is $E[\text{Prob}[\bar{c}+\Delta-c<\Delta]] = 0$ which is smaller than the expected probability of bankruptcy with a reserve price, $E[\text{Prob}[r+\varepsilon-c<\Delta]]\geq 0$. If there is strictly more than one bidder willing to place a bid, the two formats again yield different results as the winner receives the bid of the second lowest participating bidder as the payment. As the bid of each bidder for each cost term c is higher with the reserve price, the expected payment is higher as well and there is no general ranking possible.

Hence, we can distinguish three different cases: if bidders have unlimited liability, both instruments are equivalent. If the budget is such that an entry fee triggers limited liability, the reserve price fares better as is does not have a negative effect on the bidding behavior. If bidders are close to ruin, there is no general ranking possible.

4. - Discussion

In this paper the risks of procurement are analyzed in an environment where contractors can go bankrupt. When contractors

31

have uncertainty about the cost realization and limited liability, their bidding behavior is affected and they will bid more aggressively. It is shown that the revenue-equivalence principle breaks down even if the expected payments are the same. The reason is that if bankruptcy occurs, the distribution of payments becomes relevant. As a general result, the more competition the mechanism produces, the lower the expected payment and the higher the probability that the project will not be finished. But although competition is bad in terms of risk, it is good to select the more efficient contractors. Therefore, when choosing a mechanism, the procurement agency faces a trade-off between the price and the risk of non-fulfillment. Mechanisms like rationing and multi-sourcing in particular handle the trade-off quite well while others like the average-bid method, lead to undesirable results as prices can turn out to be very high. We also showed that reserve prices and entry fees are no longer equivalent.

An extension of this analysis would be to allow for asymmetries between bidders and common values with respect to the costs of the bidders. As the possibility of bankruptcy makes it desirable to have rather less competition than more, we expect that in these cases standard insights from the literature no longer hold either. E.g. as the winner's curse leads to less aggressive bidding, this might be preferred by the procuring agency. Thus, the agency might use a sealed-bid rather than an open auction.

APPENDIX

Proof for Bidding Function SBSP

Proof. The proof is straightforward and follows textbook analysis. The small costs of bankruptcy ε are assumed such that no bidder has an incentive to bid less than c. Assume that bidder i bids $b_i = c_i$ and the lowest competing bid is $b^{(2)} = min_{i \neq j} b_j$. Bidder i wins if $b_i < b^{(2)}$ and does not win if $b_i > b^{(2)}$ which gives him zero payoff.[40] The expected payoff if he wins is $\rho E\, [b^{(2)} - c_i] + (1 - \rho)\, E\, [(b^{(2)} - c_i - \Delta \mid b^{(2)} > c_i + \Delta)] - E\, [(\varepsilon \mid b^{(2)} < c_i + \Delta)]$ which is larger than zero for ε small enough. Suppose now that he deviates from bidding $b_i = c_i$ and bids $z_i = c_i$. If $b^{(2)} < c_i < z_i$, he still gets zero payoff; if $c_i < z_i < b^{(2)}$ he still gets the same payoff as bidding c_i; and if $c_i < b^{(2)} < z_i$ he looses whereas a bid of c_i would have won yielding a positive expected payoff. Now consider he bids $z_i < c_i$. If $b^{(2)} < z_i < c_i$, he still gets zero payoff; if $z_i < c_i < b^{(2)}$, he still gets the same payoff as bidding c_i; and if $z_i < b^{(2)} < c_i$ he wins and always goes bankrupt yielding a payoff of $-\varepsilon$. Thus, deviating from bidding $b(c_i) = c_i$ never increases his payoff but sometimes decreases it.[41,42]

---

[40] Because $f(c)$ is continuous we neglect ties.

[41] We assumed that bidder i knows the lowest competing bid. But the proof does not change if the lowest competing bid is random with some density function $f(\cdot)$. The proof is a standard Bayesian argument (e.g., see Matthews S., 1995), working with expected profits. Note that the bidding strategy, the expected price, and the probabilities of bankruptcy would be same in an English auction.

[42] The proof above must be slightly modified if the agency never pays more than $\bar{c}$ or the reservation price is $r \leq \bar{c}$. In this case the bidder with cost term receives his bid as the payment and this would give him always a payoff of $-\varepsilon$ if he wins (which is with probability zero). So bidding anything above $\bar{c}$ is an optimal bid for this bidder. But since he never wins, his expected payoff is zero and so we let him bid $\bar{c} + \varepsilon$.

Proof for Bidding Function FBSP, n Large

PROOF. Suppose all bidders $(j \neq i)$ follow the bidding strategy ß_{FPSB} given in proposition 2. We argue that in this case, it is optimal for bidder i to follow ß_{FPSB} as well. First, we show that under the assumption that a bidder with cost term c bids less than $c + \Delta$, it is indeed optimal for him to bid according to the equilibrium strategy. In a second step, we derive conditions under which bidding more than $c + \Delta$ is not optimal if everyone follows this bidding strategy.

In equilibrium a bidder with cost term c chooses a bid $b(c)$ which corresponds to a $\hat{c}$ with $\beta(\hat{c}) = b(c)$. Formally, such a bidder maximizes the following expression with respect to $\hat{c}$:

$$(15) \qquad \pi(\hat{c}, c) = \rho\big(\beta(\hat{c}) - c\big)\big(1 - F(\hat{c})\big)^{(n-1)}$$

where $(1 - F(\hat{c}))^{(n-1)}$ is the probability that all other bidders have cost terms higher than $\hat{c}$. For an easier notation we denote $(1 - G(c)) = (1 - F(c))^{(n-1)}$. The derivative of equation (15) with respect to a gives the following first-order condition:

$$(16) \qquad \beta'(\hat{c})\big(1 - G(c)\big) + \big(\beta(\hat{c}) - c\big)\big(-g(\hat{c})\big) = 0$$

where $-g(c) = d(1 - G(c))/dc$. In a symmetric equilibrium $c = \hat{c}$, so (16) can be rewritten as

$$(17) \qquad \frac{d}{dc}\big(1 - G(c)\big)\beta(c) = -cg(c).$$

Integrating both sides yields

$$(18) \qquad \beta_{FPSB}(c) = \frac{1}{1 - G(c)}\int_{c}^{\bar{c}} zg(z)dz = E\Big[c^{(1,n-1)}\Big|c^{(1,n-1)} \geq c\Big]$$

with the integration constant $C = 0$ for $\beta(\bar{c}) = \bar{c}$. Integration by parts gives

(19)
$$\beta_{FPSB}(c) = c + \int_c^{\bar{c}} \frac{1 - G(z)}{1 - G(c)} dz = c + \int_c^{\bar{c}} \frac{(1 - F(z))^{(n-1)}}{(1 - F(c))^{(n-1)}} dz$$

For β_{FPSB} to be smaller than $c + \Delta$, we need

$$\beta_{FPSB}(c) = c + \int_c^{\bar{c}} \frac{1 - G(z)}{1 - G(c)} dz = c + \int_c^{\bar{c}} \frac{(1 - F(z))^{(n-1)}}{(1 - F(c))^{(n-1)}} dz < \Delta$$

as a minimum requirement.

In a second step, we show that if everyone else behaves according to this strategy, it is indeed not optimal to bid more than $c + \Delta$. Assuming that a bidder bids such that he never goes bankrupt yields the following profit function

(20)
$$\pi(\hat{c}, c) = \left(\beta(\hat{c}) - c + \Delta(\rho - 1) \right) \left(1 - F(\hat{c}) \right)^{(n-1)}.$$

Maximizing this expression with respect to $\hat{c}$ and — in a symmetric equilibrium — setting $\hat{c} = c$ yields

(21)
$$\beta(c) = \frac{\beta'(c)(1 - F(c))}{(n-1)f(c)} + c - \Delta\rho + \Delta.$$

This solution for the optimal bid $\beta(c)$ is smaller than $c + \Delta$ whenever

(22)
$$\rho \geq \frac{\beta'(c)(1 - F(c))}{(n-1)f(c)\Delta}.$$

Using the fact that $(1 - F(c)) \leq 1$ and $\beta'(c) \leq 1$ we have the sufficient condition

(23)
$$n \geq 1 + \frac{1}{\Delta\rho f(c)}.$$

This also implies that the probability of having high costs

must be sufficiently small as otherwise bidding below the high-cost level would not be profit-maximizing.

Proof for Bidding Function FPSB, n Small

PROOF. We have already derived the result that bidders which bid below the threshold will bid according to the equilibrium bidding function of proposition 2. Hence, for $c > c^*$:

$$\beta(c) = c + \int_c^{\bar{c}} \frac{1 - G(z)}{1 - G(c)} dz.$$

We also showed that maximizing the profit of a bidder that never goes bankrupt (equation (20)) leads to the following differential equation (in a symmetric equilibrium):

(24) $$\beta'(c)\big(1 - G(c)\big) - \beta(c)g(g) = -cg(c) - (1 - \rho)\Delta g(c)$$

where $-g(c) = d(1 - G(c))/dc$. The last equation can be rewritten as

(25) $$\frac{d}{dc}\big(1 - G(c)\big)\beta(c) = -cg(c) - (1 - \rho)\Delta g(c).$$

Integrating both sides yields

(26) $$\beta(c) = \frac{1}{1 - G(c)} \int_c^{\bar{c}} zg(z)dz + (1 - \rho)\Delta + C$$

with the integration constant C. Integration by parts gives

(27) $$\beta(c) = c + \int_c^{\bar{c}} \frac{1 - G(z)}{1 - G(c)} dz + (1 - \rho)\Delta + C.$$

As the bid of the bidder with costs of c^* has to satisfy $\beta(c^*)$ $= c^* + \Delta$, C is:

$$\rho\Delta - \int_{c^*}^{\bar{c}} \frac{1 - G(z)}{1 - G(c^*)} dz.$$

BIBLIOGRAPHY

ARDITI D. - KOKSAL A. - KALE S., «Business Failure in the Construction Industry», *Engineering, Construction and Architectural Management*, no. 7, pages 120-132, 2000.
ANTON J. - YAO D., «Split Awards, Procurement, and Innovation», *RAND, Journal of Economics*, no. 20, pages 538-552, 1989.
ARVAN L. - LEITE A., «Cost Overruns in Long-Term Projects», *International Journal of Industrial Organization*, no. 8, pages 443-467, 1990.
BAJARI P. - TADELIS S., «Incentives versus Transaction Costs: A Theory of Procurement Contracts», *RAND, Journal of Economics*, no. 32, pages 387-407, 2001.
BOARD S., «Bidding into the Red: A Model of Post Auction Bankruptcy», *Working Paper*, University of Toronto, 2005.
BULOW J. - KLEMPERER P., «Prices and the Winner's Curse», *RAND, Journal of Economics*, no. 33, pages 1-21, 2002.
CALVERAS A. - GANUZA J. - HAUK E., «Wild Bids. Gambling for Resurrection in Procurement Contracts», *Journal of Regulatory Economics*, no. 26, pages 41-68, 2004.
ENGEL A.R. - GANUZA J. - HAUK E. - WAMBACH A., «Managing Risky Bids», to be published in *Handbook of Procurement*, Cambridge University Press, 2006.
EUROPEAN COMMISSION ENTERPRISE SECTION, «Abnormally Low Tenders», *www.europa.eu.int.*, 1999.
GANUZA J., «Los sobrecostes en las obras publicas. Un analisis economico del caso español», *Economia Industrial*, no. 318, pages 111-122, 1997.
— —, «Competition and Cost Overruns. Optimal Misspecification in Procurement Contracts», *Working Paper*, Universitat Pompeu Fabra, 2003.
GILBERT R. - KLEMPERER P., «An Equilibrium Theory of Rationing», *RAND, Journal of Economics*, no. 31, pages 1-21, 2000.
GRESIK T., «Rationing Rules and European Central Bank Auctions», *Journal of International Money and Finance*, no. 20, pages 793-808, 2001.
HARSTAD R. - BORDLEY R., «Lottery Qualification Auctions», *Advances in Applied Microeconomics*, no. 6, pages 157-183, 1996.
HENRIOD E. - LANTRAN J.M., *Trends in Contracting, Practice for Civil Works*, World Bank, 2000.
IOANNOU P. - LEU S., «Average Bid Method-Competitive Bidding Strategy», *Journal of Construction Engineering and Management*, no. 119, pages 131-147, 1993.
KRISHNA V., «Auction Theory», *Academic Press*, San Diego, 2002.
LEWIS T., «Reputation and Contractual Performance in Long-Term Projects», *RAND, Journal of Economics*, no. 17, pages 141-157, 1986.
LUPP W., *Objektivität, Transparenz und Nachprüfbarkeit der Angebotswertung bei der Vergabe öffentlicher Bauaufträge*, Univ. Diss., Munich, 1992.
MANELLI A. - VINCENT D., «Optimal Procurement Design», *Econometrica*, no. 63, pages 591-620, 1995.
MATTHEWS S., «A Technical Primer in Auction Theory», *mimeo*, Northwestern University, 1995.
MILGROM P., *Putting Auction Theory to Work*, Cambridge University Press, Cambridge, 2004.
PARLANE S., «Procurement Contracts under Limited Liability», *The Economic and Social Review*, no. 34, pages 1-21, 2003.

PECK M. - SCHERER F.M., *The Weapons Acquisition Process: an Economic Analysis*, Harvard University Press, Cambridge, 1962.

PERRY M. - SAKOVICS J., «Auctions for Split-Award Contracts», *Journal of Industrial Economics*, no. 51, pages 215-242, 2003.

ROELOFS M.R., «Common Value Auctions with Default: An Experimental Approach», *Experimental Economics*, no. 5, pages 233-252, 2002.

WAEHRER K., «A Model of Auction Contracts with Liquidated Damages», *Journal of Economic Theory*, no. 67, pages 531-555, 1995.

WAMBACH A., «A Simple Result for Revenue in Share Auctions», *Economics Letters*, no. 75, pages 405-408, 2002.

WHITE M.J., «The Corporate Bankruptcy Decision», *Journal of Economic Perspectives*, no. 3, pages 129-151, 1989.

WORLDBANK, «Closing a Business», *www.worldbank.org*, 2004.

ZHENG C.Z., «High Bids and Broke Winners,» *Journal of Economic Theory*, no. 100, pages 129-171, 2001.

Bid Average Methods in Procurement

Gian Luigi Albano · **Milo Bianchi** · **Giancarlo Spagnolo**

Consip S.p.A., Rome   Stockholm School   Consip S.p.A., Rome
                     of Economics   and
                                      Stockholm School of Economics

Procurement awarding mechanisms based on average price have been advocated to soften price competition and reduce cost overruns. We show that their theoretical support is shaky. When the bid closest to the average is awarded, firms submit identical bids, making the selection extremely costly and random, without reducing opportunistic behaviors ex-post. When instead the bid closest and below the average is awarded, the equilibrium is very sensitive to firms' production and participation costs. Either it displays tougher competition than in a first price auction, or it induces firms to randomize their bids. [JEL Classification: D44, H57]

1. - Introduction

Bid Average Methods (BAMs) award procurement contracts based on the average price submitted by competing suppliers at the tendering stage. In recent years, different countries have applied these mechanisms, mainly in construction industry, as an alternative to low-bid methods (where the awarding rule assigns a contract to the low-bid firm). The main reason why BAMs are becoming popular seems that, according to their advocates, they soften price competition, thereby reducing the likelihood of cost overrun and consequent costly renegotiation at the contract execution stage.

In this article, we provide a critical assessment of these methods. In Section 2, we describe a number of different forms BAMs have

The Authors wish to thank Laura Carpineti and Federico Dini of Consip Research Unit for their help and useful discussion.

taken in practice. Broadly speaking, these can be viewed as (variants of) two main awarding rules: in the first, the bid closest to the average wins; in the second, the winning bid is the one closest and below the average. In Section 3, we compare BAMs with other more established methods, namely beauty contests and negotiations, which may prove more suitable if one needs to soften or suppress all together price competition. In fact, a higher awarding price may help — though at a very high cost — when cost overruns are only due to suppliers' inaccurate estimates of the cost of serving the contract or to the emergence of unforeseen contingencies. However, it need not reduce the incentives for an opportunistic contractor to claim cost overruns, and require a higher compensation, once the contract has been signed.

In Section 4, we analyze in detail the distortions in bidding behavior the various forms of BAMs observed in reality tend to produce. When the bid closest to the average is awarded, firms have incentive to coordinate on a collusive equilibrium: they submit identical bids, making the selection extremely costly and random. When instead the bid closest and below the average is awarded, firms' incentive to coordinate falls. Still, the auction may display collusive behaviors since existing cartels are easier to sustain than under a standard low-bid rule. Moreover, the resulting equilibrium is very sensitive to firms' production costs. If one firm has a large comparative advantage in terms of efficiency, it will be selected, but price competition will be harsher, not softer, than with a low-bid method. Otherwise, the equilibrium will involve randomization. This may make the outcome very hard to predict by the procurement agency.

In Section 5, we analyze the suppliers' decision to submit a bid in case participation is costly. First, we show that BAMs generally increase participation, by giving some chance of winning also to less efficient firms, but equilibrium prices increase with the number of firms submitting an offer. Second, we show that when the bid closest and below the average is awarded, the outcome becomes equivalent to a simpler and more standard low-bid competitive tendering. Section 6 concludes stressing that the popularity of BAMs remains mainly a puzzle for the procurement scholar.

2. - Bid Average Methods in Procurement: Examples and Justifications

2.1 *Examples*

A: *Florida Department of Transportation (USA)*

Florida Department of Transportation (FDOT) has adopted the bid average method. This method is considered the best solution when there is ample competition. Concretely, two main scenarios are distinguished. When three or four bidders participate, the bid closest to the average is selected. When five or more contractors bid, the low bid and the high bid are excluded, and the bid closest to the average of the remaining bids is selected. If there are irregularities in the bid, the bid is thrown out, and the next closest to the average is selected.

The method is advocated for *(i)* getting the contractor to bid a true and reasonable cost for a project, and *(ii)* minimizing claims and cost overruns. Until 2001, only four FDOT projects (mainly mowing contracts) had used this technique. According to FDOT the intent of having contractors bid a more realistic cost, thereby minimizing cost overruns, has borne results, as these contracts have only overrun by 4%. FDOT expressed the view that BAM bidding is preferable when a "low bid" is anticipated to be a significant problem. This situation is likely to arise when inexperienced or unsophisticated constructors bid on small maintenance projects.

B: *State of New York (USA)*

The Procurement Services Group of the State of New York Executive Department[1] has formulated an even more convoluted awarding criterion for buying asphalt. The method of award requires a five-step procedure:

---

[1] Tendering procedure issued on 10th November 2004 for commodity group 31501 - Liquid Bituminous Materials.

1. An "average price" is calculated based on the price of all bids submitted.

2. Any bid that exceeds the "average price" by more than 50% will be made Awarding Pending.

3. A "revised average price" is calculated after removal of those over 50%.

4. Any remaining bids that do not exceed the "revised average price" increased by 10% will receive a contract award.

5. Any contractor given an "Award Pending" may become eligible for award by reducing their price(s) within the parameters of point 4.

C: Italy

The Italian National Agency for Information Technology in the Public Administration (CNIPA) pursues a variety of institutional goals. Among other things, it sets the guidelines for designing, implementing and managing acquisitions of IT solutions for the Italian Public Administration. Among the set of awarding rules suggested in CNIPA (2006)'s guidelines there is one special variant of the bid average method. More specifically, suppose that the tendering process allocates at most N ($0 < N < 100$) points to an economic offer and $(100 - N)$ to a technical offer. Consider firm i submitting an offer equal to p_i. Firm i's economic score is determined as follows: If $p_i < a * K$, then firm i gets all economic points (N); otherwise it gets

$$N * [p_{max} - p_i] / [p_{max} - a * K],$$

where p_{max} is the highest among all tenders, a is the average tender, and K is a "correction coefficient" between 0 and 1 (generally around .8 and .9).

Two features of the awarding rule are worth noticing. First, if tenders are not too concentrated and K is high enough, say .9, the CNIPA's variant of the bid award method allocates all economic points to the lowest submitted tender and to all others below the "corrected" average. Thus, it is possible that different firms submitting different offers are awarded the same number of economic points. Second, firms submitting tenders above the "corrected average" get a number of points, which decrease with the distance from the "corrected average."[2]

A second variant used in Italy, reported by Ioannou and Leu (1993), awards the contract to the firm submitting the tender closer to the average *among those below the average*.

D: Peru

Article 4.3.13 of the Peruvian regulations for bidding and contracting for public works states (translation by Henriod and Lantran (2000)):

"An award will be made in accordance with the following procedure:

1) When three or more bids have been received:

a) The average of all bids and the base budget will be calculated.

b) All bids that lie 10 percent above and below this average will be eliminated.

c) The average of the remaining bids and the base budget will then be calculated.

d) The contract will be awarded to the bidder whose bid is immediately below the second average (or, should none of the bids lie below the second average, the award will be made to the bid which more closely approximates the average.)[3]

2) If less than three bids are received, the bidding agency may cancel the process, and award the contract to the lowest bidder or to the only bidder if this were the case.

---

[2] The variant suggested by CNIPA (2006) is equivalent to a linear scoring rule with an endogenously determined threshold. For more on scoring rules see Chapter 12 in DIMITRI N. - PIGA G. - SPAGNOLO G. (eds.) (2006).

[3] We put this in parenthesis because there must have been a mistake in the translation, unless a very novel concept of average has been developed such that the average may be smaller than all its components.

2.2 Research Discussing their Properties

While it sounds intuitive that BAMs may soften price competition, little effort has been devoted so far to explore how firms respond to a rule rewarding the bidder with the most accurate guess of the average bid. To the best of our knowledge, a formal model of the bid average method has been studied only by Ioannou and Leu (1993). The authors consider a model in which N firms submit sealed bids for a contract. Production costs are assumed to be private information, and each firm's bidding function is equal to its cost plus a mark-up. In "standard" auction theory, it is customary to make certain assumptions on the distribution of private costs. In the Independent Private Value model[4], for instance, private costs are modeled as independent and identically distributed random variables. If a symmetric equilibrium is to be characterized, it is normally assumed that bidders 2 to N follow a strictly monotonic (and differentiable) bidding function. Then one looks at the necessary conditions that the bidding function must satisfy in order it to be bidder 1's *best response*. Ioannou and Leu (1993) adopt quite a different approach. They consider firms' bid-to-cost ratios as the relevant random variables and compute the probability that a specific firm bid is the closest to the average. However, this is done by making no assumptions on the shape of other firms' bidding functions. The authors instead perform a Montecarlo simulation and show that firms' expected payoffs are always higher under the bid average method than under the low-bid method.

Bid average methods are also mentioned by Liu *et* al. (2000) and discussed by Henriod and Lantran (2000) and Engel and Wambach (2004). These last authors argue that the same specification of the bid average method studied by Ioannou ad Leu (1993) pushes all firms to choose the highest possible price even when production costs are private information. Thus, firms coordinate on a focal point, which leads to a random allocation of the contract. To be sure, Ioannou and Leu (1993) also recognize

---

[4] See KLEMPERER P. (2004).

that the bid average method has a collusive drawback. However, their argument differs from the one made by Engel and Wambach (2004), which is further developed in the current paper. Ioannou and Leu (1993) point out that some firms may have an incentive to create dummy bidders that submit identical offers to their affiliated firms. Thus dummy companies and the affiliated firms pull the average towards their own price. If the dummy bidder wins the contract, it simply passes the entire project to the affiliated contractor.

3. - Why Average Price Auctions? Alternative Allocations Mechanisms

The brief survey conducted in the previous section highlights that the practice of BAMs aims mainly at softening price competition in procurement tendering processes. However, it may appear contradictory to use a competitive awarding procedure that hinges on price, coupled with an awarding rule that is meant to limit price competition. If the latter turns out to be the procurer's main concern, one could argue for other allocation mechanisms that, in most cases, do not involve any price competition at all. In what follows, we consider two alternative and established allocation mechanisms that more directly reduce price competition: beauty contest and negotiations.

3.1 *Beauty Contests*

A "beauty contest" (or comparative tender) is an allocation/selection mechanism that specifies a number of criteria according to which firms' projects are evaluated. The contractor is the firm whose project shows the best "mix" of dimensions. At a first sight, a beauty contest is not very different from a procurement tendering process with multiple criteria whereby firms' offers contain both a technical and an economic component that are evaluated according to a scoring rule. However, there are two fundamental differences between a beauty contest and a competitive tendering procedure. In the former: *i)* the rule according to which different offers are evaluated is stated in much more generic terms, leaving more discretion to the buyer in evaluating qualitative aspects that are hard to codify in a formalized way, and in refusing suspicious or unrealistic bids; and *ii)* "prices" are not a crucial aspect, while they are paramount in the latter.

3.2 *Negotiations*

An even more effective alternative, often adopted in private procurement when the good or service procured is not standardized but customized to the buyer specific needs, is that of selecting one (or very few) reputable supplier(s), known to be able to meet the demand, and to negotiate sale conditions only with him (them). In this way, competition is under direct, full control. Negotiations are also used in public procurement, particularly for complex products or services that are hard to specify contractually, and where quality has complete priority over price concerns.[5]

3.3 *Comment*

As average price auctions, these alternative allocation mechanisms soften or suppress price competition, hence leaving a larger margin to the supplier. This reduces (though does not eliminate) the likelihood of cost overrun and renegotiation, to the extent that these are linked either to suppliers' mistakes in the ex-ante estimation of their cost, or to unforeseen contingencies

---

[5] For example, NASA, and its Italian counterpart ASI, have extremely detailed and effective methodologies to guide first the preliminary supplier selection process, based on direct inspection of potential suppliers production methods and capabilities; and then structured bilateral negotiations on the characteristics of the required good or service and on its price.

occurring after the project has started.[6] In addition, these are generally better than average price auctions, which, as described in the next section, may induce very problematic bidding behaviors.

While a procurement agency may try to insure against post-contractual problems by limiting price competition, it is important to consider the serious drawbacks induced by this strategy. First, and most obviously, all these methods may be extremely costly in terms prices to be paid to the winning firm. For example, as seen in the next section, in the standard average price auction the agency might end up paying its reservation price. Second, there exist alternative methods to directly purchase insurance that are generally more effective and less costly. For example, the agency can pay a specialized surety company to bear the risk of a non-performing winning firm. This is done by issuing a bond, specifying the amount to be paid to the agency in case the contractor defaults and the surety company does not resume the contract (see Ch. 13 in Dimitri, Piga and Spagnolo, eds., 2006). Third, it is not even clear that, higher prices help reducing cost overruns and hold-up problems. Indeed, standard economic theory identifies moral hazard as a major source of these issues, and in this respect the awarding prize, being sunk, is simply irrelevant. In other words, absent reputation or fairness concerns, high awarding price does not reduce a firm ability to behave opportunistically once the contract has been signed.

Hence, the last problem is contractual, and not linked to the awarding method. It should then be resolved by choosing the appropriate contracting strategy. In particular, if lock-in and unforeseen contingencies are important, then fix-price contracts are generally not advisable. In construction industry, for instance, the most common sources of changes in building construction are defective plans and specifications, and differing conditions than expected at the construction site. Thus, the initial contract

---

[6] In the construction of a new tunnel, for instance, excavation may be delayed, and even stopped, by the discovery of a particularly resistant rock that needs specific drilling machine.

suffers from some form of incompleteness which often leads to contentious adversarial negotiations. These are likely to arise whenever the initial contract is awarded by using a fixed-price competitive tendering, while if the contract has a cost-plus (or cost-reimbursement) nature, changes to the original specifications can be almost automatically included. In fact, by adopting a cost-plus contract (CPC) the buyer agrees to reimburse all (documented) production costs related to the project. Moreover, as argued in Bajari and Tadelis (2006), the buyer should not use a competitive tendering procedure to award such a contract, since this procedure may fail to choose the most efficient supplier. Whenever possible, the agency should instead search among the most reputable firms and choose one to negotiate with and agree on the terms of the CPC.

4. - The Drawbacks of Bid Average Methods

4.1 *Pro-Collusive Aspects of the Florida Type*

Three firms compete for procuring a service. Each firm $i = 1$, 2, 3 bears a cost c_i for procuring the service. For illustration, assume that competitors know each other's efficiency levels, since for example they have been interacting in the market for quite a while.[7] However, the procurement agency cannot distinguish low-cost from high-cost suppliers. Without loss of generality, we assume that

$$c_3 > c_2 > c_1,$$

that is, firm 1 is the most efficient firm whereas firm 3 is the least efficient. The procurement agency publicly announces a reserve price $r > c_3$ which represents the highest price at which it is willing to buy the service. Firms submit sealed-bid offers (p_1, p_2, p_3). The

---

[7] Moreover, each of them knows that all others know his efficiency and so on. Formally, we are assuming that production costs are "common knowledge" among the competing firms.

winner is the firm whose bid is closest to the average of all admissible bids. Thus firm i's payoff writes

$$\Pi_i\left(p_i, a\right) = \begin{cases} p_i - c_i & \text{if} \left|p_i - a\right| < \left|p_j - a\right|, \forall j \neq i, \\ 0, & \text{otherwise} \end{cases}$$

where a is the average of all tenders, that is, $(p_1 + p_2 + p_3)/3$. Moreover, we also assume that ties are broken by using a random device that assigns equal probability to each winning offer. Notice that ties can only arise when all firms submit the same price.

The bid average method provide firms with an incentive to submit exactly the same tenders. This can be easily seen by using the following line of reasoning. Suppose that firm 1 were to believe that firms 2 and 3 are willing to submit $c_3 < p_2 = p_3 = p < r$. Does firm 1 have an incentive to submit any p_1 different than p? Notice first that if $p_1 = p$, the average $a = p$ and firm 1's payoff is $(p - c_1)/3 > 0$. Suppose, instead, that firm 1 deviates by submitting $p_1 < p$.[8] The new average is $a_1 = (1/3) p_1 + (2/3) p$. Clearly, the value p has a higher weight in the average than p_1. Thus, p is closer to the new average than p_1, which implies that firm 1 gets a payoff equal to zero.

To sum up, if any of the three firms believes that the other two competitors are willing to submit the same tender (higher than the reserve price), the remaining firm finds it profitable to submit exactly the same tender as well.[9] The resulting outcome is that the three firms will end up submitting the same tenders and the winner will selected by a random device. Our analysis suggests two main conclusions:

— The first variant of Bid-Average Method provides a clear incentive to firms to find a "focal point". This is arguably collusive, since the higher the focal point the higher firms' profit.

---

[8] This is without loss of generality. The same line of reasoning would hold with $p_1 > p$.

[9] More formally, any profile of tenders $p_1 = p_2 = p_3 = p < r$ constitutes a Nash equilibrium (in pure strategies) of the Bid-Average tendering game.

— The allocation of the contract may be inefficient since the probability that the low-cost firm is awarded the contract is 1/3.

It can also be proven that firms do not have an incentive to submit different tenders provided that they are all lower than the reserve price, but higher than the highest production cost (c_3).

4.2 *Additional Pro-Collusive Aspects of the NYS Type (Coalition Proofness)*

When firms manage to coordinate on the same bid, the variant used by the State of New York described in Section 2.1 induces the same outcome as the one generated by the BAM in Florida. To see this, suppose that the three competing firms submit the same $p \leq r$. Since the average will be exactly p, no firm will be ever given an Award Pending. Thus, there is no need to compute a "corrected average." Being all identical, bids will not exceed the average by 10%, so all firms will receive a contract award.[10]

A closer look reveals two subtler aspects of the variant used by the State of New York. First, it makes coordination feasible even when some firms accidentally do not submit the "right" bid. To see this, consider a very simple numerical example. Suppose that 10 firms try to coordinate on a price for the contract of USD 90k. Upon submitting their offers, one firm, say firm 1, "accidentally" bids USD 150k. The resulting average is then 96k, and firm 1 is given an Award Pending. The corrected average is 90k and firms 2 to 10 are given a contract award. However, firm 1 can still correct its mistake and submit the "right" bid (90k) thus obtaining a contract award as well.

The second aspect of the variant used by the State of New York concerns a pro-collusive mechanism, which is built in the awarding rule. Suppose that all potential competitors, say 10 firms, form a cartel and coordinate to submit the highest possible price, that is, the reserve price. Under the variant used by FDOT it is possible that some of the firms in the cartel, say five out of

---

[10] That is, if the State of NY is buying USD 10M of asphalt, each contractor gets 1/3 of the contract. This is equivalent ex ante to getting the whole contract with probability 1/3 according to the variant used by FDOT.

ten firms, agree to make a joint deviation by submitting a lower price. Such a deviation would consist in submitting an offer that makes the five defecting firms the sole winners. Thus, the variant of FDOT may induce coordination; it cannot prevent "joint deviations" or deviations made by sub-coalitions. Under the variant used by the State of New York, instead, if the joint deviation is such that the non-deviating firms are left above 50% of the average, they are still given an Award Pending and have still a chance of modifying their bids to react to deviating firms' offer. Thus, deviations by sub-coalitions are less profitable than under the FDOT variant.

4.3 *Instability and Collusion in the BAMs Used in Italy*

The two variants of the BAM used in Italy destroy firms' incentive to coordinate on the same price. In the variant suggested by CNIPA, this is immediately seen since all firms get a number of economic points equal to zero if they submit exactly the same price. In the second variant, whereby the winning firm is the one submitting the tender closest to the average *among those below the average*, we can also show that it is not in the firms' interest to submit the same offer.

To see this last point, assume first that when firms submit the same offers — so no bid is below the average — each firm is awarded the contract with equal probability. Consider the same three-firm environment studied in Section 4.1. Suppose again that firms 2 and 3 submit the same tender $p > r$. If $p_1 = p$ then firm 1's payoff is $(p - c_1)/3$. However, firm 1 can raise its payoff by submitting an offer just below p, say p_1'. The resulting new average would lie in the interval (p_1', p), and firm 1's offer would be the unique offer below the average. If p_1' is lower than, but sufficiently close to p (say $p - 1\text{cent}$), firm 1's deviation yields a payoff $(p_1' - c_1) > (p - c_1)/3$.

While not providing an incentive to coordinate on a focal point, this variant still makes deviations from an existing collusive agreement more costly than, say, the low-bid awarding method.

Consider a procurement contract for supplying a number of identical laptops, with a reserve price of €1,000 each. Suppose, for the sake of simplicity, that competition takes place on the price of the laptop only, so there are no technical points related to the various quality dimensions. $N > 2$ firms participate in the competitive procurement and adopt a simple collusive mechanism: firm "1" wins the contract by submitting an offer of €999/laptop while all other $(N-1)$ firms bid the reserve price.[11] Surplus is then shared. If the low-bid awarding rule is adopted, non-winning bidders can break the cartel by just offering €998. The cost of breaking the cartel is the same for all: by reducing the price by €1/laptop, any bidder is effectively able to break the agreement and win the contract.

Consider now the variant of the BAM whereby that awards the contract to the supplier whose bid is closest to the average, *but* below the average. Again, the cartel selects bidder 1 to win by submitting €999. The remaining $N-1$ bidders bid the reserve price. What is the amount a deviating bidder should submit in order to win the contract? How much does the deviation cost to him? Notice first that bidder 1 is indeed the winner since €999 is the only bid below the average, where the latter is equal to $(1/N)€999 + [(N-1)/N]€1000$. To win the competitive procurement a defecting bidder, say bidder 2, needs to place a bid such that all other bids remain above the average. It is easy to see that €998 is not low enough as under linear and lowest-bid scoring. To see this more clearly, consider the situation where $N=5$. Should bidder 2 submit €998 the average would be $(998+999+3(1000))/5 = 999.4$. With such an average, bidder 1 is still the winner. As a result, €998 is not sufficient for bidder 2 to win the competitive procurement. In order to be the winner, bidder 2 needs to bring the average below €999. Then he needs to bid a price b_{def} such that $(b_{def}+999+3(1000))/5 \leq 999$, which implies $b_{def} \leq €996$. More generally, when the number of colluding firms is N, then $b_{def} \leq (N-1)€999 - (N-2)€1000$.

---

[11] We assume in this example that prices have to be formulated as multiples of 1€.

The most interesting remark, though, is that the equilibrium outcome, i.e. the winning firm and offer, becomes very sensitive to the distribution of costs among the bidders. This is of course problematic since costs are typically unknown to the procurement agency, which will then face high uncertainty and instability. In fact, two competitive scenarios with slightly different distributions of costs may lead to extremely different outcomes. In particular, if the most efficient firm can supply at much lower costs than its competitors, it will win by offering an even *lower* bid than in the case of low-bid competitive tendering. If it cannot afford such a low bid, firms are induced to bid in a "strange" (and sometimes unpredictable) way. More precisely, in this case firms' optimal strategy would involve some randomization. Rather than a single offer, each firm would submit a probability distribution over a number of offers, i.e. firm will submit the offer p_i^1 with probability $q_i^1 < 1$, the offer p_i^2 with probability $q_i^2 < 1$, and so on.

We can see this argument in more details, considering again the environment described in Section 4.1. First, suppose that firm 1 has strong efficiency advantages with respect to the competitors. That is, let for now

$$c_1 < 2c_2 - c_3$$

In this case, an equilibrium requires firm 1 to win by submitting an offer $p_1 = 2c_2 - c_3$. In fact, suppose $p_2 = c_2$ and $p_3 = c_3$. The average bid is c_2 and firm 1 wins, while firm 2 and 3 cannot lower their bids any further.[12] In this case, the method is able to award the most efficient firm, but it is exacerbating, rather than limiting, price competition. In fact, firm 1 is bidding below the price needed to win a low-bid competitive tendering ($2c_2 - c_3 < c_2$).

Suppose instead $c_1 > 2c_2 - c_3$. The previous strategies are no

---

[12] Since firms 2 and 3 are getting zero profit, they could deviate at no cost; hence, the equilibrium is not robust. Suppose for example firm 3 submits $p_3 = r$. Now our condition becomes stricter: firm 1 will have to bid $2c_2 - r$ in order to win. Firm 3 bid is part of the equilibrium if its offer will always be above the average, even if it bids its production cost.

longer feasible, since firm 1 will not bid below its marginal cost. Instead, we argue that a strategy profile in which all firms submit a single offer with probability one cannot be part of an equilibrium. We can easily show this by contradiction. Suppose that firms submit (p_1, p_2, p_3) with probability one. Without loss of generality, consider the following strategy profile

$$c_1 < p_1 < p_2 < p_3 < r.$$

Two relevant scenarios may arise. If $p_2 < a$, firm 2 is the winner, so firm 1 has an incentive to profitably deviate by bidding marginally higher than p_2. Firms will start increasing their bids, but we know that $p_1 = p_2 = p_3 = r$ cannot be an equilibrium since all firm will then have an incentive to undercut their competitors. If instead $p_2 > a$, firm 1 is the winner, so firm 2 has an incentive to profitably deviate by reducing its bid to a level marginally higher than p_1. Firms will decrease their bids up to their marginal costs, where, given that $c_1 > 2c_2 - c_3$, the average bid exceeds $p_2 = c_2$, and we are back to the previous scenario.[13] Hence, there exists no equilibrium such that the three firms submit a single offer with certainty.

We can draw two main conclusions. First, this particular variant destroys firms' incentive to coordinate on a focal point generated by other BAMs, so the tendering procedure may have a pro-competitive effect. Nonetheless, it cannot be considered fully competitive, since collusive agreements are easier to sustain than in the case of a low-bid rule. Second, the equilibrium behaviour either requires the most efficient firm to submit a very low bid (hence intensifying rather than softening price competition) or it involves randomization (hence producing an unpredictable outcome from the procurement agency's viewpoint as well). In essence, similar competitive scenarios may generate very different awarding prices.

---

[13] Note that the same argument applies to the cases where either $p_1=p_2<p_3$ or $p_1<p_2=p_3$.

5. - In Further Research of a Rationale: BAMs and Costly Participation

The discussion so far has assumed that each firm, even when expecting to make zero profit, was submitting a bid. Moreover, all offers were important for the description of the equilibrium, since in BAMs the winning bid depends on all other submitted bids. We can now relax this assumption, leaving each firm the possibility to decide whether or not to participate in the competitive tendering. To make the discussion interesting, we consider the case where participation is costly. When submitting a bid, each firm has to pay some $\varepsilon > 0$, which can be thought as an entry fee or, more generally, as the cost to be spent in order to acquire information about the auction and to decide the bidding strategy in a sensible way. Given this ε, it is clear that no firm will participate if it expects zero profit in equilibrium, i.e. if it will have to bid at its marginal cost or if it has zero probability of getting the prize. This simple observation changes somewhat the results in the previous sections, as we now describe in more details.

Consider first the method where the winner is simply the bidder closest to the average. As discussed in Section 4.1 firms will submit the same offer, somewhere between the highest production cost and the reserve price. These are still equilibria in a game with costly participation, if ε is low enough, but we now have an even larger set of possible outcomes. In fact, suppose there are n potential competitors, ordered in term of efficiency:

$$r > c_n > c_{n-1} > \dots > c_2 > c_1$$

One can show that there exists an equilibrium where only the first k most efficient firms enter and bid c_{k+1}. For example, one can have that firm 1, 2 and 3 enter and bid c_4. Given this, no other firm is willing to enter, since in order to win, it will have to bid c_4, which never exceeds its production cost. The average bid will then be c_4 and, for the same reason explained in Section 4.1, no participating firm has incentive to deviate. Whether this more efficient equilibrium or some other will actually take place is something one cannot say a priori. This depends on how firms manage to coordinate, which incentives they have to do so, hence in particular on the distribution of production costs and reservation price.[14]

Notice however that in any equilibrium at least three firms will submit a bid.[15] Hence, BAMs generally increase participation, by giving some chance of winning also to the less efficient firms. Moreover, having a large number of competing firms now is not good news for the procurement agency: the higher the participation the higher will be equilibrium prices, i.e. the further we will move from the most efficient outcome.

Despite affecting participation and the set of possible outcomes, costly entry does not change the essential feature described above: simple average method pushes towards homogeneity of bids, thereby strongly limiting (or destroying) the ability to screen and opening up to the possibility to extremely costly collusive behaviours.

Now consider the variants of BAMs used in Italy. In this case, a small entry cost makes a great difference, revealing once again the instability of this method. In fact, the "strange" outcomes described in Section 4.3 disappear: irrespective of the strength of its efficiency advantage, firm 1 will win the auction by bidding (slightly below) c_2. Given firms' incentives to bid slightly below the average, bids will keep decreasing and the most inefficient firms will then prefer not to participate (and not waste the ε). In equilibrium, only firm 1 will bid and will make an offer exactly sufficient to keep all the other firms, and in particular firm 2, out of the competition. Hence, we get the very same outcome of a low-bid competitive tendering. At this point, it is not clear why one should use a method producing the same outcome as the most standard tendering format. After all, awarding rules should aim

---

[14] These determine for example whether firms 1, 2, 3 prefer getting 1/3 of a smaller prize (c_4) rather than increasing the prize (up to r) but then having to share it with a larger pool of participants.

[15] If only firm 1 and 2 are participating, they both have the incentive to increase their bid. This would not change their chance of winning (1/2) but it would increase the size of the prize. By bidding higher than c_3, however, they will attract firm 3 into the competition.

at simplicity, which is a way to improve transparency and reduce costly litigations; hence, this variant of BAMs cannot be defended because of equivalence with low-bids methods.

6. - Conclusion

We have reviewed the increasingly popular Bid Average Methods and their strategic implications, which have proven often in contradiction with what claimed by their advocates. The major reason behind the adoption of BAMs is that they are supposed to soften price competition, push competing firms to coordinate on a "true and reasonable" bidding price, and hence reduce *ex-post* transaction costs linked to delay and wasteful renegotiations following cost overrun. We have argued that there are no theoretical arguments to support these claims. If anything, standard economic analysis would instead predict that firms will coordinate to bid on the highest admissible price. We have also shown that a variant of BAMs, where the winner is the one closest and below the average, may be very sensitive to the specific features of the strategic environment (distribution of production costs, participation costs...) hence generally quite unpredictable from the procurement agency viewpoint. At best, its outcome can be replicated by a simple low-bid tendering format.

More generally, the awarding price affects ex-post cost overrun and renegotiation problems only if they are linked to innocent mistakes and exogenous shocks, and not at all when these originate from opportunistic behaviour of suppliers. In any case, these are better handled through cost-plus-contracts, surety bonds, or alternative awarding methods described in Section 3.

A possible line of defence of BAMs may still be that there are situations where none of the proposed alternatives is viable. For example, given public procurement regulation to enhance accountability and prevent corruption, one may need to insure against "excessive" price competition while not being able to: identify the most suitable contractor and privately negotiate with it; rely on any surety firm; evaluate discretionally the qualitative aspects of the offer... Hence, in a sense, despite giving up most of the benefits of competition (and in particular failing to select the most efficient firm and pay the lowest price) BAMs would represent a "compromise" between a number of conflicting requirements and constraints. It is clear however that, even accepting this line of reasoning, one cannot advocate any general role for these methods, being they dependent on a particular situation, where many conditions need to be satisfied simultaneously.

In conclusion, our analysis has not revealed any convincing and general way to rationalize the fundamental tension inherent to BAMs, which soften price competition while at the same time using a competitive awarding rule. For these reasons, BMAs remain largely a puzzle, which calls for further attention by scholars and scrutiny by practitioners.

BIBLIOGRAPHY

BAJARI P. - HOUGHTON S. - TADELIS S., «Bidding for Incomplete Contracts: An Empirical Analysis», *NBER, Working Papers*, vol. 12051, 2006.

CNIPA, «Appalto pubblico di forniture ICT: manuale applicativo», *I Quaderni*, vol. 24, 2006.

DIMITRI N. - PIGA G. - SPAGNOLO G. (eds.), *Handbook of Procurement*, Cambridge University Press, forthcoming, 2006.

ENGEL A.R. - WAMBACH A., «Risk Management in Procurement Auctions», University of Erlangen-Nuernberg, *Working Paper*, 2004.

HENRIOD E. - LANTRAN J.-M., «Trends in Contracting Practice for Civil Works», World Bank, [On-line], Available at *www.worldbank.org*, 2002.

IOANNOU P. G. - LEU S.S., «Average-Bid Method: Competitive Bidding Strategy», *Journal of Construction Engineering and Management*, vol. 119, pages 131-147, March 1993.

KLEMPERER P., *Auctions: Theory and Practice*, Princeton University Press, 2004.

LAI K.K. - LIU S.L. - WANG S.Y., «Multiple Criteria Models for Evaluation of Competitive Bids», *IMA, Journal of Mathematics Applied In Business and Industry*, vol. 11, no. 3, pages 151-160, 2000.

MCAFEE P. - MCMILLAN J., «Bidding for Contracts: a Principal-Agent Analysis», *RAND, Journal of Economics*, vol. 17, pages 326-338, 1986.

OHIO DEPARTMENT OF TRANSPORTATION AND TRAUNER CONSULTING SERVICES, INC., *Six-State Survey of Construction Administration Practices and procedures*, 2001.

II - EFFICIENCY IN PROCUREMENT

Combinatorial Procurement Auctions: A Collusion Remedy?

Anders Lunander - **Jan-Eric Nilsson**
Örebro University   Swedish National Road
                         and Transport Research Institute,
                         Borlänge

This paper presents the outcome of an experiment where the standard one shot sealed bid procurement auction for two identical goods provides the benchmark. Inducing scale economies a combinatorial auction is applied on the situation with non-linear costs. The mechanisms are first run without, and then with the possibility for subjects to communicate prior to bidding. There are two human and one computer bidder in each period. It is demonstrated that the combinatorial mechanism is able to enhance efficiency and that subjects are less inclined to cooperate under the combinatorial auction than under the standard bidding format.
[JEL Classification: D44, D78]

1. - Introduction

Many public procurement auctions comprise a large number of identical or similar contracts allocated at the same time. One example is the procurement of services for cleaning local community offices, schools and homes for elderly etc. During all 2002, Stockholm City Council for instance invited bids for 168 separate objects of this nature. Another example is the procurement of contracts for road maintenance activities. The Swedish road authority annually lets about 50 similar contracts

The Authors are grateful for comments on previous versions from Lance Brännman, Arne Andersson and participants at the 2003 North American Meeting of the ESA. Funding from the Swedish Competition Authority, the National Rail Adminstration and from Vinnova is gratefully acknowledged.

for painting of road markings. Moreover, the authority solicits bids for some 100 large road pavement renewal projects per year.

One concern with the simultaneous letting of many similar contracts is that entrepreneurs' costs may not be linear in the number of contracts awarded. Because of capacity constraints, small firms can have low initial costs that increase with the number of contracts while large firms, with extensive capacity, can have considerable scale economies in winning an increasing number of contracts. As a result, a standard one shot, sealed bid procurement auction may fail to allocate contracts efficiently. In such cases, the use of more flexible bidding mechanisms, like the simultaneous ascending (descending) auctions or combinatorial auctions may increase efficiency and lower the procurer's cost.[1]

A second concern is that the sequential or (almost) simultaneous letting of a large number of similar contracts facilitates coordination of bidder behavior. The contracts may be awarded for short time periods, often for one year at a time. This makes it possible for colluders to punish possible deviators from an agreement no more than one year after that a break of an agreement takes place. Anecdotal evidence also suggests that bidders sometimes win a larger number of contracts than they have capacity to handle and therefore have to negotiate with the bidders that have not won contracts — i.e. that have spare capacity — to be able to honor their submission. *Ex post* communication of this sort lowers the barrier for *ex ante* contacts at subsequent events.

Collusion and bid rigging schemes is a serious problem in many auctions and the number of studies within the auction literature addressing different aspects of collusive behavior grows (see for example summaries in Pesendorfer, 2000; Krishna, 2002; and Aoyagi, 2003). Inspired by the allocation of spectrum licenses in the US, much of this work focuses bidding behavior in ascending, multiple-object auctions when bidders collude by signaling or communicating.[2]

---

[1] See LUNANDER A. - NILSSON J.E. (2004) for a listing of some studies.

[2] For studies on signalling in a single object environment, see for example SHERSTYUK K. (1999, 2002).

Kwasnica (2000) provides an analysis of collusion in a one-shot setting, and in particular the choice of cooperative strategies in private values, sealed bid auctions. He looks at bidding behavior when bidders are allowed to engage in pre play communication in situations with multiple objects. In his experiment five subjects bid in five simultaneous single object first price sealed bid auctions. Subjects were allowed to communicate between periods, but they were neither allowed to reveal their private values nor to discuss the use of side payments. He found that bidders formed collusive agreements and — in this restricted set of alternatives — tended to use bid rotation as strategy, that is, each of the five bidders was selected to be the sole bidder on one contract each.[3] A related theoretical study is Aoyagi (2003), modeling a dynamic bid rotation scheme where bidders collude through communication in repeated one-shot auctions. In this environment, bidders that communicate can compensate each other through dynamic bid rotation instead of using side payments.

Based on a wind-tunnel experiment, the present paper studies the vulnerability of different auction mechanisms to collusive behavior. In particular, we consider the role of pre play communication in three types of sealed bid procurement auctions where the procurer seeks to acquire multiple contracts with cost complementarities. The purpose of the paper is to see whether bidding behavior in general, and the choice of cooperative strategies in particular, is affected by the option to submit bundle bids, given complementarities and the presence of an automata bidder. In other words, do bidders have more difficulties to collude under a combinatorial auction than under standard simultaneous sealed bid auction?[4]

---

[3] See also GOSWANI G. *et* AL. (1996) for an experiment on the effect of pre play communication in uniform-price and discriminatory auctions of share.

[4] Within the multiple objects auction environment, very few studies have investigated cooperative agreements in combinatorial auctions. KELLY F. - STEINBERG R. (2000) describe a combinatorial auction procedure which essentially is a simultaneous multiple-round auction, but where bidders are allowed to submit package bids at a later stage of the auction. The mechanism is designed to make it more difficult for signaling with prices and thus to reduce the possibility of collusion.

We therefore compare allocation efficiency, procurer costs and participants' behavior under three different mechanisms. The first is a standard one shot sealed bid auction; the second is the same mechanism but with scale efficiencies in the number of contracts awarded; and the third is a combinatorial auction also with scale economies in the number of contracts. Each session starts with eight periods with the base-line design followed by a number of periods where subjects are able to communicate via a chat line prior to bidding in each period. Our results provide some support to the a priori conjecture that subjects are less able and/or inclined to form collusive agreements in a combinatorial auction than in the standard first price auction when synergies are present. Also, the combinatorial auction generates higher efficiency and lower procurement cost.

Our conjecture is that the combinatorial environment curbs the motive for bidders to set up and maintain a cartel. One reason is that a bidder can exploit cost synergies using bundle bids rather than by way of colluding. Even though the exposure problem inherent in the standard auction partly can be circumvented in our setting by means of a bidders' agreement, the option to submit a package bid may still be the preferred way to take advantage of the synergies. If colluders communicate ex ante to establish who should win each round, mutual trust is necessary and, moreover, if colluding by taking turns, the "wrong" party would win every now and then. A second and complementary reason for bidders to choose the narrow path, is that the calculation of an optimal collusive bid strategy when it is feasible to submit both single bids and a combinatorial bid, even in our simple environment with only two objects up for bidding, is not straight forward.

An important difference between our environment and that of previous experiments on collusion in multiple object auctions is that we, except for the human subjects, also make use of a computerized bidder that cannot be part of any collusive agreement. This mimics the potential threat from outsiders that the members of a cartel have to take into account when forming cooperative agreements. A price paid for increasing the realism of the setting is that it gets more difficult to isolate the bidders' behavioral pattern. In the absence of the computer, it would have been easier for bidders to collude which would may have made the (possible) impact of collusion on outcome more articulate.

The paper starts with a description of the experimental design (section 2), results in terms of efficiency and costs are presented in section 3, section 4 analyses bidding behavior and section 5 concludes.

2. - The Experimental Design

Three core features of our procurement experiment are the non-linearity of costs, the risk for collusion and the possibility to use combination bids. The cost aspect is handled in the following way. Subjects were invited to submit bids for two identical objects, A and B. The two bids are submitted simultaneously. Under the first treatment, the standard one-shot sealed bid auction, bids on A and B were evaluated independently and contracts awarded to the lowest bidder. Costs c_i, $i = A, B$ were induced by independent draws from a uniform distribution with the support [200, 300]. Under the second and third treatments, subjects had scale economies. This was implemented by letting the cost per object decrease with 10 or 20 percent (two different scale parameters were tested) if the same subject won both items. Profits (π) for a bidder j submitting the lowest bid $\tilde{b}_i^j$ on both objects A and B and therefore awarded both contracts was therefore $\pi^j = \sum_i (\tilde{b}_i^j - c_i^j)$ under treatment one, $\pi^j = \sum_i (\tilde{b}_i^j - \alpha \times c_i^j)$ under treatment two and $\pi^j = \tilde{b}_{A+B}^j - \sum_i \alpha \times c_i^j$ [or in case the bidder won with his two single bids $\pi^j = \sum_i (\tilde{b}_i^j - \alpha \times c_i^j)$] under treatment three; α is the scale factor ($\alpha = 0.8$ or 0.9).

The second feature of the experiment was to design a structure that allowed for collusion. In order to make it as simple as possible for bidders to collude, only two physical subjects were submitting bids for the contracts. In addition, bids submitted by a computer were used to avoid making the collusion sessions trivial. Subjects were informed that the computer would always submit a bid with $\hat{b} = 100 + 2/3\, c$ with c independently drawn from the same distribution as for the human subjects.[5] A draw of 240 would therefore generate a bid of 260 and the computer would never bid below 233 or above 300. The computer had no scale economies in the number of contracts awarded.

The collusion design was benchmarked against an initial number of periods where bidders could not communicate, where after a chat line was opened in order to facilitate collusion. Subjects were informed about different ways to cooperate; *(a)* after observing the cost draw, they could agree about which bid that each was to submit; *(b)* they could agree to take turns, and; *(c)* they could let one win all periods and share profits after leaving the classroom. The risk of being tricked by the other party was also emphasized.[6] No penalties for collusion were metered out.

The experiment's third feature was the possibility to use combination bids as a means to reduce the extent of collusion. Under the third treatment, the two human subjects were therefore given the possibility to submit bids not only on A and B in isolation but also on the combination AB. The bidder(s) behind the combination of bids that generated the lowest cost — i.e. awarding A and B to different subjects or both going to the same — was designated to be the winner.

To summarize, before each bidding period the subject was informed about which two independent costs draws that had been made for her. The subject knew that the other human subject and the automated bidder were given draws from the same distribution but did not know the draws of the others. Subjects were also informed that all cost draws had been made in advance and were stored in our computer. To simplify comparisons, the same draws were used across all sessions.

Based on this information, bids were to be submitted in order to maximize profits with no restrictions on bids, i.e. any strategy — not only the ones provided as examples — could be employed. Our

---

[5] This is the predicted risk neutral Nash equilibrium when $n = 3$ and costs drawn from $U \sim [200, 300]$. In the absence of theoretical predictions in environments with non-linear costs, we imposed this bid function in all three treatments on the computerized bidder in order to maintain constancy across the sessions.

[6] The reason for providing this information was to ensure that all subjects in the experiment had access to equal information about possible bidding strategies.

first treatment used the standard simultaneous first price sealed bid mechanism to award contracts and the second treatment introduced non-linearities in costs but still used the standard bidding principle. Also the third treatment had cost non-linearities but in addition, human subjects were given the possibility to submit bids not only on A and B in isolation but also on the combination AB. After each round of bidding, everyone was informed about who won at which price, but only the winner(s) could calculate profits.

Each session was initiated with two (trial) periods with an exchange rate of 0.5 followed by eight non-communication periods with the exchange rate 1.5. The session was then finalized with another eight periods plus a variable number of periods where communication was allowed, still with the 1.5 exchange rate. The final number of periods ($U \sim [1, 6]$) was decided by the experiment leader throwing a dice, which was not shown to the subjects until after the conclusion of the experiment. This was done to make subjects uncertain about which period was the final, i.e., to curb the risk for backward induction.

Bidders' show-up fee was SEK 150, with SEK 100 being a guarantee amount and SEK 50 a buffer against losses; also this part of the fee was to be kept if such losses were not incurred. Importantly, each human player in the auction was a team of two physical individuals. We did this in order to make it feasible for the two to talk to each other, and so to enhance the chance that they grasped the nature of the problem put to them. All earnings were therefore to be split between the two, all being economics students at Örebro University. Actual earnings for the two-hour sessions ranged from SEK 250 to 1200.[7]

3. - Results: Efficiency and Costs

A total of 14 experimental sessions were concluded during spring and fall semesters 2002. Table 1 summarizes the number of sessions allocated to each treatment and the number of periods concluded.

---

[7] At the time of the experiments, the price for a US$ was about SEK 9.

TABLE 1

NUMBER OF SESSIONS AND NUMBER OF PERIODS
UNDER DIFFERENT TREATMENTS

Treatment	# Sessions	Thereof with scale parameter		# periods with no chat	# periods allowing for chat	Total # periods	
I. Standard	4	–	–	32	52		84
II. Standard with non-linear costs	5	0.9	3	24	38	62	
		0.8	2	16	28	44	106
III. Combinatorial with non-linear costs	5	0.9	3	24	43	67	
		0.8	2	16	27	43	110
Sum	14			112	188		300

Results from the two initial trial periods in each session have been omitted throughout the analysis. We start by describing efficiency (3.1) and cost (3.2) properties of the mechanisms in this section. Section 4 will then report about bidding behavior and communication within each of the three mechanisms.

3.1 Efficiency

Table 2 summarizes efficiency, as defined by equation *(1)*, under the three treatments. This normalized efficiency measure provides a better fit than the standard measure to handle possible idiosyncrasies in the random draw of bidders' costs. A is the actual costs for the winners of fulfilling contracts, M is the lowest induced cost of fulfilment and N is the expected induced cost of a random allocation. For each period, N is computed as the total sum of the induced cost of all possible allocations of the two contracts among the three bidders. This sum is then dived by the number of possible allocations, which are (3^2) 9.

(1)
$$E = 1 - \frac{A - M}{N - M}$$

Table 2

EFFICIENCY ACROSS MECHANISMS[*]

Mechanism	Average efficiency - all periods	n	Average efficiency - periods with no communication	n	Average efficiency - periods allowing for communication	n
I. Standard	0.92	84	0.9	32	0.93	52
II. Standard with non-linear cost						
All	0.73	106	0.74	40	0.72	66
$\alpha = 0.9$	0.76	62	0.75	24	0.76	38
$\alpha = 0.8$	0.68	44	0.71	16	0.67	28
III. Combinatorial with non-linear cost						
All	0.89	110	0.91	40	0.88	70
$\alpha = 0.9$	0.86	67	0.88	24	0.85	43
$\alpha = 0.8$	0.95	43	0.97	16	0.93	27

[*] See Appendix for a table with std. dev. and t-tests of mean efficiency across mechanisms.

The possibility to communicate does not have any significant effect on efficiency in neither of the treatments. However, the introduction of scale economies in a standard first-price auction significantly reduces efficiency; only an average 73 percent of potential gains are actually realized in contrast to 92 percent when there are no scale economies. When the possibility to submit combination bids is introduced in treatment III, efficiency goes back to about 90 percent: Efficiency is significantly higher with the combinatorial than with the standard auction when synergies are present. This confirms the favorable qualities of the combinatorial auction demonstrated in previous studies, e.g., Lunander and Nilsson (2003).

3.2 Costs

We use the winners' profits, i.e. $\pi_{i,k} = \sum_i (b_{i,k} - c_{i,k})$, to measure the procurement cost in each period k. Excluding the instances where computerized bids won, regression equation *(2)* is run on payments (bidders' profits) under treatment I, controlling for periods allowing communication ($D = 1$ with communication, 0 otherwise).

$$(2) \qquad \pi_{i,\,k} = \alpha_0 + \alpha_1 D_i + \beta_0 \text{Cost}_{i,\,k} + \beta_1 \left(D_i \times \text{Cost}_{i,\,k} \right) + u_{i,\,k}$$

The results show that neither the intercept (α_1) nor slope (β_1) coefficients representing communication possibilities are significant. Hence, the possibility to communicate prior to bidding has not made it possible to squeeze out more money (to increase the procurement cost) from the procurer under treatment I.

Graph 1 illustrates the earnings under treatment II and III in 104 periods (40 periods without and 64 periods with communication), the vertical line indicating where in the sequence of periods the chat line was opened. Payments under the combinatorial mechanism are centered on SEK 20 throughout the periods and the possibility to communicate after period eight seems to have had little effect on procurement costs. The last observation also applies to treatment II, but the distribution of payments is more scattered. Also, in a number of periods, winning bidders in the standard mechanism (treatment II) incurred losses due to the exposure problem.

TABLE 3

ESTIMATED PAYMENTS TO SUBJECTS UNDER TREATMENT I[*]

Parameter	Estimate	t-ratio
α_0	87,50	8,86
β_0	–0,32	–7,62
α_1	16,75	1,097
β_1	–0,06	–0,93
N	131	
R^2	0,44	

[*] SEK, robust standard errors.

GRAPH 1

PAYMENTS UNDER TREATMENT II AND III
IN IDENTICAL PERIODS

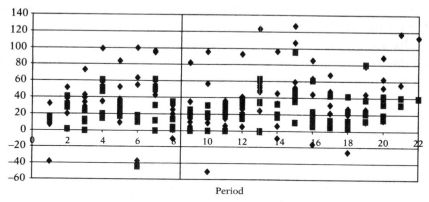

Period

◆ Standard with non linear cost   ■ Combinatorial

TABLE 4

COMPARISON OF AVERAGE PERIOD PAYMENTS (SEK) TO SUBJECTS

Environment	Treatment		Number of periods	Test statistics $(t\text{-}ratio)^*$
	III. Combinatorial	II. Standard with non linear cost		
Whole sample				
Chat	25.40	41.35	64	3.77
No chat	19.68	38.98	40	3.32
Synergy 0.9				
Chat	21.39	30.84	38	3.10
No chat	19.0	32.17	24	1.93
Synergy 0.8				
Chat	31.27	56.73	26	2.43
No Chat	20.69	49.19	16	2.64

* *t-tests* for equal mean values across mechanisms.

Table 4 summarizes payments in the two mechanisms, for the whole sample and separated for weak and strong synergies. In spite of that winning bidders in some periods under treatment II incurred substantial losses — which decreases the mechanism's reported cost — it is clear from table 4 that the combinatorial auction generated significantly lower profits for bidders (i.e. lower payments) than the standard mechanism. When the synergy effect of winning both contracts increases from $\alpha = 0.9$ to $\alpha = 0.8$, the results suggest that the increase in procurement cost of using the standard mechanism is greater than the corresponding increase in the combinatorial mechanism.

5. - Observed Bidding Behavior

Results summarized in tables 2 and 4 indicate that the combinatorial auction outperforms the standard mechanism both in terms of efficiency and costs to the procurer even if bidders are allowed to collude. In order to provide a deeper understanding of differences between environments without and with communication, this section gives an analysis of individual's bidding behavior under the respective mechanisms.

We use the following definitions of how bidders have used the option to communicate in order to reach a collusive agreement. The first is to *divide the market*. The two human bidders then decide to take one contract each. The second type of agreement is referred to as *bid rotation*. Bidders agree that one of them is to win both contracts. Sometimes the designated loser abstains from bidding altogether, and at other instances a 'high' bid is submitted, sometimes even SEK 300, the highest possible bid.[8] The third type of observed collusive agreement is *side payment*, where one of the bidders adjusts bidding behavior in exchange for receiving remunerations afterwards. Finally, *no agreement* refers to situations where pre-play communication is not observed or where the parties have been unable to strike a deal.

Table 5 summarizes observed *ex ante* collusive behavior — if any — under the three treatments. The information is obtained from the logged chat traffic between the two human bidders prior

---

[8] In the analysis, we have coded non-bidding as if the bid is SEK 300.

TABLE 5

TYPES OF PRE-BIDDING COMMUNICATION
UNDER THREE TREATMENTS

Type of agreement	Treatment I		Treatment II		Treatment III	
	# periods	%	# periods	%	# periods	%
No agreement	10	19	29	44	46	66
Divide the market	36	69	14	21	5	7
Bid rotation	4	8	9	14	19	27
Side payments	2	4	14	21		.
Number of periods	52	100	66	100	70	100

to bidding in each period collated against the bids that were subsequently submitted. In some cases but not always, information about private costs for each contract was revealed during the communication phase. There were some situations where one bidder may have tried to fool the other, but this may alternatively have been due to that the parties did not fully understand the implications of competing against the automated bidder. Even if communication is cheap-talk the table provides information about what sort of thinking that was going on.

Before commenting on the results of the table, and before going into the analysis of bidding without and with having the possibility to communicate, a couple of notes on bidding relative to theoretical predictions are warranted. To provide a benchmark, Graph 2 provides information about bidding behavior under treatment I with no communication while table 6 reports the estimated linear relationship with and without communication. Using the relevant parameter values, the RNNE bid function is $\beta_i^j(c) = 100 + 0{,}67c$. Much in the same way as the standard findings in most experiments with first-price sealed bid (procurement) auctions within the private values model, bids are significantly below the RNNE prediction.

75

TABLE 6

WINNING BIDS AND COSTS IN TREATMENT I[*]

Parameter	Periods			
	not allowing for communication	t-ratio	allowing for communication	t-ratio
α_0	87.50	9.22	104.25	8.98
β_0	0.68	16.18	0.62	12.71
N	52		79	
R^2	0.84		0.62	

* SEK, robust standard errors.

GRAPH 2

TREATMENT I. OBSERVED AND PREDICTED BIDS
IN PERIODS WITH NO COMMUNICATION (SEK)

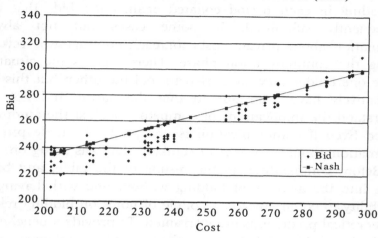

For those subsets of bids where it is feasible to benchmark observed behavior against a theoretical prediction, the same pattern prevails also under treatments II and III, i.e. individuals consistently seem to be risk averse. Due to space restrictions, we will not present any further analysis on this, but such results are available on request. It should also be noted that we have no

76

theoretical predictions about optimal bidding behavior when costs are non-linear, neither under the standard nor under the combinatorial treatment. It is therefore not feasible to undertake a standard comparison of predicted relative to observed behavior. The subsequent analysis is therefore primarily concerned with comparing bids under alternative treatments.

5.1 *Standard Auction with Linear Cost (Treatment I)*

Table 3 above demonstrated that the option to communicate did not have a significant effect on the size of the bidders' profits. Although treatment I bidders to a large extent formed collusive agreements (divided the market; cf. table 5) these have had little effect upon the designated winner's profits. However, table 7 shows that there is a small but significant difference between average mark-up on cost from bids submitted under the first eight periods (no communication allowed) with the average mark-up on cost from all bids submitted in the subsequent periods (communication allowed).

In order to see if repeated interactions matter, we also test the link between bidding behavior in previous and subsequent periods. We use the observed communication between the human bidders logged in the chat files to test if the likelihood for a collusive agreement in the current period can be explained by bidders' communication in previous periods and to some extent by the distribution of the induced costs. The binary logit equation estimated is given by eq. *(3)*.

TABLE 7

AVERAGE MARK-UP ON COST IN TREATMENT I - ALL BIDS

Periods	Mean mark-up	Std.dev	n
No communication allowed	1.055	0.048	128
Communication allowed	1.070	0.069	208
t-test for equal means	–2.08		

$$(3) \quad Agreement_k = \alpha + \beta_1\, Agreement_{k-1} + \beta_2\, Agreement_{k-2} +$$

$$+ \beta_3\, Low + \beta_4\, Each + \beta_5\, (Low \times Each) + \varepsilon_k$$

$Agreement_k$ takes the value 1 if a collusive agreement is made in the written communication prior to bidding in periods k, $k-1$, $k-2$ and 0 otherwise. *Low* refers to min $c^j_{i,\,k}$, that is the lowest of the four randomly induced cost in each period. The lower the induced cost is on any of the human bidders' contracts, the higher the probability is to beat the computerized bidder, giving the bidders incentives to engage in collusive bidding. *Each* is a dummy variable which takes the value 1 if both bidders find their lowest induced cost placed on different contracts, i.e., $c^1_{A,k} < c^2_{A,k}$ and $c^2_{B,k} < c^1_{B,k}$, or $c^1_{B,\,k} < c^2_{B,\,k}$ and $c^2_{A,\,k} < c^1_{A,\,k}$, and 0 otherwise. Given that the bidders find themselves with absolute advantages on a contract each, an agreement to try to divide the market seems plausible. Finally, *Low × Each* combines the two effects.

The high propensity to engage in collusive behavior in treatment I is to some extend reflected in the estimates. Only ten scattered periods saw no agreement, but each of these ten periods was followed by a period where an agreement took place. Therefore, the two lagged dummy variables $Agreement_{k-1}$ and $Agreement_{k-2}$ perfectly predict the success of an agreement in period k.

TABLE 8

DEPENDENCY IN COLLUSIVE AGREEMENTS BETWEEN PERIODS
- TREATMENT I

Variable	Estimate	p-value
$Agreement_{k-1}$	Predicts success perfectly	.
$Agreement_{k-2}$	Predicts success perfectly	.
Low	−0.02	0.773
Each	123.05	.
Low × Each	−0.48	0.001
Constant	5.80	0.698

5.2 *Standard Auction With Non Linear Cost (Treatment II)*

In periods where collusive agreements have been reached, table 5 (above) indicates that all three classes of collusion strategies have been discussed under treatment II, with side payments concentrated to one specific session. Most striking is that the number of *ex ante* agreements has been reduced when the complexity of the problem put to the bidders has increased.

Table 9 provides the regression results from both no-communication periods and periods allowing for communication,

TABLE 9

BIDDING BEHAVIOR UNDER TREATMENT II[*]

Parameter	All bids Periods		Winning bids Periods		Pooling winning bids
	not allowing for communication	allowing for communication	not allowing for communication	allowing for communication	
Whole sample					
α_0	51.4	76.9	89.78	154.11	$\alpha_1 = 0$
	(5.54)	(7.60)	(4.04)	(12.04)	**(2.51)**
β_0	0.78	0.72	0.60	0.34	$\beta_1 = 0$
	(19.57)	(18.07)	(5.97)	(6.12)	**(-2.27)**
N	160	268	72	120	
R^2	0.71	0.46	0.50	0.24	
Synergy 0.9					
α_0	51.57	39.77	62.87	75.91	$\alpha_1 = 0$
	(5.52)	(6.72)	(3.28)	(6.09)	**(0.57)**
β_0	0.79	0.86	0.74	0.69	$\beta_1 = 0$
	(20.04)	(37.28)	(8.71)	(12.62)	**(-0.46)**
N	96	156	43	69	
R	0.81	0.83	0.73	0.66	
Synergy 0.8					
α_0	51.14	129.24	112.71	205.77	$\alpha_1 = 0$
	(2.81)	(5.90)	(3.22)	(11.64)	**(2.39)**
β_0	0.76	0.52	0.47	0.11	$\beta_1 = 0$
	(9.62)	(6.01)	(3.00)	(1.58)	**(-2.10)**
N	64	112	29	51	
R	0.63	0.19	0.36	0.04	

[*] SEK, robust standard errors, *t-ratios* in parenthesis.

using eq. *(2)*. Both the results from including all bids and when only winning bids are included are presented. The reason for making this distinction is that any form of collusion means that an assigned looser submits a bid with poor information, i.e. which may defy any systematic analysis which tries to capture the logic of these bids. Even if only a few bids are rigged in this way, this may destroy the possibility to derive any valuable information from the dataset of all bids. In both datasets the estimated bidding behavior resembles the bidding behavior we observed in treatment I; the intercept of the estimated slope increases whereas the coefficient decreases when subjects are given the option to communicate prior to bidding.

The rightmost column in table 9 indicates a difference in bidding behavior across periods not allowing for chat and allowing for chat, respectively. When subjects can communicate, they seem to be changing their behavior, at least when synergies in the number of contracts awarded are large.

We have also applied regression equation *(3)* to test the presence of serial correlation in observed agreements across periods. Given the choice of explanatory variables, table 10 indicates that the probability for a collusive agreement in the current period (k) only depends on whether the bidders reached a collusive agreement in period $k - 1$ but that no other explanatory variable is significant.

TABLE 10

DEPENDENCY IN COLLUSIVE AGREEMENTS BETWEEN PERIODS - TREATMENT II

Variable	Estimate	p-value
Agreement$_{t-1}$	1.24	0.048
Agreement$_{t-2}$	0.86	0.161
Low	0.04	0.415
Each	10.48	0.40
Low × Each	−0.05	0.418
Constant	−9.90	−0.90

80

5.3 *Combinatorial Auction (Treatment III)*

Table 5 showed that our chat recordings indicate far fewer collusive agreements being formed under the combinatorial mechanism than in the other two mechanisms. In most of the cases where an agreement was reached, one of the bidders was designated to bid for both contracts against the computerized bidder's two single bids. Bid data also indicate that the designated bidder in general only submitted the package bid for AB and not any single bid.

In each of the no-communication periods both human bidders submitted a combinatorial bid for AB. Graph 3 shows that the mark-up over cost was rather modest, on average 7,5 percent, which is likely to be below equilibrium.[9] Except for their package bid on AB, the bidders could also submit a single bid on contract

GRAPH 3

SINGLETON BIDS UNDER TREATMENT III IN PERIODS NOT ALLOWING FOR COMMUNICATION

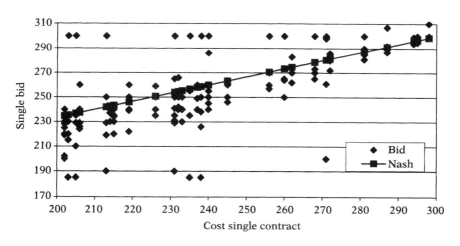

___

[9] Note that the average RNNE mark-up in a simple environment (without synergies) is about 8%, given our random costs for contract A and contract B (see Graph 2).

A and a single bid on contract B. These bids are illustrated in figure 6 where also the «virtual» Nash behavior, i.e. interpreting singleton bids as if no combination bid could be submitted, is indicated.

Table 11 reports the estimated coefficients from both treatment I and III, using these singleton bids. Pooling the data we cannot reject the hypothesis of identical intercepts and coefficients. Thus, when submitting singleton bids in the combinatorial auction, bidders' adopt the same strategy as they do in a standard auction, neglecting the interdependence between their single bids and their combinatorial bids. A number of subjects have, however, either refrained from submitting singleton bids or submitted singleton bids equal to the highest possible bid by the computerized bidder (SEK 300).

Making use of eq. (2), we investigate the impact of allowing pre-play communication on bidding behavior. In this, we focus only on the observed package bids.

Table 12 presents the same sort of comparison as table 9 above. Pooling the winning bids (last column) we cannot reject the hypothesis of identical bidding behavior in periods without and with communication. We therefore conclude that subjects seem to be less inclined or able to engage in cooperative bidding

TABLE 11

ESTIMATED BID FUNCTION FOR SINGLE BIDS IN TREATMENTS I AND III, PERIODS NOT ALLOWING FOR COMMUNICATION[*]

Parameter	Treatment	
	Standard auction (I)	Combinatorial auction (III)
α_0	68.21	63.77
	(12.28)	(4.80)
β_0	0.77	0.79
	(35.15)	(15.34)
N	128	156
R^2	0.92	0.57

[*] SEK, robust *t-ratio* in parenthesis.

TABLE 12

BIDDING BEHAVIOR UNDER COMBINATORIAL AUCTION[*]

Parameter	All bids Periods		Winning bids Periods		Pooling winning bids
	not allowing for communi- cation	allowing for communi- cation	not allowing for communi- cation	allowing for communi- cation	
Whole sample					
α_0	77.02	217.69	106.87	160.40	$\alpha_1 = 0$
	(2.21)	(5.20)	(3.97)	(6.50)	(1.47)
β_0	0.89	0.59	0.78	0.69	$\beta_1 = 0$
	(10.19)	(6.42)	(11.80)	(12.43)	(−1.16)
N	80	140	38	63	
R^2	0.61	0.19	0.80	0.72	
Synergy 0.9					
α_0	108.18	231.84	138.60	215.99	$\alpha_1 = 0$
	(1.92)	(4.47)	(2.55)	(7.50)	(1.27)
β_0	0.83	0.56	0.73	0.57	$\beta_1 = 0$
	(6.17)	(5.07)	(5.76)	(9.01)	(−1.12)
N	48	86	22	39	
R^2	0.53	0.18	0.65	0.70	
Synergy 0.8					
α_0	130.56	182.63	173.14	191.56	$\alpha_1 = 0$
	(4.56)	(1.78)	(6.38)	(3.04)	(0.27)
β_0	0.73	0.68	0.60	0.60	$\beta_1 = 0$
	(8.73)	(2.67)	(8.90)	(3.76)	(−0.001)
N	32	54	16	24	
R^2	0.44	0.10	0.86	0.36	

[*] SEK, *t-ratio* in parenthesis.

in a combinatorial auction that when the standard auction format is used. In combination with the number-count in table 5 above, this provides support for our maintained hypothesis that the possibility to submit combinatorial bids makes it more difficult to collude.

Finally, again using eq. *(3)* to establish the correlation of collusive agreements between periods in treatment III, the estimates only give support for correlation between the current period (k) and the period before $(k-1)$.

TABLE 13

DEPENDENCY IN COLLUSIVE AGREEMENTS ACROSS PERIODS -
TREATMENT III

Variable	Estimate	p-value
$Agreement_{k-1}$	2.00	0.009
$Agreement_{k-2}$	1.02	0.165
Low	−0.08	0.179
Each	−22.05	0.119
Low × Each	0.10	0.114
Constant	14.35	0.240

6. - Summary

A couple of previous studies have demonstrated that combinatorial bidding is better at establishing efficient allocations than the standard one shot, sealed bid institution when there are non-linearities in the number of contracts awarded to a bidder. The research reported here indicates that the possibility to submit combinatorial bids also may have an impact on the possibility to collude. By allowing for combination bids it gets more difficult for colluders to agree on a policy which boosts their earnings at the expense of the procurers' costs or of efficiency. We can therefore think about this augmentation of the bidding space as an additional policy device for reducing the chances of collusion formation or increasing the chances of an existing collusion to break down (see Coate, 1985).

When analyzing actual bidding behavior during the experiments, we have been startled by that the introduction of a possibility to communicate does not generate more collusion than we actually see. The detailed analysis of bidding behavior has however established that there indeed is a difference between bids submitted under the standard mechanism (treatment II, table 9) between periods without and with chat possibilities. This difference disappears when the possibility to submit package bids is introduced in treatment III (table 12). This is confirmed when counting the number of collusive agreements reached under the respective treatments. Moreover, there is a cost difference between no-chat and chat treatments. Our main result is therefore that the standard one shot, sealed bid procurement auction provides possibilities for collusion which evaporates under the new set of bidding rules.

One reason for that the impact of communication on efficiency and cost still is small could be that our environment is a bit "kind" in this respect; since there are only three bidders and two contracts to be awarded, there are not so many incorrect allocations that can be established. Another possible reason is that since the outside (automata) bidder disturbs any collusive agreement, it is difficult for the two colluders to establish a solution where they both win reasonably many times. It is an obvious challenge for further research to test whether or not our conclusion is robust against alternative experimental designs.

Although we inadvertently created an environment where it is fairly difficult to collude — where participants can only to a degree make use of the possibility to coordinate behavior — it has still been possible to establish that combinatorial bidding affects behavior and enhances efficiency. Real applications of combinatorial auctions may involve ten or more contracts and therefore a large number of feasible bid combinations. In addition, the number of bidders is often more than three. This means that there may be an even better efficiency-enhancing potential for the mechanism under real-life conditions than in our stylized lab.

TABLE A1

EFFICIENCY ACROSS MECHANISMS
(STANDARD DEV IN PARENTHESIS)

Mechanism	Average efficiency - all periods	n	Average efficiency - periods with no chat	n	Average efficiency - periods allowing for chat	n
Standard	0.92 (0.15)	84	0.9 (0.19)	32	0.93 (0.12)	52
Standard with linear cost						
Synergy 0.9+0.8	0.73 (0.39)	106	0.74 (0.37)	40	0.72 (0.72)	66
Synergy 0.9	0.76 (0.30)	62	0.75 (0.33)	24	0.76 (0.28)	38
Synergy 0.8	0.68 (0.49)	44	0.71 (0.42)	16	0.67 (0.53)	28
Combinatorial with linear cost						
Synergy 0.9+0.8	0.89 (0.20)	110	0.91 (0.15)	40	0.88 (0.25)	70
Synergy 0.9	0.86 (0.23)	67	0.88 (0.18)	24	0.85 (0.26)	43
Synergy 0.8	0.95 (0.15)	43	0.97 (0.19)	16	0.93 (0.19)	27

TEST OF MEAN EFFICIENCY ACROSS MECHANISMS

H_0: Efficiency$_{Comb.}$ = = Efficiency$_{Standard\ with\ non\ linear\ cost}$	t-ratio	Combinatorial n	Standard with non linear cost n
All periods (both $\alpha = 0,9$ and $\alpha = 0,8$)	3,79	110	106
Periods with chat line closed	2,69	40	40
Periods with chat line open	2,81	70	66
All periods when $\alpha = 0,9$	2,11	67	62
Periods with chat line closed	1,69	24	24
Periods with chat line open	1,57	43	38
All periods when $\alpha = 0,8$	3,49	43	44
Periods with chat line closed	2,45	16	16
Periods with chat line open	2,43	27	28

TEST OF MEAN EFFICIENCY ACROSS SIZE OF SYNERGY

H_0: Efficiency$_{\alpha = 0,8.}$ = = Efficiency$_{\alpha = 0,9}$	t-ratio	n $\alpha = 0,9$	n $\alpha = 0,8$
Standard with non linear cost			
All periods	1,04	62	44
Periods with chat line closed	0,34	24	16
Periods with chat line open	0,82	38	28
Combinatorial			
All periods	2,27	67	43
Periods with chat line closed	1,92	24	16
Periods with chat line open	1,38	43	27

BIBLIOGRAPHY

AOYAGI M., «Bid Rotation and Collusion in repeated Auctions», *Journal of Economic Theory*, vol. 112, 2003.

BRUSCO S. - LOPOMO G., «Collusion via Signaling in Simultaneous Ascending Bid Auctions with Heterogeneous Objects, with and without Complementarities», *Review of Economic Studies*, vol. 69, 2002.

COATE M., «Techniques for Protecting Against Collusion in Sealed Bid Markets», *The Antitrust Bulletin*, 1985.

CRAMTON P. - SCHWARTZ J.A., «Collusive Bidding: Lessons from the FCC Spectrum Auctions», *Journal of Regulatory Economics*, vol. 17, 2000.

GOSWANI G. - NOE T.H. - REBELLO M.J., «Collusion in Uniform-Price Auctions: Experimental Evidence and Implications for Treasury Auctions», *The Review of Financial Studies*, vol. 9, no. 3, 1996.

KELLY F. - STEINBERG R., «A Combinatorial Auction with Multiple Winners for Universal Service», *Management Science*, vol. 46, 2000.

KRISHNA V.J., *Auction Theory*, Academic Press, 2002.

KWASNICA A., «The Choice of Cooperative Strategies in Sealed Bid Auctions», *Journal of Economic Behavior & Organization*, vol. 42, 2000.

KWASNICA A.M. - SHERSTYUK K., «Collusion and Equilibrium Selection in Auctions», *mimeo*, Department of Economics, University of Hawaii at Manoa, 2003.

LUNANDER A. - NILSSON J.E., «Taking the Lab to the Field: Experimental Tests of Alternative Ways to Procure Multiple Contracts», *Journal of Regulatory Economics*, vol. 25 (1), 2004.

PESENDORFER M., «A Study of Collusion in First-Price Auctions», *Review of Economic Studies*, vol. 67, 2000.

PHILLIPS O.R. - MENKHAUS D.J. - COATNEY K.T., «Collusive Practices in Repeated Auctions: Experimental Evidence on Bidding Rings», *American Economic Review*, vol. 93, 2003.

PORTER H.R. - ZONA J.D., «Ohio School Milk Market: An Analysis of Bidding», *RAND, Journal of Economics*, vol. 30, 1999.

SHERSTYUK K., «Collusion without Conspiracy: An Experimental Study of One-Sided Auctions», *Experimental Economics*, vol. 2 (1), 1999.

— —, «Collusion in Private Ascending Price Auctions», *Journal of Economic Behavior & Organization*, vol. 48, 2002.

Auction Formats and Award Rules in Swedish Procurement Auctions

Sofia Lundberg

Umeå University

This paper provides an empirical analysis of outcomes from Swedish procurement auctions given award criterion and auction format. The auctions are single-unit sealed bid auctions or their simultaneous counterpart and contracts can be awarded to the lowest bidder or in accordance with qualitative criteria. The empirical results provide no evidence of differences in winning bids depending on the auction format. The award rule on the other hand matters; a horizontal comparison shows higher winning bids on contracts awarded to other than the lowest bidder. The effect of bidder interaction and bidder identity is also considered. [JEL Classification: D44, H57].

1. - Introduction

The main purpose of this paper is to empirically compare the outcomes of two different auction formats, single-unit and simultaneous sealed bid auctions of interior cleaning service contracts and the two award rules that can be applied within public procurement in Sweden. This is an empirical study based on a unique data set with 758 contracts from procurements at the local government level in Sweden from the period 1991 to 1999.

Public procurement in Sweden answers to the Public Procurement Act (LOU 1992:1528), which states, in accordance

Financial support from the Swedish Competition Authority is gratefully acknowledged as insightful comments from Linda Andersson, Johan Lundberg, Gustavo Piga, Lars Westin, and seminar participants at the 32nd congress of the Economic Association for Research in Industrial Economics in Porto.

with the standards applied within the European Union (EU), that sealed bidding is applied and that the lowest bidder or the bid considered as the economically most advantageous bid should be awarded the contract. The winner is paid in accordance with his/her bid and the contracts are in general fixed-price contracts. In the auctions studied here there is one contract per object or premises (a school, an office, etc.) to be cleaned. The local governments can arrange procurements selling one contract only, for example interior cleaning of a school. This is referred to as a single-unit auction. Alternatively, more than one contract can be offered in a simultaneous auction where combinatorial bids are not allowed. The evaluation of the bids should be made contract by contract in the simultaneous auctions. In other words, the bid from a firm on one contract should be independently evaluated relative to the bids placed by that firm on the other contracts auctioned in one and the same procurement. It is not necessary for the bidder to place bids on all contracts auctioned in the same procurement, but in the cases studied here they generally do.

Although Swedish procurement auctions only have the character of first-price sealed bid auctions (to be explained below) support for expecting a difference in winning bids explained by auction format can be found in the literature. An important theoretical difference between the single-unit and the simultaneous first-price auctions is that the former are under the assumption of private costs efficient, while the latter are not necessarily[1]. One bidder could end up with all the contracts auctioned simultaneously although this bidder does not necessarily have the lowest cost for the realization of some of the contracts. Results by Krishna and Tranæs (2002) show that given combinatorial bidding simultaneous first-price auctions can result in efficient allocations. However, as mentioned above there are no combinatorial bids present in the procurements studied here. As a consequence, the contracts that are auctioned under the simultaneous first-price format were not necessarily offered to the

---

[1] See BIKHCHANDANI S. (1999) for a theoretical presentation of the simultaneous first-price auction.

bidder who had the lowest cost for realization of the contract. Since bids are dependent on costs there could be a difference in the price paid to the winning bidder depending on the auction format. The first hypothesis that will be studied in the present paper is that contracts auctioned under the single-unit format demand a lower price than simultaneously auctioned contracts.

Furthermore, publicly procured contracts in Sweden can be awarded to other than the lowest bidder. A higher bidder than the lowest bidder could be contracted if it is considered to be the economically most advantageous bid with respect to price, quality, environmental aspects, service, maintenance, and so forth. This is the quality that makes these procurement auctions different from standard first-price sealed bid auctions. These criteria should be posted in advance of the bidding[2], but the importance attached to each criterion in the evaluation is unknown to the bidders prior to the bidding in the procurements studied here. Great importance given to price can in practice lead to the lowest bid being the award rule. The law, as it was written during the time period studied, gave the contracting entity a lot of freedom choosing the award rule after the bids were submitted. Today, this has changed and is more formalized and the scoring rules have to be revealed in the contract notice. However, the application of different models for scoring rules is wide and their implementation can still be unclear[3]. As such, the issues studied here still have validity.

The application of two award rules without the pre-announcement of the scoring rules could complicate the bidders' strategies. It is reasonable to assume a trade-off between posting a regular first-price auction bid and increasing the probability of being the lowest bid in case of a high importance given to price, or a less aggressive bid hoping for higher weighting awarded to qualitative criteria (i.e. the economically most advantageous bid award rule). This would increase the profit to the bidder if he/she wins the contract. However, there is always the risk that the local government will go for the lowest bid leading to a loss of the

---

[2] They should be specified in the contract notice.
[3] ANDERSSON A. - LUNANDER A. (2004).

contract. A significant effect of award rule on the winning bids would indicate that this trade off exists and is applied. Furthermore, allocation of contracts to other than the lowest bidding bidder is inefficient since low bids are associated with low costs. This feature of the institutional rules governing Swedish procurement auctions has, to my knowledge, not been empirically analyzed or theoretically modeled in previous studies. The latter is left to further research to deal with. To summarize, the second hypothesis to be tested in the present paper is that contracts awarded according to the lowest bid criterion command a lower price than contracts allocated with the economically most advantageous bid criterion.

Vickrey (1961, 1962) was the first to formalize auction theory and since then, the contributions to this area have been considerable, both with respect to theoretical issues, empirical papers, as well as applied studies. The number of different formalized auction formats has with time become substantial. There are several variants of both single-unit auctions and multi-unit auctions. When it comes to comparisons of different auction formats there are a numerous number of papers to choose among, and many of them are theoretical. The comparisons mainly focus on differences within single-unit auction formats (e.g. Lucking-Riley, 1999), or within different multi-unit auctions (e.g. Engelbrecht-Wiggans, 1988; Szentes and Rosenthal, 2003), such as the discriminatory pay auction and the uniform pay auction[4]. Krishna (2004) provides an exposition of different auction formats and the adherent theory. However, there are exceptions that compare single-unit auctions to multi-unit auctions. For example, Wilson (1979) compares the prices from auctions of one indivisible good (unit auctions) to auctions of one divisible good (share auctions). The uniform price auction is

---

[4] Under both these auction formats the units are identical and the highest bidder wins. But, in the discriminatory price auction the winning bidders pay the sum of their bids on the units they are awarded. As a contrast, in the uniform price auction, the winning bidders pay the market-clearing price. That is; the price at which the bidders' demand equals supply. The winners are awarded units in accordance with the number of competing bids that they have overbid (see KRISHNA V., 2004).

compared to the second price auction in List and Lucking-Reiley (2000). The bids from the two auction formats are compared with experimental auctions of sports cards. Comparisons of outcomes of different auction settings based on experiments within a common value setting can be found in Lunander and Nilsson (2004). The present paper assumes private values. As for comparisons of single-unit and simultaneous first-price auctions Alsemgeest, Noussair and Olson (1998) provide results from an empirical study based on experiments. The bidders compete for one or two (identical) units.

This paper contributes to the previous mentioned literature with an empirical comparison of the outcome of single-unit sealed bid auctions (that can have the character of first-price sealed bid auctions) to its simultaneous counterpart and award criteria based on a rich data set with procurements at local government level in Sweden. The 758 contracts concern interior cleaning of different public premises such as schools and day care centers. This has important policy implications for local governments regarding how they should auction their contracts and evaluate the bids. The effect of different auction formats on the winning bid is estimated in the same way as MacDonald, Handy, and Plato (2002) estimated the competitive effect on winning bids in US commodity procurements. However, these procurements did not have diversity in auction format since all contracts were auctioned by single-unit first-price auctions. Another difference is the incorporation of bidder interaction effects on the winning bid. The computation of the interaction variables follows Gupta (2002).

The rest of this paper is organized as follows; a description of the bidding environment is given in Section 2. This is followed by a presentation of the data with a discussion of possible implications given by the bidding environment and variable definition in Section 3. The empirical approach and regression are presented in Section 4 followed by presentation and interpretation of the results. Section 6 contains a summary and discussion and finally there is an appendix with tables of descriptive statistics.

2. - A Simple Model

The bidders' costs for completing an interior cleaning service contract are assumed to be private and independent. That is, the firms privately know their own cost to complete the contract with certainty and this is independent of the competitors' costs. It is reasonable to assume that the level of uncertainty regarding the cost for completing an interior cleaning service contract to be negligible. The firm knows the square meters to be cleaned, the cleaning frequency, the type of building, and resources demanded to do so. These details are given in the contract notice and technical specification given to the bidders when the procurement is announced. The contracts are therefore considered to be well defined and not complex. This is further supported by information from interviews with three firms acting on this market. They reported the contract notice and technical description to be detailed enough in order for them to place bids that reflects their true cost for completing the contract. It is therefore reasonable to assume that the cost for the interior cleaning of one square meter is independently drawn from a commonly known distribution. This cost is to be regarded as a basic interior cleaning cost for one square meter to be cleaned. Additional costs due to heterogeneity in contracts and bidding environment should be added to the basic interior cleaning cost. It is assumed that the bidders draw one cost for each contract auctioned in a single-unit or a simultaneous sealed bid auction. If there are multiple contracts at stake, the cost for completing each contract is assumed to be independent of the costs for completing the other contracts auctioned simultaneously. This is reasonable due to the evaluation process in these procurements, which is described above. It is further assumed that the bidders in the market for interior cleaning services know each other well due to the local character of the market (firms compete in general within regions[5]). Therefore, it is assumed to be no uncertainty about the number

---

[5] The geographical area corresponding to the municipality in which the contract is auctioned defines the region.

of bidders. So in each auction $i = 1, ..., n$ commonly known bidders compete for contract k, where $k = 1, ... K$ is the number of contracts and the auction format is either single-unit auctions ($k = 1$) or simultaneous auctions ($1 < k \leq K$).

Bidder i could place a bid on a contract k in accordance with the traditional equilibrium bid function for the sealed bid first-price auction, b_{ik}, or another bid, b'_{ik}, than that depending on her belief about award rule or equally, the weights attached to price and qualitative criteria, where $b_{ik} \leq b'_{ik}$[6]. This belief is reflected in a probability attached to each award rule. The probability that the lowest bid will win is denoted λ_{ik} and the probability that some other bid than the lowest bid will win is $(1 - \lambda_{ik})$. Then the expected bid from bidder i is

(1)
$$E\,[b'_{ik}] = b_{ik} + (1 - \lambda_{ik})\,\theta_{ik}$$

where θ_{ik} is a price mark up given the expectation of the economically most advantageous award rule. For $\lambda_{ik} > 0$ the bid from bidder i on contract k will be higher than the bid given in accordance with the standard equilibrium bid function based on the basic interior cleaning cost corresponding to a given quality and competition level. The profit to bidder i given that he/she is awarded the contract and the lowest bid award rule is applied is lower than the profit if he/she wins with a higher bid under the economically most advantageous award rule.

The bid from bidder i on each contract k, is further assumed to be a function of procurement characteristics (PC_k), the basic cost for interior cleaning of one square meter, c_k the number of bidders n_k, and municipality characteristics, MC_k.

(2)
$$b'_{ik} = b'_{ik}\,(PC_{ik}, c_{ik}, n_{ik}, MC_{ik})$$

The bid is the demanded annual price per square meter to be cleaned. Returning to expression *(2)*, a motivation to consider

---

[6] The derivation of the standard equilibrium bid function and the necessary assumptions are for example presented in DONALD S. - PAARSCH H.J. (1993).

possible differences in winning bid due to auction format can be found in auction theory[7]. If the bidders follow the bidding strategy given by the equilibrium bid function for first-price sealed bid auctions their bids will decrease in costs. All things equal, if a significant difference in winning bids is found between the auction formats, bidders behave differently depending on the format. This could indicate that the supposed independency among simultaneously auctioned contracts is questionable. This is the first hypothesis that will be empirically tested. The second hypothesis concerns the potential effect on the winning bid from the award rule. As mentioned in the introduction, the bidders' uncertainty about the selection criteria or award rules prior to bidding could affect the bidding behavior and result in an efficient contract allocation. Should they go for the lowest possible bid hoping for price as the only selection criteria or a less aggressive bid increasing profit in the case of their winning the contract? If contracts selected on the basis of price are found to demand a significantly lower price than contracts allocated according to the economically most advantageous bid criterion this could be evidence of such a trade-off.

3. - Data

The empirical analysis is based on a data set from public procurements of interior cleaning contracts carried out by Swedish local governments during the time period 1991 to 1999[8]. The data was collected from a survey of all Swedish local governments asking them for documents regarding procurements of interior cleaning service contracts[9]. The response rate was 79.5 percent. According to the survey, in 59 out of 229 municipalities the local government had procured this service during the time

---

[7] See, for example, KRISHNA V. (2004).

[8] Actually, there were three municipalities that contributed with procurements from 1990 and 1991 (4 contracts) and these are included in the data.

[9] The documents are the contract notice, technical specification, list of tenders, and decision protocol.

period[10]. The remaining local governments reported in-house production and many of them stated that they were ready to start to procure interior cleaning services, or were discussing doing so. In Sweden, this is a political decision, which makes this study even more interesting because it has policy implications that could be important not only for those who have already put their in-house production unit up for competition, but also for the local governments that are about to do so[11]. There are three settings in the data. The number of procurements is 131, consisting of 758 contracts and a total of 5,926 bids were placed on these. The variables of main interest in this paper are the winning bids (endogenous variable), the auction format, and the applied award rule (procurement characteristics). The other control variables are procurement-, winner-, and municipality characteristics.

The Procurement characteristics (PC): Dummy variables for auction format (*single* = 1) and award rule (*lowest bid* = 1) are included in the empirical analysis. The single-unit auction is the most common auction format in the data. It counts for 61.8 percent of the procurements. However, a majority of the contracts, 87.6 percent, were auctioned under the simultaneous auction. The economically most advantageous award rule is in general given in the announcement of the contracts in the data. The weighting attached to the criteria was only occasionally made public prior to the bidding (in 2.3 percent of the cases). In only two of the procurements was the lowest bid award rule posted prior to the bids being placed. Despite this, 39.2 percent of the contracts were assigned to the lowest bidder. The lowest bid rule is more common under the single-unit (68.8 percent) than the simultaneous auction (24.6 percent). All the four procurement procedures given by law[12] are represented in the data set. These are aggregated into a dummy variable in the estimations. The dummy variable takes the

---

[10] Fiftyone of those were usable.
[11] There have been some changes in the Public procurement act after the time period during which these procurements took place. But, the results and issues discussed in the present paper are still interesting and have policy implications for present and future procurements.
[12] The Public Procurement Act (1528:1992).

value one if the contract is auctioned in procurement with a total estimated value under the threshold value and zero otherwise (*simplified* = 1)[13]. High values are created by big contracts in terms of total square meters to be cleaned and/or many contracts auctioned simultaneously. All procurement procedures have the character of seled bid auctions and will hereafter be referred to as such. See table A1 in the appendix for frequencies and description of the different procurement procedures. See Lundberg (2005) for more information about the procurement procedures and an analysis of the choice of procurement procedure.

The contract period and type of cleaning premises are also accounted for. The cleaning premises could be a school, a day care center, an office etc. There is one contract for each cleaning premise. The effect of contract type is measured with dummy variables and school contracts are the reference category. See Table A2 in the appendix for a complete presentation of all the contract types.

The bidders (X): A well-established result in auction theory is that the competition within a first-price auction affects the bid. A higher degree of competition does in general lead to lower bids and thereby lower payment from the local government to the winning bidder (see e.g. Laffont, 1997). This motivates the inclusion of the number of bidders in the empirical analysis, where the number of bidders is treated as exogenous. This variable is assumed to be decreasing. Since it is reasonable to believe that the competitive effect decreases after a certain number of bidders have entered the auction this variable is non linear. The number of bidders per contract in the data set varies between 1 and 37 and is on average 7.8. From Table 1 it is evident that the single-unit auctions in the data attract on average significantly less bidders than the simultaneous auctions. There is, however, no significant difference in the average winning bid with respect to auction format. Interesting differences are also found in winning bids depending on the award rule. Winning bids are measured in Swedish kronor per square meter to be cleaned in the 1994 price

---

[13] The threshold value is 200,000 Euro.

TABLE 1

DESCRIPTIVE STATISTICS, NUMBER OF BIDDERS
AND WINNING BID WITH RESPECT TO PROCUREMENT SETTING

Procurement setting	Variable	Minimum	Maximum	Mean	Standard deviation	N
All	No. of bidders	2	37	7.83	3.90	756
	Winning bid	13.03	1069.51	132.83	76.63	
Single-unit	No. of bidders	2	37	6.69	4.77	93
	Winning bid	13.03	1069.51	130.85	114.69	
Simultaneous	No. of bidders	2	18	7.99	3.73	663
	Winning bid	22.36	664.80	133.10	69.78	
Lowest bid wins	No. of bidders	2	17	6.73	3.09	296
	Winning bid	13.03	1069.51	111.86	76.44	
Economically most advantageous bid wins	No. of bidders	2	37	8.54	4.19	460
	Winning bid	22.36	664.80	146.32	73.75	

level[14]. The bids are pure price bids; it is not possible to divide them in to a price part and a part reflecting soft (qualitative) parameters.

The bidding firms in the data are heterogeneous in size. There are five national firms who compete against smaller local firms where the former dominate the market for interior cleaning services in Sweden. Another dominant bidder category is the municipalities' in-house production units[15]. The two most dominating national firms were together with in-house production units assigned 68 percent of all contracts in the data. The five national firms and in-house production units received 75 percent of all contracts. Little was left to the other smaller local firms. Further, in-house production units are the most successful bidder category with a success rate of approximately 50 percent (see Table A3 in the appendix). In accordance with Bajari and Hortacsu (2003), the effect of bidder heterogeneity is measured with firm

---

[14] The winning bids are normalized to a cleaning frequency of 260 days per year.

[15] There is one in-house production unit for each municipality. These are treated as one bidder category.

specific dummy variables for the five dominating firms and the in-house production units. The other smaller firms are used as reference category. See Table A4 in the appendix for descriptive statistics on winning bids contingent on bidder identity.

The municipality characteristics (MC): The population density, political situation, and unemployment per capita are used as municipality characteristics. The political situation is measured as the share of seats in the local council assigned to the social-democratic and leftwing parties. The population density is calculated as the population divided by land area. The average municipality in the data has a population density of 284.29, a local council where the left wing parties are assigned 45 percent of the seats, and an unemployment rate of approximately 8 percent. These variables are assumed to reflect the business environment within the municipality and the character of the local government running the auction. More information on the municipality characteristics can be found in Table A5 in the appendix.

4. - The Empirical Model and Estimation

The payment from the local government to the winning bidder is equal to his/her bid and assumed to be determined by expression *(2)*. Following MacDonald, Handy, and Plato (2002) the winning bid, b_k on an interior cleaning service contract, k, is a function of matrices with procurement-, winning bidder-, and municipality characteristics, respectively.

$$(3) \qquad b_k^l = b_k^l (PC_k, X_k, MC_k)$$

In addition the potential effect of interaction among bidders is included in the empirical analysis. Interaction is a relevant issue since the data set covers a time period of six years and the local character of the market. The interaction effect is measured by the two interaction measures from Gupta (2002). The first one, $r1_k$, is the average of $C1_i$ which is the number of unique competitors J facing bidder i in relation to the total number of competing bids

$n_k - 1$ facing bidder i on each contract k, over all contracts and procurements $p = 1, \ldots P$ in a municipality.

$$(4) \qquad C1_i = \frac{J}{\sum\limits_{k=1}^{K} \sum\limits_{p=1}^{P} (n_{kp} - 1)}$$

$$(5) \qquad R1_k = \frac{\sum\limits_{i=1}^{N} C1_i}{n_k}$$

Low values on $C1_i$ indicate that bidder i is frequently interacting with the same bidders. The measure is distributed between 0 and 1. A high value on $r1_k$ is the same as low interaction among bidders and more competitive bids (Gupta, 2002). The second interaction measure, $r2_k$, is the average of $C2_i$, defined as the number of unique competitors J facing bidder i in relation to the total number of contracts that bidder i has submitted bids on over all contracts and procurements in a municipality.

$$(6) \qquad C2_i = \frac{J}{\sum\limits_{p=1}^{P} k_p}$$

$$(7) \qquad R2_k = \frac{\sum\limits_{i=1}^{N} C2_i}{n_k}$$

Many unique competitors facing bidder i in relation to the number of contracts where i has been an active bidder explain a high value on $C2_i$. Low values on $r2_k$ indicate high interaction among bidders and reasons to suspect collusion and higher winning bids as a result. This interaction measure is empirically distributed between 0.08 and 29.39. More descriptive statistics on both interaction measures are found in Table A6 in the appendix. The use of the two different interaction measures is motivated since it is possible for a bidder to be active on many contracts but not interacting with the same bidders and vice versa. The time series in the data is incomplete; there are local governments that did not deliver documents regarding all procurements for the requested time period. So the interaction variables are measures of the observed minimum level of the interaction among bidders within each municipality.

Two regression equations will be estimated. There are separate equations for each measure of bidder interaction.

$$(8) \qquad b_k^i = \alpha_1 + PC_k\beta_{1PC} + X_k\beta_{1X} + MC_k\beta_{1MC} + \beta_{1r1}r1_k + \varepsilon_{1k}$$

$$(9) \qquad b_k^i = \alpha_2 + PC_k\beta_{2PC} + X_k\beta_{2X} + MC_k\beta_{2MC} + \beta_{2r2}r2_k + \varepsilon_{2k}$$

The bidders' cost for completing the contract is the by piecewise pseudo maximum likelihood estimated cost (Donald and Paarsch, 1993) under the assumption of Pareto distributed costs. The error term is assumed to reflect unobservable things that can affect the bid and assumed to be normally distributed. The regression equations are estimated with ordinary least square.

5. - Results

The estimation results are presented in Table 2. From the table it is obvious that the award rule matters for the size of the winning bid in these procurements. As one perhaps would expect the winning bids are significantly lower if the lowest bid award rule has been applied instead of the economically most advantageous award rule. But this was not *ex ante* given since bids are determined (vertically) within each auction. This result supports the hypothesis that the bidder's strategy is affected by the award rule. The auction format has no significant effect on the winning bid. One interpretation is that bids on simultaneously auctioned contracts are submitted independently of each other as if they were auctioned one by one.

It is clear that contract type matters for the size of the price.

Table 2
ESTIMATION RESULTS

Variable	Expression (8)		Expression (9)	
	β	t-value	β	t-value
Constant	79.93	6.46	79.23	6.62
Auction format (single = 1)	−3.97	−0.76	−2.28	−0.44
Award rule (lowest bid = 1)	−32.81	−14.37	−33.01	−14.48
Procurement procedure (simplified = 1)	−6.59	−1.58	−6.51	−1.55
Contract period	−0.00	−0.24	−0.00	−0.29
Child care contracts	16.19	5.00	16.22	4.96
Care contracts	1.74	0.45	2.33	0.61
Office contracts	17.57	3.15	17.51	3.17
Other contracts	12.84	1.93	12.75	1.92
Number of bidders (n)	−3.39	−4.48	−3.79	−4.67
Number of bidders squared (n^2)	0.09	3.80	0.12	3.52
Cost $(\hat{c})$	0.86	33.95	0.87	34.03
Firm 1 winner	6.52	1.78	6.23	1.71
Firm 2 winner	15.34	3.30	15.18	3.27
Firm 3 winner	0.45	0.08	0.91	0.15
Firm 4 winner	−3.68	−0.70	−3.59	−0.69
Firm 5 winner	17.61	3.96	16.78	3.77
In-house winner	8.12	2.54	7.65	2.40
Population density (*density*)	0.00	1.68	0.01	2.16
Political situation (*red*)	−41.38	−2.86	−38.59	−2.75
Unemployment rate (*unemp*)	−2.79	−4.18	−2.68	−4.02
$r1$	−1.58	−0.24	–	–
$r2$	–	–	−1.16	−1.43
R^2_{adj}		0.75		0.75
N		756		756

Winning bids on child care, office, and the other types of premises[16] contracts are significantly higher than on school

[16] The other premises parameter is significant on the 10 percent level.

contracts. A Wald test shows that health care contracts demand lower winning bids than contracts regarding child care premises (ten percent significance level). The test statistics from the Wald test are presented in Table A7 in the Appendix.

The parameters specific to firms show that bidder identity matters for the size of the winning bids. A contract given to firm 2, firm 5, or in-house production units commands a higher price than a contract given to some of the smaller firms in the data. Table A8 in the appendix provide test statistics from Wald tests where the coefficients from the firm dummy variables are tested against each other.

A look at the parameters for municipality characteristic shows that these have a significant effect on the winning bids. Contracted firms in more densely populated municipalities have submitted higher bids than in sparsely populated municipalities. The parameter for political situation is negative and significant and so is the unemployment rate parameter. The higher the unemployment rate, the lower the winning bids. Consequently, the business environment and the character of the local government matters for the amount paid to the winning bidder. The estimation results do not indicate any effect on the winning bids from bidder interaction indexes.

The explanatory power of the two models is high, they both produce R^2_{adj} values of 75 percent. Descriptive statistics for the estimated and observed winning bids are found in Table 3. From the table and from Graph 1, which shows predicted and observed

TABLE 3

DESCRIPTIVE STATISTICS, NUMBER OF BIDDERS
AND WINNING BID WITH RESPECT TO PROCUREMENT SETTING

Procurement setting Variable	Minimum	Maximum	Mean	Standard deviation	N
Observed winning bid	13.03	1,069.51	132.83	76.63	756
Estimated winning bid (r1)	-0.38	1,043.94	133.10	66.89	748
Estimated winning bid (r2)	0.15	1,045.92	133.10	66.90	748

winning bids versus number of bidders, it is clear that the model describes the data reasonably well. The two models generated predicted mean winning bids that correspond well to the observed mean winning bids. The parameter estimates in Table 2 is corrected for heteroscedasticity in accordance with White's corrected covariance matrix. The winning bids have also been estimated according to different specifications of bidder types, for example the two most dominating firms (firm 1 and firm 2) have been aggregated into one dummy variable together with the in-house production units. An alternative model specified with a dummy variable for all five dominating firms and one for the in-house production units has also been tested. The estimation results for the other parameters are robust for the different model specifications. A trial with the natural logarithm of the continuous variables was also made, but gave a worse model fit than a linear approach.

The overall conclusion is that these types of contracts should be awarded to the lowest bidder given that this does not lower the standards of quality and there is no indication of effect of auction format.

GRAPH 1

ESTIMATED WINNING AND OBSERVED WINNING BIDS VERSUS NUMBER OF BIDDERS, PLOT AND DISTRIBUTION

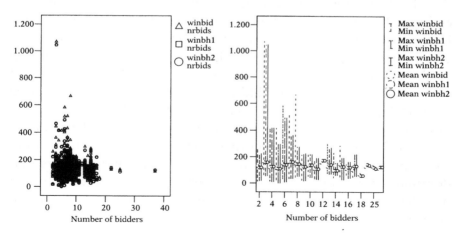

6. - Summary and Discussion

The aim of this paper is to analyze the outcome from Swedish procurement auctions of interior cleaning service contract given different award criteria and auction format. The contracts can be auctioned in single-unit sealed bid auctions or their simultaneous counterpart. There is a theoretical difference in the likelihood of the auction being efficient depending on the auction format, indicating a possible difference in outcome (the price paid to the winner). The empirical results provide no evidence of differences in winning bids depending on the auction format. The logical conclusion is that the bids on contracts auctioned simultaneously are indeed submitted independently of each other. The bids on simultaneously auctioned contracts should be and are evaluated independently of each other and the results indicate that the bidders act in accordance with this. The award rule on the other hand matters for the winning bids. Contracts can according to the Swedish Public Procurement Act (1992:1528) be awarded to other than the lowest bidder in accordance with a qualitative criterion motivated as the economically most advantageous bid. There can be a mix of contracts assigned to the lowest bidder and other than the lowest bidder within a simultaneous auction. A horizontal comparison of winning bids show higher bids on contracts awarded to other than the lowest bidder. The paper also considers the effect of interaction among bidders. There is no evidence of collusive behavior among bidders in terms of how frequently they interact with each other in relation to how many competitors they face or how frequently they participate in the auctions. According to the results, the business environment and character of local government as well as the bidder identity matters for the price paid to the winner. Contracts assigned to the in-house production units are more expensive than contracts given to smaller firms or some of the other dominating firms. This is particular interesting since the in-house production units is one of the bidder types that dominates the market for public interior cleaning contracts and has the highest success rate in terms of likelihood of winning a contract.

APPENDIX TABLES

TABLE A1

DESCRIPTION OF THE PROCUREMENT PROCEDURES

Procurement Mechanism	Description	N	Lowest bid award	Single-unit auction
MECHANISMS APPLICABLE UNDER THE THRESHOLD VALUE				
Simplified	All potential suppliers are allowed to bid. The contracting entity can invite some or all bidders to a negotiation after the auction.	129	82	63
Direct	No bidding process. Not an auction	–	–	–
MECHANISMS APPLICABLE OVER THE THRESHOLD VALUE				
Open	All potential suppliers are allowed to bid	315	137	13
Restricted	Only potential suppliers invited by the contracting entity are allowed to bid	255	64	8
Negotiated	As restricted. but the contracting entity can invite some or all bidders to a negotiation after the auction.	59	15	10
N		758	298	94

107

DESCRIPTIVE STATISTICS, WINNING BIDS GIVEN CONTRACT TYPE

Variable	Statistics					
	Sample	Min	Max	Mean	σ	N
School	All	22.83	412.59	108.10	41.97	319
	Single	59.96	311.40	100.96	46.20	32
	Simultaneous	22.83	412.59	108.88	41.49	287
Child care	All	46.50	664.80	168.42	80.23	302
	Single	84.24	413.24	154.58	56.63	32
	Simultaneous	46.50	664.80	170.06	82.34	270
Care	All	26.76	191.75	101.16	35.85	27
	Single	43.47	154.59	99.22	33.41	11
	Simultaneous	26.76	191.75	102.49	38.46	16
Office	All	32.19	283.74	104.40	62.55	65
	Single	53.36	207.59	113.21	56.34	10
	Simultaneous	32.19	283.74	102.80	63.96	55
Other	All	22.36	239.47	110.38	52.93	34
	Single	78.51	196.76	137.63	83.62	2
	Simultaneous	22.36	239.47	108.68	52.02	32

STATISTICS ON BIDDING BEHAVIOR AND SUCCESS RATE FOR NATIONAL FIRMS AND IN-HOUSE PRODUCTION UNITS (PERCENT IN PARENTHESIS)

	Number of placed bids		Number of wins		Success ratio	
	All	Simultaneous	All	Simultaneous		
Firm 1	698 (92.1)	620 (93.4)	196 (25.9)	172 (25.9)	0.28	0.28
Firm 2	561 (74.0)	507 (76.4)	98 (12.9)	80 (12.0)	0.17	0.16
Firm 3	338 (44.6)	321 (48.3)	23 (3.0)	20 (3.0)	0.07	0.06
Firm 4	51 (6.7)	48 (7.2)	22 (2.9)	21 (3.2)	0.43	0.44
Firm 5	83 (10.9)	65 (9.8)	4 (0.5)	1 (0.2)	0.05	0.02
In-house	437 (57.7)	371 (55.9)	218 (28.8)	202 (30.4)	0.50	0.55
N	758	664	758	664	758	664

DESCRIPTIVE STATISTICS, WINNING BIDS GIVEN BIDDER IDENTITY

Variable	Statistics					
	Sample	Min	Max	Mean	σ	N
Firm 1	All	22.83	413.24	121.29	50.20	196
	Single	54.11	413.24	119.83	70.65	24
	Simultaneous	22.83	338.28	121.49	57.66	172
Firm 2	All	31.77	365.71	129.99	58.19	98
	Single	62.19	165.85	116.47	25.70	18
	Simultaneous	31.77	365.71	133.03	62.96	80
Firm 3	All	82.91	443.67	163.41	92.24	23
	Single	115.23	225.24	163.50	56.23	3
	Simultaneous	32.19	443.67	163.40	97.57	20
Firm 4	All	56.82	264.45	140.06	66.51	22
	Single	82.66	82.66	–	–	1
	Simultaneous	56.82	264.45	142.80	68.88	21
Firm 5	All	102.56	190.01	131.94	39.36	4
	Single	102.56	118.33	112.58	8.71	3
	Simultaneous	190.01	190.01	–	–	1
Smaller firm	All	13.03	1,069.51	153.04	100.61	241
	Single	13.03	1,069.51	135.31	185.36	30
	Simultaneous	42.44	664.80	155.57	82.29	211
In-house production	All	22.36	581.57	124.60	62.16	218
	Single	53.36	311.40	157.33	62.33	16
	Simultaneous	22.36	581.57	122.00	61.56	202

DESCRIPTIVE STATISTICS, MUNICIPALITY CHARACTERISTICS BY AUCTION FORMAT

Variable	Statistics					
	Sample	Min	Max	Mean	σ	N
Population Density	All	4.60	2,808.02	284.29	486.52	758
	Single	4.60	2,808.02	361.94	701.08	94
	Simultaneous	8.75	2,749.69	273.30	447.59	664
Red	All	0.18	0.67	0.45	0.13	758
	Single	0.18	0.67	0.45	0.09	94
	Simultaneous	0.21	0.66	0.45	0.13	664
Unemployment rate	All	1.76	13.96	8.16	2.52	758
	Single	1.76	11.28	7.99	2.00	94
	Simultaneous	3.90	13.96	8.18	2.59	664

DESCRIPTIVE STATISTICS, INTERACTION MEASURES

Statistics	$r1_k$	$r2_k$
Mean	0.16	1.01
Std.deviation	0.22	1.79
Percentiles		
Minimum	0.02	0.08
5	0.02	0.08
10	0.03	0.16
25	0.04	0.32
50	0.07	0.48
75	0.13	1.05
Maximum	1.00	29.39
N	756	756

WALD TEST. $\chi^2(1)$-STATISTIC FOR CONTRACT CATEGORIES. RESULTS FROM ESTIMATION OF EXPRESSION (8)/(9)

	Child care	Health care	Office	Other
Child care	–	3.16*/2.92*	0.06/0.05	0.29/0.32
Health care		–	3.12*/2.86*	1.37/1.20
Office			–	0.39/0.40
Other				–

* Significant at the 0.10 level.

WALD TEST. $\chi^2(1)$ - STATISTIC FOR DOMINATING BIDDERS. RESULTS FROM ESTIMATION OF EXPRESSION (8)/(9)

	FIRM 1	Firm 2	Firm 3	Firm 4	Firm 5	In-house
Firm 1	–	2.18/2.27	0.47/0.36	1.33/1.23	0.30/0.28	0.16/0.12
Firm 2		–	2.39/2.19	3.93**/3.86**	0.01/0.01	1.68/1.84
Firm 3			–	0.12/0.15	0.65/0.56	0.77/0.59
Firm 4				–	0.98/0.89	1.78/1.60
Firm 5					–	0.23/0.21
In-house						–

** Significant at the 0.05 level.

BIBLIOGRAPHY

ALSEMGEEST P. - NOUSSAIR C. - OLSON M., «Experimental Comparisons of Auctions Under Single- and Multiunit Demand», *Economic Inquiry*, no. 36(1), 1998, pages 87-97.

ANDERSSON A. - LUNANDER A., «Metoder vid utvärdering av pris och kvalitet vid offentlig upphandling. En inventering och analys av utvärderingsmodeller inom offentlig upphandling», *Konkurrensverkets uppdragsforskningsserie 2004:1*, Report written for the Swedish Competition Authority, in Swedish, 2004.

BAJARI P. - HORTACSU A., «Are Structural Estimates of Auction Models Reasonable? Evidence from Experimental Data», National Bureau of Economic Research. Inc., *NBER, Working papers*, 9889, 2003.

BIKHCHANDANI S., «Auctions of Heterogeneous Objects», *Games and Economic Behavior*, no. 26(2), 1999, pages 193-220.

DONALD S. - PAARSCH H.J., «Piecewise Pseudo-Maximum Likelihood Estimation in Empirical Models of Auctions», *International Economic Review*, no. 34(1), 1993, pages 121-48.

ENGELBRECHT-WIGGANS R., «Revenue Equivalence in Multi-Object Auctions», *Economic Letters*, no. 26(1), 1988, pages 15-9.

GUPTA S., «Competition and Collusion in a Government Procurement Auction Market», *Atlantic Economic Journal*, no. 30(1), 2002, pages 13-25.

KRISHNA K. - TRANÆS T., «Allocating Multiple Units», *Economic Theory*, no. 20(4), 2002, pages 733-50.

KRISHNA V., *Auction Theory*, San Diego, USA, Academic Press, 2004.

LAFFONT J-J., «Game Theory and Empirical Economics: The Case of Auction Data», *European Economic Review*, no. 41(1), 1997, pages 1-35.

LIST J.A. - LUCKING-REILEY D., «Demand Reduction in Multi-unit Auctions: Evidence from a Sportscard Field Experiment», *American Economic Review*, no. 90(4), 2000, pages 961-72.

LUCKING-RILEY D., «Using Field Experiments to Test Equivalence between Auction Formats: Magic on the Internet», *The American Economic Review*, no. 89(5), 1999, pages 1063-80.

LOU, *The Public Procurement Act in Sweden*, (1992:1528), 1992.

LUNANDER A. - NILSSON J-E., «Taking the Lab to the Field: Experimental Tests of alternative Mechanisms to procure Multiple Contracts», *Journal of Regulatory Economics*, no. 25(1), 2004, pages 39-58.

LUNDBERG S., «Restrictions on Competition in Municipal Competitive Procurement in Sweden», *International Advances in Economic Research*, no. 11, 2005, pages 353-66.

MACDONALD J.M. - HANDY C.R. - PLATO G.E., «Competition and Prices in USDA Commodity Procurement», *Southern Economic Journal*, no. 69(1), 2002, pages 128-43.

SZENTES B. - ROSENTHAL R.W., «Three-object Two-bidder Simultaneous Auctions: Chopsticks and Tetrahedra», *Games and Economic Behavior*, no. 44(1), 2003, pages 114-33.

VICKREY W., «Counterspeculation, Auctions, and Competitive Sealed Tenders», *Journal of Finance*, no. 16(1), 1961, pages 8-37.

— —, «Auctions and Bidding Games in Recent Advances in Game Theory», in MORGENSTERN O. - TUCKER A. (eds.), *Proceedings of a Conference*, Princeton, Princeton University Press, 1962.

WILSON R., «Auctions of Share», *Quarterly Journal of Economics*, no. 93(4), 1979, pages 675-89.

III - CONTRACTING IN PROCUREMENT

On the Economics of Subcontracting

Achim Wambach · **Gero von Grawert-May**
University of Cologne   TWS-Partners, Munich

In a situation where firms compete for a contract of an agency and subcontract part of this contract it is shown that:
(i) If the timing of subcontracting is determined by the firms, then the more efficient firms subcontract after the award, while the less efficient firms subcontract before the award.
(ii) Depending on the market structure, using a Dutch auction can be preferable to an English auction when subcontracting takes place before the award.
(iii) To foster competition among subcontractors, a firm should not always subcontract even if subcontractors are cheaper than producing in-house.
(iv) The agency when deciding on the timing of subcontracting faces a trade-off between a competition enhancing effect and an efficiency effect. [JEL Classification: D44, L24]

1. - Introduction

Subcontracting is a pervasive phenomenon in everyday business relations. Morcos (2003) reports that in 2001 subcontracting among the EU-15 was valued at 635 billion Euros. Kamien *et* al. (1989) cite a study which reports that in the automobile industry in Europe and the US about 50% of the final product is subcontracted. In a more recent study, Grossman and Helpman (2002) note that only 37% of the production value of an American car is generated in the US. An estimation by the Confederation of Finnish Industry and Employer in 1996 yields that subcontracting was about 50% of

The Authors thank Susanne Ludewig-Greiner for research assistance and Gregor Berz and Andreas Engel for helpful comments.

115

the value of Finnish manufacturing products (cited in Morcos, 2003).

An industry has evolved in supporting firms which intend to subcontract, where the focus lies on legal issues in relation to subcontracting. In the US, courses are offered training decision makers on how to establish and manage successful subcontracts and showing advantages and disadvantages of subcontracting. In Europe, trade shows focussing on subcontracting and its suppliers have been established.[1] To foster international subcontracting, the United Nations Industrial Development Organizations' Industrial Subcontracting and Supply Chain Management Program has been establishing Subcontracting and Partnerships Exchanges (SPX) on a world wide basis since 1982.

In this paper we focus on particular economic issues in the context of subcontracting.

The economic environment we investigate is the following: An agency intends to award a contract. Examples are the construction of an airport, the installation of a new telecommunications network, exhibition construction, automotive engineering or civil engineering (e. g. construction of tenements or commercial buildings). There are several firms or general contractors competing for this contract. For technological or economical reasons these firms have to subcontract part of their work. We only consider vertical subcontracting, i.e. the potential subcontractors are not among the group of firms.[2] There are several potential subcontractors competing for the subcontract at each firm.

We are interested in the interaction between the contest for the subcontract and the contest for the contract. In particular, we are concerned with the following questions:

1. If a firm has to decide whether to subcontract before or after the award, what are the relevant factors for this decision? How will a firm decide?

---

[1] E.g. October 17-19, 2006 PROCEED — European Center for Subcontracting, Industrial Supply and Services in Metz (*http://www.proceedexpo.com/*) or April 4-5, 2006, European Subcontracting Meeting in Lyon: Metal, Electronics, Plastics (*http://www.eventseye.com/fairs/event_tc99_1_1.html*).

[2] For an analysis of horizontal subcontracting, see KAMIEN M.I. *et* AL. (1989) and GALE *et* AL. (2000).

2. If a firm has taken the decision on when to subcontract —
how should it subcontract? Is an English auction better than a
Dutch auction or vice versa?

3. If a firm can choose the amount of subcontracted products/
services — how much should it subcontract?

4. In several states (see the discussion below), the agency can
decide whether subcontracting has to take place before or after
the award. What factors determine this decision? How should the
agency decide?

In the next section, we describe the economic environment in
more detail and outline the relevant economic parameters. In
section 3, we shed light on the timing decision; section 4 is
concerned with the subcontract-procurement design. Section 5
turns to the question on how much to subcontract, while in section
6, we will discuss the decision problem the agency faces. In section
7, we summarize and conclude. Sections 3 and 4 are based in parts
on the works by Wambach (Wambach 2006*a*, 2006*b*); section 6 is
based on the work by Marechal and Morand (2003).

2. - The Economic Environment

Players

There are three groups of players: First, there is the agency,
which intends to award a contract. Second, there are the firms
which compete for the contract. Third, there is the group of
potential subcontractors. As mentioned above, we consider vertical
subcontracting only, which implies that the group of firms and
the group of subcontractors are distinct.

Market for Subcontractors

While all firms are suitable to do the work for the agency, this
must not be the same for the subcontractors with respect to the work
at each firm. We consider two extreme cases. First, every subcon-

tractor can do the work for every firm. This implies, for example, that if several firms subcontract before the award, each time all subcontractors compete against each other. In the second case — although there is competition at each firm — each subcontractor can work for a single firm only. As an example, consider the case of two competing firms of which one is located in the US and the other in Europe. If the subcontract has to be provided locally, then for the US firm only American subcontractors will be relevant, and respectively for the European firm only European subcontractors. Another reason might be technological standards: If competing technologies e.g. in software are in use, then subcontractors can only work for firms which have compatible systems.

Timing

A firm which intends to apply for the contract has two possibilities with regard to the timing of subcontracting. First, it may subcontract after the award and only in case of winning the award. In that case, the economics of subcontracting is like in any other procurement, so that standard auction theory results apply. The second alternative is to subcontract before the award *conditionally* on winning the award. That is to say the firm and the subcontractor specify the subcontract consisting of a price and a description of the work. However, the price will only be paid and the work will only be done if the firm wins the award. This interdependence between the two contests (for the contract and for the subcontract) distinguishes the economics of subcontracting from standard procurement. And, as we will see later on, will lead to results which differ from standard auction theory.

Amount of Subcontracting

Note that throughout the work, it is assumed that ex-ante all firms are symmetric with respect to their need for subcontracting. As argued above, subcontracting is pervasive in many industries so we do not justify the assumption on the need for subcontracting further. With regard to the amount of subcontracting, we distinguish two cases. In the first one, the amount of subcontracting is exogenously given while in the second one, this is a choice parameter of the firm. Although the latter is the more realistic scenario, we assume in several cases that subcontracting is exogenously given to concentrate on other aspects involved.

Efficiency Effects of Later Subcontracting

When talking to practitioners, it seems to be the case that they expect that subcontracting after the award is efficiency enhancing. Actually, in their opinion subcontracting after the award leads to lower prices, which however is quite similar for the purpose of this paper. There are several potential reasons for this efficiency enhancing effect. A first reason, given to us by practitioners, is that subcontractors just do not quote as aggressive if they do not know whether they will get the order for sure (which would be the case, if subcontracting takes place after the award). One reason for this might be that the quoted price of the subcontractor is determined by negotiations within the company of the subcontractor, i.e. between the sales force and the management. Fighting internally for better prices will only be worthwhile for the sales person if this leads to a new order, but not if this just leads to some vague business prospect. Although firms — if subcontracting before the award — negotiate prices somewhat down after the award, it could be argued that by doing this they will not recoup the potential cost reduction, as the threat of picking another subcontractor is not available anymore. As a second efficiency enhancing effect of later subcontracting, one might argue, that after the award the precise technological requirements are much better known, so that the subcontract can be specified in much more detail. This has two cost reducing effects. First, the subcontractor knows what to expect in more detail so that it puts a lower "risk-premium" (e.g. for later changes) into its offer. Second, if the subcontract is less well specified, the lowest cost subcontractor might be the one having the lowest average costs (among all possible specifications). With more detailed specification, the winning subcontractor will not be the supplier with the lowest average cost on all specifications but the one with the lowest cost on the actual specification. A third reason for efficiency effects of subcontracting later might be the better understanding of the claims management possibilities, as argued in Marechal and Morand (2003). These authors assume that after the award of the contract, the winning firm has much better knowledge on the possibilities to do claims management. Although claims management is a zero sum game with respect to efficiency, this knowledge on claims management is used by the firms in Marechal and Morand (2003) to optimize their subcontracting strategy. This in turn might be efficiency enhancing.

To illustrate the different aspects involved in subcontracting, we discuss an example taken from the building industry.

Case Study

An Asian Country wants to source a new major airport. A small number of international firms are invited to bid for the contract. In order to construct, plan and build the airport, these firms need to subcontract goods and services to local and international suppliers. Firm X is one potential contractor. The firm faces different numbers of subcontractors and market situations in each product category, e.g. some categories are characterized by high global demand and high capacity utilization, whereas suppliers in other categories have plenty of free capacity. In some categories many suppliers compete for the subcontract while others have monopolistic/oligopolistic structures. The agency's tender does not perfectly specify important aspects of the logistical questions. In addition, the country in which the airport is located imposes high duties on imported goods and services, which could be evaded by joint ventures of international subcontractors with local companies. In order to establish these cost saving joint ventures, subcontractors need to assess their chances of winning the subcontract as early as possible with a minimum of uncertainty.

3. - When to Subcontract?

As we have argued in section 2, subcontracting after the award might be efficiency enhancing, e.g. because the project is better known at this stage. However, subcontracting before the award gives the firm better information about the costs of the subcontractor. This information can be used in the preparation of the bid for the award. Accordingly, there seems to be a trade-off between earlier and later subcontracting. In the first part of this section, we discuss several theoretical results on the timing of subcontracting. In the second part, we report on the case mentioned above and describe how the timing decision was made.

The cost for the subcontractor represents a crucial element in the cost estimate being the basis for the bid preparation in the contest for the contract. Firms which subcontract after the award have to take the expectation for the costs of the subcontractor into their cost breakdown. In the contrary, firms negotiating with their subcontractors before the award, know the exact price they have to pay for the subcontractor. However, they forgo the efficiency gains of later contracting. In this environment, Wambach (2006 a) shows that the less efficient or high cost firms are better off, if they subcontract earlier while the more efficient or low cost firms are better off subcontracting later.

The reason for this result is as follows: If a firm is a high cost firm, it will have a low chance of winning the contest for the award. If such a firm subcontracts earlier, it might realize that the subcontractor is cheaper than initially expected. This in turn will make the firm more capable to compete with the low cost firms having to calculate with the higher expected costs. The low cost firms, on the other hand, are better off subcontracting later in order to take advantage of the efficiency gains.

As another result, it turns out that firms which subcontract later shade their bid in the contest for the contract downwards. E.g.

if the contest takes the form of an English auction, firms should under normal circumstances stay in the auction until the price reaches their expected costs. However, in this case it makes sense to stay even longer. By realizing that a competitor is still in the contest, a firm should reason that this competitor might be someone who subcontracted earlier and learnt that the subcontractors have very low costs, at least lower than expected. By taking this into account, the expectation of the price the firm has to pay for the subcontractor will be revised downwards, which explains the more aggressive bidding behaviour.

Apart from the efficiency gains of subcontracting later, there is another argument against subcontracting earlier, however only if the auction design is not chosen optimally (see also section 4.2). Assuming that the number of subcontractors is less than or equal to the number of firms, subcontracting after the award is unproblematic, as there is enough competition among the subcontractors. However, subcontracting before the award might give rise to a subtle form of strategic demand reduction (see e.g. Brusco and Lopomo, 2002). Consider the case where there are exactly as many subcontractors as firms: If each subcontractor demands a relatively high price at one firm (which is different for each subcontractor), and a very high price at all the other firms, then every subcontractor will be chosen at one firm. As the firms have (in a symmetric scenario) a similar chance of winning the contract, each subcontractor has a chance of getting the final subcontract. In effect, the subcontractors coordinate on lottery tickets — everyone has a chance of winning. By (tacitly) coordinating on relatively high prices, the price in case of winning is quite attractive.

This behaviour might be stable in equilibrium by the following argument. If everyone behaves as described, then all the firms have to pay the same high price for the subcontractor. As this applies to all firms, it does not influence the firms' chances of winning the contract. As for the subcontractors, they now have a chance of winning the final award, but at very good conditions for them. Accordingly, rather than competing at every firm, which will lower the prices for the subcontract, it might be optimal to stay at one firm, demand a high price, and hope that this firm will win the final contest. Note that this reasoning only works if all the other subcontractors also stay at one single firm and demand a high price as well. As we will argue below, this will not be the case if firms subcontract via a first price sealed bid auction. However, if contractors source via an English auction, then with a similar argument along the lines of Wambach (2006c), such a form of strategic demand reduction might be an equilibrium outcome.

Case Study

Firm X which is competing for the contract to build the airport knows that sourcing after the award would lead to the lowest achievable prices, but sourcing before would enable the firm to estimate its costs more precisely and to submit a better bid. Depending on the market situation in each product category in which the firm intends to subcontract part of the work, the firm decides on a different sourcing strategy. In some cases the situation is clear cut:

If e.g. the firm faces a monopoly without having chances to modify its technology in order to end this dependency or to create competition by other means, it has established a partnership with the monopolist in order to obtain parts of its economies of scale.

In other cases it is less obvious how to proceed, as the trade-off described above arises. The firm decides on a two-stage procedure: Before the contest for the award, subcontractors are asked for quotes on the basis of which a shortlist of subcontractors will be established. In case of winning the contract, the firm intends to make an auction only with the subcontractors on the short list. The competing subcontractors are made aware that such a shortlist will be made, which in turn makes them bid more aggressively. This procedure allows the firm to get a rather good idea about its cost situation for its own bid and at the same time to take advantage of the cost lowering efficiency effects of finally subcontracting after the award (see Option 3 in the diagram below).

SUBCONTRACTING: MAJOR NEGOTIATION OPTIONS

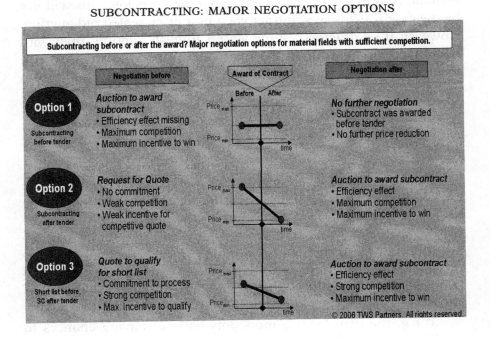

4. - How to Subcontract?

In this section we are concerned with the question on how a firm should subcontract, i.e. which form of competition it should employ. After reporting theoretical results on the design for the subcontract contest, we will discuss the case study and the applied auction design.

Let us start with the unproblematic cases, i.e. those cases where standard analysis applies. First, if subcontracting takes place after the contract contest, only the winning contractor will search for a subcontractor. Thus the contest for the subcontract boils down to a typical procurement situation in which all the standard results from auction theory apply. In particular, revenue equivalence holds. Second, suppose that subcontracting takes place before the competition of the contract, the pool of potential subcontractors being the same for all firms and this pool being sufficiently large. Then a subcontractor winning the subcontract at one firm is probably the one with the lowest costs. Therefore, it will also win the subcontract contest at the other firms. In this case, the situation is again the standard procurement case, as the strategic effect, which we discuss below — namely to bid more aggressively so that the firm has a higher chance of obtaining the contract — is missing, as the subcontractor influences all firms in the same way.

So we now turn to the strategic effects in this context. There are two effects which we will analyse in more detail. First, we discuss the case in which the pool of subcontractors are distinct for each firm, e.g. because the firms (and the required subcontractors) are located in different countries. Second, the case of a small number of subcontractors will be discussed.

4.1. *Distinct Pool of Subcontractors*

Wambach (2006*b*) shows that if subcontractors do not compete at different contractors, then a first price sealed bid (FPSB) auction (or a Dutch auction) fares better than a second price sealed bid (SPSB) auction (or an English auction). This implies that the well known result from auction theory, the revenue equivalence result, breaks down. The reason is that in a SPSB auction subcontractors bid their costs, so the price is equal to the second lowest cost. In a FPSB auction, however, the subcontractors take into account that if they make a smaller bid, this will make "their" firm more competitive in the final award competition. Thus bidding more aggressively has two positive effects: First, it increases the probability that the subcontractor is chosen among the group of subcontractors. Second, it increases the probability that their contractor is chosen among the group of contractors. As a final result, subcontractors bid more aggressively compared to the case where the latter effect is not present. In Wambach (2006*b*) it is shown that the expected price will then be lower than the expected second lowest costs.

This logic, namely that the bid of the subcontractor becomes more aggressive because the subcontractor participates in the contest the firm faces, can be pushed even further. The firm might announce that for any price reduction in the auction for the subcontract, it will lower the price in the contest for the award by e.g. x% more than this reduction. This would align the incentives of the subcontractor even stronger to the incentives of the firm. In Wambach (2006*b*) the optimal mechanism is discussed.

4.2. *Few Subcontractors*

As we have argued in section 3, if there are only few potential subcontractors (less or equally many subcontractors than firms) the subcontractors might engage in strategic demand reduction, if the sourcing for the subcontract takes places before the award of the contract. However, for this collusive arrangement to work, contractors have to negotiate with the subcontractors in a parallel way. Ideally (from the point of view of the subcontractors), there will be n parallel English auctions, so that each subcontractor can see whether its competitors behave as expected, namely to bid only at a single firm, and react in case they do not do so. As in the conventional discussion on collusion in auctions (see e.g. Krishna, 2002, page 151 ff) such an arrangement is much harder to sustain if the auction takes the form of a FPSB auction. To see this, note that if the subcontractors tacitly agree that e.g. subcontractor A should work with firm 1 and subcontractor B with firm 2, and if both firms make a FPSB auction, then it might be easy for subcontractor B to undercut subcontractor A at firm 1, as A is expected to hand in a high offer. Accordingly, by undercutting A, subcontractor B can become the winner at both firms. As A anticipates this, it might make a similar low bid at firm 2 (and reduce its bid at firm 1). Therefore, the overall result is that collusive demand reduction will not work.

To illustrate this, suppose subcontractors A and B compete for subcontracts of two firms, X and Y. A and B have identical costs of 50. Both firms award their subcontracts by a FPSB auction. A and B agree that each of them makes a bid to only one firm at the price of 250. For simplicity, we assume that the only alternative bid is 150. If A and B collude and behave according to its agreement, their payoffs are 100 each — both have a 50% chance of winning the final subcontract in which case they make a profit of 200 (northwest corner of the table below). If subcontractor A colludes by submitting a bid of 250 to only one firm while subcontractor B defects by submitting a bid of 250 to the other firm and a bid of 150 to the firm subcontractor A is bidding for, B will win the final contract for sure. Either its firm will get the contract in which case B will make a profit of 200, or A's firm, which will also choose B as its subcontractor, as B made a better offer, will win the contract in which case B makes a profit of 100. The expected profit is thus 150. A on the other hand has a profit of 0 (northeast corner of the table). The situation is similar vice versa if B sticks to the collusive agreement and A defects (southwest corner of the table). How would the subcontractors behave in a FPSB auction? If one subcontractor thinks the other colludes, its payoff is higher if it defects. Accordingly, defecting is the better strategy for A and B, in case they think the other one colludes. In case both expect the other to defect, it is optimal to bid the lower price at both firms. They then have an equal chance of winning the final subcontract in which case they make a profit of 100. So the expected profit is 50 (southeast corner of the table). This is the standard Prisoners' Dilemma situation — although strategic demand reduction (each subcontractor only bidding at one firm) would be jointly optimal, individual profit maximization leads both subcontractors to compete aggressively at both firms.

GRAPH 2

INCENTIVES TO COORDINATE ON HIGH PRICES

127

Case Study

Before the award of the airport-contract, firm X requested quotes from all potential national and international subcontractors. Depending on the market structure, this took the form of either single quotes only or a quote-bidding process, where respective best quotes were revealed to competing subcontractors and better offers could be made. The firm linked the quality of the subcontractors' quotes to their chances of winning the subcontract in the final auction after the award, i.e. subcontractors with better offers and higher quality obtained an advantage for the sourcing process which was to follow in case of winning the award.

The final awarding of the subcontracts was to take place after the awarding of the contract. Again, in the different product categories the final design was made to depend on the market structure (e.g. number of suppliers, free capacities) and product characteristic (e.g. scale economics) in that particular market. Subcontractors having offered good conditions before the award obtained an advantage in the final process, either in form of a final bid, or in form of a bonus during the negotiation.

5. - How Much to Subcontract?

In some situations a firm has some leeway to decide on the amount of subcontracting, i.e. the decision which part of the work is given to an outside firm and which part will be done in-house. There is huge literature on the decision whether to outsource or not, which goes way beyond the scope of this article (see e.g. Holmstrom and Roberts, 1998).

Here we want to discuss one particular aspect of the decision on how much to subcontract, namely its implication for the auction format.

As a first rule it appears sensible to subcontract whenever the costs of subcontracting are cheaper than the cost of producing the product/service in-house. Although the costs of the subcontractors are in general not known, such a rule can easily be implemented by using an auction among subcontractors where the own costs of producing the product/service serves as a reservation price. I.e. the winner of the auction only obtains the subcontract if its offer was below the reservation price. In this way, it can be assured that only subcontractors having lower costs than producing in-house will obtain the subcontract.

The firm could do even better: There is a well-known result in auction theory (see e.g. Krishna, 2002, p. 71) which states that to maximize the revenue, a firm should set a reservation price even lower than its own costs of producing the product/service in-house. This might well lead to the inefficient situation where the best subcontractor has costs lower than the in-house costs but larger than the reservation price, so it will not obtain the subcontract and the firm will produce the product/service itself. However, due to the aggressive reservation price subcontractors with lower costs are forced to compete stronger, which in turn will lead to better prices on average.

6. - How to Regulate Subcontracting?

We now discuss the case in which the agency can decide whether subcontracting has to take place before or after the award.

This possibility exists in particular in the context of public projects. According to Marechal and Morand (2003), in the US, each bidder is required to submit the potential subcontracting plan before the award of contracts that exceed $500,000 ($1,000,000 for construction). Contract authorities in Canada and the EU may ask the tenderer to specify the proportion of subcontracting in his bid, or they may allow him to choose the proportion of subcontracting after the contract is awarded.

In general, the agency when taking the decision has to take account of two effects: The efficiency effect and the competition effect. As for the *efficiency effect* which we argued above, later subcontracting leads to an efficiency gain. It should be in the interest of the agency to let contractors use these efficiency gains

129

for the following reason: If contractors anticipate that they will have lower costs by subcontracting later, they will bid more aggressively in the contest for the award, which in turn leads to lower prices for the agency. Second, there is a *competition effect*. To obtain low prices, the agency is interested in strong competition among the firms. However, competition is stronger, the more equal the firms are.

Marechal and Morand (2003) point out that if the efficiency gains of subcontracting later are not the same for all firms, but e.g. increase if firms have lower costs, then by subcontracting later firms will in effect become more heterogeneous. This would then be an argument in favour of letting all firms subcontract before the award. In Marechal and Morand (2003) this increased heterogeneity arises because after the award firms know better how to do claims management. It is quite plausible that these profits from claims management are higher, the lower the costs of the firm are, thus increasing the heterogeneity between firms. However, to make the claim that subcontracting before is better than after the award, one has to show that the increase in profit — due to better fine tuning of the claims management after the award compared to before the award — is larger, the smaller the costs are.

7. - Conclusions

A general contractor who intends to bid for a contract faces several problems with regard to his subcontracting strategy. It is shown that there is a trade-off between subcontracting earlier and later. While the firm would like to subcontract before the award to know its costs more precisely, subcontracting after the award might lead to efficiency gains, as the technical requirements are better known at this stage and because subcontractors bid more aggressively if they know that by winning the contest they have a contract for sure (which would not be the case if subcontracting takes place before the award).

We discuss the economics of subcontracting earlier and later and provide a case study in which a hybrid mechanism — partial subcontracting before the award, a final contest after the award — was used in order to solve the trade-off.

In addition to this timing condition, the firm also has to decide on how to subcontract. Subcontracting after the award is like standard procurement. By subcontracting before the award, new issues arise. First, measures to avoid strategic demand reduction by the subcontractors should be employed. Second, a mechanism letting the subcontractor participate in the firm's contest for the award might fare better than a standard English auction.

BIBLIOGRAPHY

BRUSCO S. - LOPOMO G., «Collusion Via Signalling in Simultaneous Ascending Bid Auctions with Heterogeneous Objects, with and without Complementarities», *Review of Economic Studies*, no. 69, 2002, pages 407-36.

GALE I.L. - HAUSCH D.B. - STEGEMAN M., «Sequential Procurement with Subcontracting», *International Economic Review*, vol. 41, 2000, pages 989-1020.

GROSSMAN G. - HELPMAN E., «Outsourcing in a Global Economy», *NBER, Working Paper*, no. 8728, 2002.

— — - — —, «Outsourcing versus FDI in Industrial Equilibrium», *NBER, Working Paper*, no. 9300, 2002.

HOLMSTROM B. - ROBERTS J., «The Boundaries of the Firm Revisited», *Journal of Economic Perspectives*, no. 12, 1998, pages 73-94.

KAMIEN M.I. - LI L. - SAMET D., «Bertrand Competition with Subcontracting», *RAND, Journal of Economics*, no. 20, 1989, pages 553-67.

KRISHNA V., *Auction Theory*, Academic Press, San Diego, 2002.

MARECHAL F. - MORAND P.-H., «Pre vs. Post-award Subcontracting Plans in Procurement Bidding», *Economics Letters*, no. 81, 2003, pages 23-30.

MORCOS J.-L., «International Subcontracting versus Delocalization», *http://www.unido.org/file-storage/download/?file_id=18187*, 2003.

WAMBACH A., *When to Subcontract — Pre or Post-award?*, mimeo, University of Cologne, 2006a.

— —, *How to Subcontract?*, mimeo, University of Cologne, 2006b.

— —, *Bargaining and Auctions with Unknown Preferences of the Principal*, mimeo, University of Cologne, 2006c.

Efficiency of Procurement Procedures for Medical Devices

Calogero Guccio - **Giacomo Pignataro** - **Ilde Rizzo**
Università "Mediterranea"   Università di Catania   Università di Catania
di Reggio Calabria

The paper investigates the efficiency of procurement for medical devices. Differentiation of products in this market, due to doctors' preferences for specific technologies, might reduce the number of suppliers and the potential positive impact of auctions relative to negotiations. Using a large official dataset on technological equipment purchased by Italian hospitals in the period 1995-2005, we run an empirical analysis of the differential impact of procurement procedures on the purchasing price, controlling for several factors like product differentiation and number of suppliers. The policy implication is that incentives are needed for managers and doctors when auctions cannot ensure efficiency in procurement. [JEL Classification: H57, I18, C13].

1. - Introduction

In Italy, the National Health Service expenditure for goods and services covers different typologies of items: 16% is for standardized and conventional goods and services, common to any branch of the public sector; 31% is for goods and services that can be also consumed in other branches of the public sector, but present peculiar features in the health care sector (for instance,

The Authors are grateful to Claudio Giuricin, Marina Trampus and to the "Agenzia per i Servizi Sanitari Regionali - Friuli Venezia Giulia" for the availability of the data used in their analysis. The usual disclaimer applies. Even if the paper is the result of the joint work of the Authors, sections 4 and 5 are attributable to Calogero Guccio.

133

cleaning services for hospitals); 53% is only consumed in the health care sector (for instance, drugs, medical equipment) (Catalano - Gallo, 2003). Within the above expenditure, according with the latest data available, in 2002 medical devices accounted for 4,035 million Euros (Cerbo and Morgese, 2004).

The quantitative dimension of the above expenditure is relevant and, therefore, any improvement in its efficiency and effectiveness may have a significant impact in economic as well as financial terms. From this point of view, a crucial role is plaid by the set of procurement rules. Indeed, in the economic literature as well as in the political debate, great attention is paid to such an issue.

In what follows no attempt is made to analyze in depth such a wide issue but attention will be focused only upon some of the most significant theoretical aspects, to stress their relevance for the procurement of medical devices. In section 2 the role of rules and of competition in procurement will be compared to the role of incentives; section 3 will offer an overview of the main features of the market for medical devices; in section 4, a description of the data set will be offered and some statistics will be computed. In section 5 we will run an empirical analysis of the differential impact of procurement procedures on the purchasing price and will offer some comments on the results. Few concluding remarks will be presented in section 6.

2. - Rules vs. Incentives in Procurement

Procurement objectives can be stated saying that Government aims at obtaining "value for money", including the quality dimension in the concept of value[1]. The possibility of fulfilling this objective depends on:
— the selection of the private contractor;
— the specification of the contract;
— the enforcement of the contract.

---

[1] We are not taking into account the allocative issues, i.e. the choice of the object of the contract.

The economic issues involved in procurement are very well known and are mainly related to asymmetric information, both in the form of adverse selection (i.e. the problem of choosing the best private contractor) and of moral hazard (i.e. the problem of preventing opportunistic behaviour in the implementation of the contract). Procurement rules should be designed to address and overcome the above problems.

In Italy, procurement is characterized by many strict rules. No attempt is made here of analyzing the Italian legislation[2] and only few key general features will be recalled. Italian procurement rules specify how decisions should be taken (for instance, "award to the lowest bidder,") or what process has to be followed in making a decision (for instance, "do not accept late proposals", "evaluate proposals only based on the evaluation criteria in the solicitation"). Rules attempt to positively dictate every step, which the contracting authority must follow, and every factor, which it must take into account, so that bureaucratic discretion is reduced to the lowest possible level[3]. On these grounds, preference is given to competition[4]: procurements should be widely advertised and evaluated strictly on criteria announced in advance. Sealed bids are used to prevent collusion among the participants and to ensure transparency[5]. In other words, competition is promoted as much as possible, as a tool to select the most convenient bidder[6]. As far as the specification of the contract is concerned, cost plus contract are not allowed to prevent opportunistic behaviour of private contractors. Since December 1999, the Italian Government has

---

[2] Italian rules are under transformation: very recently new rules have been devised and a law was passed (*Codice dei contratti pubblici di lavori, servizi, forniture*) to implement the Directive n. 2004/18/Ce.

[3] This is what Kelman S. (2002) calls "objectification" in decision-making (when there are no rules, bureaucrats should be driven by considerations that can be stated independent of human judgment, preferably in quantitative terms). As Kelman points out these features strongly characterized the USA procurement before the legislative reforms passed in 1994, 1995 and 1998.

[4] Open and restricted procedures are the rule and negotiated procedures can be adopted only in well defined circumstances.

[5] As Piga G. and Zanza M. (2004) show, EU public procurement auctions exhibit some common features.

[6] This is in line with the more traditional results of the economic literature on auctions. For an overview of this literature see Klemperer P. (1999).

developed a program for electronic public procurement, integrated into the program of rationalizing public spending for goods and services.

Indeed, the "philosophy" underlying the above mentioned procurement rules does not always seem to align itself with the economic reality of procurement: emphasis is placed on competition as a tool to ensure the selection of the best contractor on the assumption that it ensures also the minimization of the costs for the purchasing authority[7]. However, procurement rules aimed at ensuring competition might not be effective in producing the expected final outcome. As Kelman (1990) stresses, the use of sealed bids, i.e. purchasing with anonymous sellers, is in contrast with any purchasing practice in the industrial sector since it makes difficult to establish any relationship between the purchaser and the seller. It follows that customers and suppliers cannot enjoy the value deriving from long term, continuing relationships such as those characterising private sector industrial purchasing[8], though the undesirable lock-in effect should be not undervalued. Potentially relevant incentives for good performance, such as a promise to award future contracts, are ruled out. These shortcomings might be especially relevant when centralized procurement procedures are used.

Indeed, the scope of the above consideration is particularly relevant in the case of non standardized and complex supplies and services[9], since commercial factors in the selection of the contractor can turn up as strategic[10] and the phase of the enforcement of the contract is crucial. Indeed, procurement rules establish a rigid framework: the purchasing authority can rely upon past experience, financial viability, technical ability, previous performance in similar works but cannot base its choice

---

[7] Expected total costs do not necessarily decrease when the number of bidders increases: the administrative costs as well as the costs for the preparation of the bid should not be undervalued.

[8] The advantages of such a kind of relationship have been stressed by WILLIAMSON O.E. (1985).

[9] This issue has been explored by LAPECORELLA F. - RIZZO I. (2002) for public works.

[10] An extensive analysis of this issue is provided by KELMAN S. (2002) and DENHARDT K.G. (2003).

on other relevant considerations such as previous performance with the same authority, reputation for excessive claims, trade record in the same or in other authorities. In other words, the firm reputation cannot be used as an evaluation criterion and the subjective judgement of the purchasing officer is left out.

The negative implications of such an approach have been put forward by Rizzo (1992, 1994); more recently, Dini and Spagnolo (2004) underline the relevance of reputation for e-public procurement and Doni (2005) outlines possible ways for including the reputation as an evaluation criterion in Italian procurement[11], emphasising that attention should be paid in evaluating the trade off between the need for giving more incentives to firms for the implementation of the contract and the reduction of competition.

The rules, which prevent any discretional evaluation of the purchasing officer, are usually justified also as ways to avoid abuse, particularly corruption (Rose-Ackerman 1999). However, this is not necessarily the case; Celentani and Ganuza (2002) show that corruption may well be increasing in competition and empirical evidence shows that rules do not prevent dishonest agents from pursuing their own interest. At the same time, a rigid regulation may negatively affect the outcome of the public decision-making process because it induces bureaucrats to shirk, since they do not face any incentive to improve their performance.

Rizzo (2001) outlines that a way of addressing these problems might be to allow procurement officers to make discretional decisions and, at the same time, to make them liable for the outcome achieved through the procurement process. From this point of view, to prevent opportunistic bureaucratic behaviour, indicators, such as standard costs, should be used to evaluate procurement officers performance[12].

The above arguments have different weights according to the features of the markets involved; *ceteris paribus*, the benefits of auctions are likely to be higher the greater the degree of competition

---

[11] In countries like, for instance, UK, France and US, the role of reputation is not disregarded (see DONI N., 2005).

[12] Standard costs are expressely mentioned in the Italian *"Codice dei contratti pubblici di lavori, servizi, forniture"*.

characterizing the market, since it allows for the spontaneous production of information, useful to overcome the above mentioned adverse selection problem. Therefore, in order to investigate how different procurement procedures perform in the purchasing of medical devices, a close analysis of such market is needed.

3. - The Market for Medical Devices

The market for medical devices is a mixed market. «Medical device products can be grouped into medical high-tech products and more conventional products. The segment of high tech products is composed of sophisticated devices designed for specific therapeutic and diagnostic uses. These are associated with costly and risky R&D activities, clinical trials, administrative and regulatory procedures for marketing clearance. The market of more conventional devices consists of items such as syringes, gauze, and intravenous products as well as a wide range of other conventional diagnostic and therapeutic products. This segment is associated with low margins and high volumes» (Pammolli et al., 2005)[13].

The features of the market are, of course relevant, for the purchasing decisions of health care organizations and for their performance. When considering the market for conventional products, which are usually standardizable and homogenous, it is reasonable to think that purchasing procedures like auctions, run by single purchasers or at a some centralized level, can produce satisfactory outcomes for the purchasers, in terms of prices paid for the items they purchase, while maintaining a good control of their quality[14].

---

[13] PAMMOLLI F. et AL. (2005) estimate the size of this market at over €184 billion. Expenditures on medical devices represent a relevant share of total health care expenditures: in Europe, 6.2 percent of total health care expenditure goes to medical devices, while in US and Japan the same indicator is at 5.1 percent. They also estimate that "... for a subset of the total aggregate show that the they constitute at least 0.8 percent of total production of the EU-25 manufacturing sector and 1.2 percent of total EU-25 manufacturing employment".

[14] NICITA A. and PAMMOLLI F. (2003) provide a survey of the main pros and contras of centralized purchasing, above all with respect to those related to the modification of the market power on the demand side.

As for the high-tech section of the market, its products tend to have completely different characteristics. They are usually sophisticated products that need to be used by specialized professionals, generally doctors. There may exist, in other words, a complementarity between medical technology and doctors, which can be relevant for the latter in as much as the practice with a given medical equipment will affect the ability and the costs of using it. Learning-by-doing can indeed be relevant in the use of high-tech medical devices. The potential complementarity between doctors and single medical devices may have an impact on the market structure, since producers can strategically exploit this feature. It is well known that product differentiation does not only respond to the objective of adapting supply to consumers' preferences, but it is also a way of softening price competition among firms, through a segmentation of the market and the exercise of market power. Even if the purchasing authority lies in the hands of the administrators of health care organizations, who cannot be interested in the differences among products, one has to consider the role of doctors in the decision-making process within these organizations. They are those who start the purchasing process, by requiring the availability of some technology, and who also advise the management on the best devices to buy. However, the relationship between doctors and administrators is generally characterized by asymmetry of information, above all as far as the characteristics of a sophisticated equipment is concerned[15].

Product differentiation tends to be confirmed by data collected by the Italian *Osservatorio Prezzi e Tecnologie*, for a sample of Italian hospitals. In Italy there are classes of products, such as the ecotomograph, which count 104 different products, with an average of 33 products per class. Differentiation will shrink the size of the market and will weaken the potential benefits of procurement procedures, like auctions.

---

[15] It must also be considered that it could be in the administrator's interest to buy the device that is more familiar to doctors, since it will reduce the costs of its utilization.

There is also another impact of product differentiation on the purchasing procedures that need to be considered. Centralized procurement may bring about several benefits, among which the saving in transaction costs, due to the reduction in the number of identical purchasing procedures implemented by different purchasers. With highly differentiated markets, however, centralization will not result in the reduction of procedures that one could expect in the case of standardized products. Moreover, in the case of standardized and homogenous products, centralization increases the size of the market that the winner of the centralized auction will serve and, therefore, will induce the Bertrand behaviour of the firms, with the expected positive effects on prices, for the buyers. Again, product differentiation will weaken these effects and will reduce the convenience of centralized procurement. Forcing centralized purchasing for these type of products may create the risk emphasized by Nicita and Pammolli (2003), that is the competition among products characterized by a different degree of technological innovation can reduce the capacity to recover R&D costs, thus reducing the incentives of the bidders to invest in further innovation.

Finally, it also needs to be considered that firms may try to segment the market dynamically, through innovation and the introduction of new products, as an alternative way of exercising market power. Even if new products may reduce the benefits of complementarity with an existing device for its users, however, another effect on the doctors' side needs to be acknowledged. It is the well known technological bias that brings doctors to wish to work with the latest and sophisticated technology, to produce what Pauly and Redish (1973) call "Cadillac-quality medicine". Pammolli *et* al. (2005) have estimated the intensity of the R&D activity for the different medical devices, in several countries. They find that « high-tech segments (*in-vitro* diagnostics on top of all) present the highest R&D intensity, while traditional low-tech segments (laboratory apparatus and furniture, surgical appliance and supplies) the lowest». Here again, this feature of the market will reduce the potential benefits of procurement procedures like auctions, for its effect on the number of potential bidders.

Altogether, therefore, we should expect that some features, characterizing the market for high-tech medical devices will tend to create segmentation and concentration of markets and, as a consequence, will reduce the welfare enhancing properties of procurement procedures like auctions or of centralized purchasing.

Furthermore, it is also worth noting that the segmentation of the market and the existence of what we have named as complementarity between doctors and «specialised» medical equipment, may have an impact on the nature of the relationship between single purchasers and suppliers. When the time comes to renovate some equipment, if doctors will push their managers to buy a product realised by the same producer and, probably, distributed by the same firm, the purchasing relationship assumes a potential long term nature, which is better exploited within a negotiating procedure, as argued in the previous section. Besides, the equipment requires maintenance interventions and consumable parts, whose costs can be relatively relevant and whose purchase can be better dealt with within a long-term contract negotiated with the producer.

Then, the characteristics of some medical devices are such that, in principle, there seem to be good reasons why negotiations could work more efficiently than auctions. The empirical analysis carried out in the following sections will try to test the existence of such benefits from negotiations relative to auctions within a sample of purchases of different medical devices, realised by Italian hospitals and local health care authorities.

4. - Data and Methods

The empirical objective of this paper is to check whether auctions turn to be efficient procedures when used for the purchase of medical technologies, given their specific characteristics and features of the decision-making process of health care organisations.

This paper adds to a growing empirical literature on the

efficiency of procurement procedures[16]. A recent paper by Kjerstad (2005) shows that, for medical and surgical articles, auctions do not necessarily produce lower prices than negotiation. Bonaccorsi *et* al. (2000) find that negotiation is preferred whenever quality is a relevant feature of the good to be purchased. Bajari *et* al. (2003), with reference to private sector building contracts, find that auctions perform poorly and negotiated procedures are preferable when projects are complex and there are few available bidders.

The following empirical analysis is based on a large dataset collected by the Italian *"Osservatorio Prezzi e Tecnologie"*, on medical devices. We use data on procedures run in the period 1995-2005 by a sample of 38 Italian public health care organisations, both hospitals and local health authorities (ASL). The data set is organised according to a detailed classification system of medical devices, based on categories (Angiographic catheters, Diagnostic reagents, Filters for haemodialysis, Orthopaedic prostheses, Pacemakers, Technical equipment, X-ray films), classes, grouping homogenous products as far as their technological characteristics are concerned (e.g. ecotomograph within the category of technical equipment) and single products[17].

Table 1 shows the composition of the sample used in our analysis, in terms of the number of purchases for each category. For each purchase, the following data are available: price, purchasing date, the seller and the type of procurement procedure. In addition, only for technical equipment, the number of bidders is also available.

Some limitations of the available data need to be underlined at this stage, since they impact on the empirical analysis. First of all, the observations available for each single identical product are very few and, therefore, the regression analysis will be carried out only at the class level. Within the class, however, products can be considered homogeneous from the technological point of view, the

---

[16] For a methodological survey see ATHEY S. - HAILE P.A. (2006).
[17] The classification system was developed by Consorzio per l'Area di ricerca di Trieste. For further details, see *http://www.assr.it/Opt.htm#tecnologie*.

TABLE 1

COMPOSITION OF THE SAMPLE

Product category	Number of Classes	Number of purchases	Average purchases per class
Angiographic catheters	9	2,422	269.11
Diagnostic reagents	58	3,641	62.78
Filters for haemodialysis	1	801	801.00
Orthopaedic prostheses	14	2,002	143.00
Pacemakers	1	1,039	1,039.00
Technical equipment	36	1,965	54.58
X-ray films	11	1,931	175.55
Total	130	13,801	106.16

Source: our elaboration on data from *Osservatorio Prezzi e Tecnologie - Agenzia per i Servizi Sanitari Regionali.*

implicit assumption being that their homogeneity is also with respect to their use[18].

Second, the data set does not offer information about the features of the purchasing authority (dimension, location, institutional characteristics) and, therefore, we cannot investigate how they impact on the efficiency of procurement procedures as well as on their choice.

Procurement procedures included in the data set are divided into two different groups: auctions (open and restricted procedures according to EU Directive) and negotiations. Awarding criteria in auctions are the lowest price and the most economically advantageous offer. Negotiation appears to be the most used procedure. As Graph 1 shows, it is used in the 72.03% of the sampled purchases.

Since the main objective of the paper is to investigate about the efficiency of different procurement procedures, we show, in Table 2, some statistics on the prices of the purchases in the different

---

[18] Since the data set is based on the technological characteristics of products and not on their functions it might be possible, however, that some products, though belonging to different classes, might be substitutes because they perform the same function.

GRAPH 1

DISTRIBUTION OF PROCUREMENT PROCEDURES BY CATEGORY

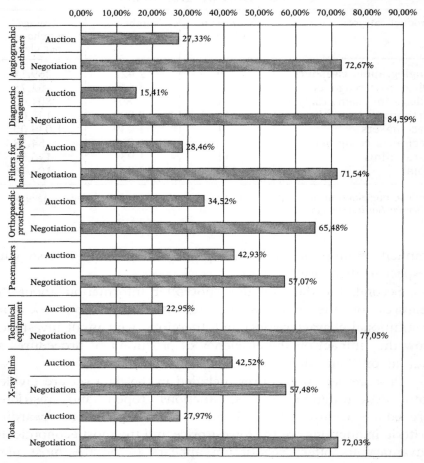

Source: our elaboration on data from *Osservatorio Prezzi e Tecnologie - Agenzia per i Servizi Sanitari Regionali.*

categories, differentiated by procurement procedures. Prices show a marked variability within each type of procedure in all categories, as shown by the values of standard deviation, and relevant differences, on average, between procurement procedures[19].

---

[19] The marked price variability across the two procurement procedures, in the case of medical equipment, is likely to depend, among the other things, on the existing legal constraints on the use of negotiations.

Table 2

SUMMARY STATISTICS OF PRICES

Product category	Procurement procedure	No. of purchases	Mean price (Euro)	Std dev. price (Euro)
Angiographic catheters	Auction	662	19.5	12.8
	Negotiation	1,760	38.8	29.8
	Total	2,422	33.5	27.7
Diagnostic reagents	Auction	561	155.6	209.3
	Negotiation	3,080	202.7	330.5
	Total	3,641	195.5	315.3
Filters for haemodialysis	Auction	228	25.7	22.8
	Negotiation	573	35.1	26.8
	Total	801	32.4	26.1
Orthopaedic prostheses	Auction	691	828.9	789.2
	Negotiation	1,311	738.1	721.2
	Total	2,002	769.5	746.4
Pacemakers	Auction	446	2,604.3	895.9
	Negotiation	593	2,584.1	927.6
	Total	1,039	2,592.8	913.8
Technical equipment	Auction	451	155,898.9	324,872.5
	Negotiation	1,514	26,678.3	60,928.4
	Total	1,965	56,336.6	173,194.8
X-ray films	Auction	821	104.7	187.5
	Negotiation	1,110	161.5	234.0
	Total	1,931	137.4	217.3
Total	Auction	3,860	18,714.2	121,649.5
	Negotiation	9,941	4,404.3	25,587.3
	Total	13,801	8,406.6	68,198.9

Source: our elaboration on data from *Osservatorio Prezzi e Tecnologie - Agenzia per i Servizi Sanitari Regionali.*
Notes: All values are converted into 2,000 Euro constant prices.

As for the latter difference, it must be reminded that, within each category, there are different classes and, within each class, several products. Then, a better understanding of the differences in prices between the procurement procedures, within each category, can be given by the relative deviation of a product's price with respect to the average price for identical products (IP) and

TABLE 3

SUMMARY STATISTICS OF THE INDICATORS OF PERFORMANCE
OF PROCUREMENT PROCEDURES

Product category	Procurement procedure	Average value of IP	Std dev. IP	Average value of IC	Std dev. IC
Angiographic	Auction	−8.07	23.25	−36.99	37.14
catheters	Negotiation	4.67	21.33	21.38	84.45
	Total	1.19	22.59	5.43	78.97
Diagnostic	Auction	−0.26	19.13	−8.26	102.24
reagents	Negotiation	1.28	19.72	9.08	124.77
	Total	1.04	19.64	6.41	121.72
Filters for	Auction	−2.76	23.57	−18.65	71.77
haemodialysis	Negotiation	1.73	20.70	10.79	84.69
	Total	0.45	21.64	2.41	82.26
Orthopaedic	Auction	−0.53	14.95	1.93	62.23
prostheses	Negotiation	0.97	22.25	0.29	71.89
	Total	0.45	20.04	0.85	68.70
Pacemakers	Auction	0.11	11.31	0.56	34.59
	Negotiation	0.27	11.57	−0.24	35.78
	Total	0.21	11.45	0.10	35.26
Technical	Auction	2.61	18.46	13.31	71.93
equipment	Negotiation	−0.89	21.94	−1.87	63.43
	Total	−0.08	21.24	1.61	65.77
X-ray films	Auction	−14.12	58.68	−25.12	87.16
	Negotiation	5.91	38.87	13.74	122.88
	Total	−2.60	49.29	−2.78	110.79
Total	Auction	−4.37	32.26	−12.02	73.35
	Negotiation	1.99	23.36	8.49	98.05
	Total	0.21	26.31	2.76	92.27

Source: our elaboration on data from *Osservatorio Prezzi e Tecnologie - Agenzia per i Servizi Sanitari Regionali.*

to the average price in the class (IC)[20]. Table 3 shows the different values of the two indicators for each product category.

---

[20] The indices are obtained as follows:

$$IP = \frac{P_h - \overline{P_h}}{\overline{P_h}}; \quad IC = \frac{P_h - \overline{P_j}}{\overline{P_j}}$$

where P_h is the price paid for a product h in the class j, $\overline{P_h}$ is the average price of product h, and $\overline{P_j}$ is the average price of all the products in the class j.

Overall, auctions seem to perform better than negotiations for all categories but technical equipment. Therefore, an appropriate econometric analysis is required to control for the different factors that can affect the differences in prices, to ascertain whether the procurement procedure has a clear and systematic impact on prices.

5. - Regression Analysis and Results

The efficiency of the different procurement procedures is tested by regressing the price paid in the purchases on the type of procurement procedure, while controlling for other factors. To reduce potential heteroscedasticity we adopt a log transformation of the dependent variable (the price)[21].

One of the factors that may affect the prices paid by purchasers is the competitive extension of the market, as measured by the number of suppliers. As it was previously mentioned, the available data are different for the technical equipment and for the other products, since we know the number of bidders only for the former. We, therefore, attempt to estimate the extension of the supply by considering, for each class, the number of registered suppliers in the class, referred to in what follows as potential bidders (POTBID). Table 4 shows average values and the standard deviation for each category.

Moreover, to control for the effects of residual heterogeneity within each class, as arising from the different quality of the same products, we will employ a proxy variable, computed as the average price of each product standardized for the average price of its class[22]. We also add some dummies to represent the

---

[21] The estimated model is also called semi-elasticity model, since the interpretation of the estimated values of the coefficients is in terms of percentage change in the dependent variable corresponding to a one per cent increase in the independent variable (see WOOLDRIDGE J.M., 2003). An exception occurs when a dummy variable is employed, in which case the percentage change in the dependent variable is given by $e^{\beta} - 1$ (see KENNEDY P., 2003).

[22] The variable QUALCOST is the *ratio* of the average price for a product h in the class j $\bar{P}_h$ to the average price for all products in the class j $\bar{P}_j$.

147

TABLE 4

NUMBER OF SUPPLIERS BY CATEGORY

Product category	Average number of suppliers	Std dev. No. of suppliers
Angiographic catheters	9.0	2.6
Diagnostic reagents	11.6	4.2
Filters for haemodialysis	18.0	0.0[*]
Orthopaedic prostheses	20.6	7.6
Pacemakers	12.0	0.0[*]
Technical equipment	14.8	8.7
X-ray films	6.5	2.5
Total	12.6	6.7

Source: our elaboration on data *Osservatorio Prezzi e Tecnologie - Agenzia per i Servizi Sanitari Regionali.*
[*] Only one class of products in this category.

procurement procedure (NEGOTIATION), the category (CATEGORY) and the class of the product being purchased (CLASS). Finally, we add a variable to capture the changes of prices over time (T). Table 5 presents the variables and Table 6 shows some summary statistics employed[23].

TABLE 5

VARIABLES IN THE ESTIMATED MODELS

Dependent Variable	
LN_PRICE	log of unit price (converted into 2000 Euro constant prices)
Explanatory Variables	
POTBID	total number of potential bidders for each class
BIDDERS	total number of actual bidders (only for equipment)
QUALCOST	proxy for quality variation within class
NEGOTIATION	dummy variable with value 1 if negotiation and 0 for auction
CATEGORY$_z$	dummy variables for $z - 1$ category ($z = 1, ..., 7$)
CLASS$_j$	dummy variables for $j - 1$ class ($j = 1, ..., 129$)
T	time variable

[23] Given that the variable POTBID is constant within a class and changes only across classes, the use of a dummy for each class creates perfect multicollinearity. To avoid this problem, we need to give up a further dummy in the regressions (130-1-1).

Table 6

SUMMARY STATISTICS OF THE VARIABLES USED IN THE ANALYSIS

Variable	Mean	Std. Dev.	Min	Max	Observa-tions
PRICE	8,406.63	68,198.86	0.26	3,264,082.00	13,801
POTBID	12.60	6.74	2.00	32.00	13,801
QUALCOST	1.02	0.87	0.00	17.45	13,801
NEGOTIATION	0.72	0.45	0.00	1.00	13,801
CATEGORY					
Angiographic catheters	0.18	0.38	0.00	1.00	13,801
Diagnostic reagents	0.26	0.44	0.00	1.00	13,801
Filters for haemodialysis	0.06	0.23	0.00	1.00	13,801
Orthopaedic prostheses	0.15	0.35	0.00	1.00	13,801
Pacemakers	0.08	0.26	0.00	1.00	13,801
Technical equipment	0.14	0.35	0.00	1.00	13,801
X-ray films	0.14	0.35	0.00	1.00	13,801
BIDDERS	5.76	5.49	1.00	50.00	1,066

Source: our elaboration on data *Osservatorio Prezzi e Tecnologie - Agenzia per i Servizi Sanitari Regionali.*

Since the sample is quite large, it seems reasonable to use a pooled regression, controlling for a set of dummy variables[24]. We run two different regressions: in the first one, we consider dummies at the category level, while in the second one dummies are introduced at the class level. Thus, a general formulation of the models estimated can be written as follows:

(1)
$$LN\_PRICE_i = \beta_0 + \beta_1\ POTBID_i +$$
$$+ \beta_2\ QUALCOST_i + \beta_3\ NEGOTIATION_i$$
$$B_4\ T_i + \beta_{z-1}\ CATEGORY_{z-1,\,i} + \varepsilon_i$$

(2)
$$LN\_PRICE_i = \beta_0 + \beta_1\ POTBID_i +$$
$$+ \beta_2\ QUALCOST_i + \beta_3\ NEGOTIATION_i$$
$$B_4\ T_i + \beta_{j-1}\ CLASS_{j-1,\,i} + \varepsilon_i$$

---

[24] Using robust standard errors (White H., 1980).

where $z - 1$ refers to category ($z = 1, ..., 7$), $j - 1$ refers to class ($j = 1, ..., 129$) and ε is the disturbance term.

Table 7 shows the results of the regressions, when considering the data for all the purchases included in the dataset.

TABLE 7

REGRESSION RESULTS FOR ALL PURCHASES

	[1] LN_PRICE	[2] LN_PRICE
CONSTANT	3.381*** (0.047)	4.302*** (0.084)
POTBID	−0.010*** (0.002)	−0.164*** (0.012)
QUALCOST	0.727*** (0.026)	0.729*** (0.022)
NEGOTIATION	0.114*** (0.021)	0.269*** (0.015)
T	−0.070*** (0.005)	−0.072*** (0.003)
CATEGORY	yes	no
angiographic	−0.692*** (0.036)	
diagnostic	0.577*** (0.041)	
filters	−0.529*** (0.045)	
prostheses	2.511*** (0.050)	
pacemakers	3.971*** (0.042)	
equipment	5.899*** (0.056)	
CLASS	no	yes
Observations	13,801	13,801
R-squared	0.8380	0.9208
F-test	F(10, 13790) = 32680.2 Prob>F= 0.0000	F(132, 13668) = 5389.72 Prob>F=0.0000

Notes: White heteroskedasticity-consistent standard errors are reported in parentheses. ***, ** and * denote significance at 1, 5 and 10 per cent levels, respectively.

The results of the estimation of the two models show a substantial consistency as far as the signs and the significance of the coefficients' estimates are concerned[25].

The results also show that, considering the purchases for all the products in the dataset, negotiations are less efficient than auctions, both when we control for the different categories and for the different classes. The estimated differential impact of negotiations on prices is relevant, accounting for a 12.07% increase in price relative to auctions, when controlling for categories, and for a 30.34% increase, when controlling for classes[26].

The extent of competition, as measured by the number of potential suppliers, as expected, is negatively correlated to prices. Each additional potential bidder is estimated to decrease prices by 1.0%, when controlling for categories and by 16.4%, when controlling for classes. Such a result may suggest caution toward the use of highly centralized procurement systems to the extent that they may reduce competition in the market, since they increase the size of the tender and, therefore, shrinks the number of firms that are able to participate. It is also worth noting the effect of time on prices. They are estimated to decrease by 7% per year and the coefficient is highly significant. Available data, however, do not allow for ascertain whether prices decrease through time because purchasing authority become more efficient or because the prices in the market decrease.

However, the number of potential suppliers in a class cannot give a precise idea of the actual competition for each purchase. Data on the actual number of bidders for each purchase are available only for some of the purchases of technical equipment (1,066 observations over a total of 1,965 purchases of technical equipment). Therefore, it is interesting to estimate the impact of

---

[25] The difference in the magnitude of the estimates of some coefficients between the two models is related to the different variability of prices, when controlling for categories and for classes. The coefficients of categories must be interpreted considering that the base group is X-ray films.

[26] The size of the effect is computed taking into account what explained in footnote 21.

actual competition, as measured by the number of bidders for each purchase, on the prices of technical equipment. The results of these other regressions are shown in Table 8[27].

The estimation of the impact of competition gives the same result as the one obtained for all the purchases, even if, when we do control for the different classes of products, the coefficient for BIDDERS is not significant. This implies that prices are affected by potential competition, regardless of the procedure adopted, and

TABLE 8

REGRESSION RESULTS FOR THE PURCHASES OF TECHNICAL EQUIPMENT

	[1] LN_PRICE	[1.a] LN_PRICE	[2] LN_PRICE	[2.a] LN_PRICE
CONSTANT	10.110*** (0.172)	10.128*** (0.172)	8.900*** (0.059)	8.760*** (0.058)
POTBID	−0.016*** (0.003)		−0.007*** (0.002)	
BIDDERS		−0.030*** (0.006)		−0.003 (0.003)
QUALCOST	0.835*** (0.084)	0.833*** (0.081)	0.894*** (0.043)	0.893*** (0.043)
NEGOTIATION	−1.205*** (0.113)	−1.272*** (0.116)	−0.047** (0.023)	−0.056* (0.030)
T	−0.038 (0.028)	−0.049* (0.028)	0.003 (0.008)	0.002 (0.008)
CLASS	no	no	yes	yes
Observations	1,066	1,066	1,066	1,066
R-squared	0.2872	0.2906	0.9418	0.9415
F-test	$F_{(4, 1061)}$= =54.41 Prob>F=0.0000	$F_{(4, 1061)}$= =60.42 Prob>F=0.0000	$F_{(38, 1027)}$= =1388.10 Prob>F=0.0000	$F_{(38, 1027)}$= =1,360.84 Prob>F=0.0000

Notes: White heteroskedasticity-consistent standard errors are reported in parentheses. ***, ** and * denote significance at 1, 5 and 10 per cent levels, respectively.

[27] Models [1.a] e [2.a] employ the variable BIDDERS instead of POTBID. Moreover, the regression is carried out on 36 classes, i.e. those corresponding to medical equipment.

that such an effect is not overcome by the actual competition effect[28].

What is interesting in this new regression is the sign of the impact of the procurement procedure used in the purchases. When we consider only the purchases for technical equipment, negotiations perform better than auctions, and the coefficient estimates are strongly significant. The apparently contradictory result can be explained by the different characteristics of technical equipment with respect to the other products in the dataset. Technical equipment are usually complex goods, not easily substitutable with each other; therefore, their complementarity with doctors, discussed in section 3, can be handled better by a negotiated procedure. Moreover, for technical equipment, the enforcement of the contract might be crucial, especially if the installation and/or the maintenance is part of the contract itself; therefore, as it was stressed in section 2, the reputation of the contractor can turn up as a strategic element of selection. The fact that for technical equipment the buyer-seller relationship is relevant can explain the positive impact of negotiations on prices — a procedure which, indeed, favours such a relationship. In fact, under negotiation, potentially relevant incentives for good performance, such as a promise to award future contracts, are likely to arise and this can explain the positive impact on prices.

6. - Conclusions

The empirical analysis employed is primarily descriptive. However we believe that it shows an important aspect in procurement: the relationship between the complexity of products and the efficiency of the procurement procedure used.

The above results, far from offering clear cut conclusions, simply show that caution should be used when considering

---

[28] We aware of the potential interaction taking place between the variables negotiation and bidders. However, as already described in the text, at this stage of our analysis it was not possible to adopt the approach suggested by Kjerstad E. (2005) because of the lack of information about the purchasing authority.

auctions as the best tool. Indeed, the relationship buyer-seller, as expressed by negotiation, matters and has a positive impact on the procurement performance, when the purchase of complex goods, like medical equipment, is involved. From this point of view, a policy implication stemming from the analysis, though at this early stage, is that attention should be paid to the design of proper incentives schemes to ensure that the discretional choices exerted in negotiation lead to produce efficient results.

The dataset does not include information on the characteristics of the purchasing authorities nor on their relationship with the supplier, i.e. to what extent contracts are awarded to the same suppliers; further interesting developments might come from a closer analysis in this direction.

BIBLIOGRAPHY

Athey S. - Haile P.A., «Empirical Models of Auctions», Yale, Cowles Foundation, *Discussion Paper*, no. 1562, 2006.

Bajari P. - McMillan R. - Tadelis S., «Auctions versus Negotiations in Procurement: An Empirical Analysis», Cambridge, Massachusetts, *NBER, Working Paper*, no. 9757, 2003.

Bonaccorsi A. - Lyon T. - Pammolli F. - Turchetti G., «Auctions vs. Bargaining: An Empirical Analysis of Medical Device Procurement», Pisa, Italy, Sant'Anna School of Advanced Studies, Laboratory of Economics and Management (LEM), *LEM Papers Series 1999/20*, 2000.

Catalano G. - Gallo P., *L'acquisto di beni e servizi a livello decentrato: l'evoluzione della normativa e lo stato di attuazione dell'introduzione del nuovo modello di e-procurement*, mimeo, Roma, Italy, Commissione Tecnica Spesa pubblica, 2003.

Celentani M. - Ganuza J.J., «Corruption and Competition in Procurement», *European Economic Review*, no. 46, 2002, pages 1273-303.

Cerbo M. - Morgese P., *Le tecnologie biomediche nelle strutture del servizio sanitario nazionale*, mimeo, Roma, Italy, Agenzia per i Servizi Sanitari Regionali, Roma, 2004.

Denhardt K.G., «The Procurement Partnership Model: Moving to a Team-Based Approach», available on line at *http://www.businessofgovernment.org*, 2003.

Dini F. - Spagnolo G., «Meccanismi reputazionali e mercati elettronici: problematiche economiche e possibili soluzioni per il public procurement», *Quaderni Consip*, no. 2, 2004.

Doni N., «L'affidamento mediante gara di contratti pubblici: l'importanza della reputazione», *Politica Economica*, vol. XXI, no. 2, 2005, pages 307-35.

Kelman S., *Procurement and Public Management: The Fear of Discretion and the Quality of Government Performance*, American Enterprise Institute, Washington D.C., 1990.

Kelman S., «Remaking Federal Procurement», Harvard, Mass., The John. F. Kennedy School of Government, *Working Paper*, no. 3, 2002.

Kennedy P., *A Guide to Econometrics*, MIT Press, Cambridge, Massachusetts, Fifth Edition, 2003.

Klemperer P., «Auction Theory: A Guide to the Literature», *Journal of Economic Surveys*, vol. 13, no. 3, 1999, pages 227-86.

Kjerstad E., «Auctions vs. Negotiations: A Study of Price Differentials», *Health Economics*, vol. 14, no. 12, 2005, pages 1239-51.

Lapecorella F. - Rizzo I., «La regolamentazione del mercato dei lavori pubblici: alcune indicazioni di policy», in Piacentino D. - Sobbrio G. (eds.), *Stato o mercato? Intervento pubblico e architettura dei mercati*, Franco Angeli, Milano 2002, pages 201-18.

Nicita A. - Pammolli F., «La centralizzazione delle procedure pubbliche di acquisto per beni e servizi «complessi»: quale valutazione economica delle opportunità e dei rischi?», *Note CERM 6/04*, 2003.

Pammolli F., *Medical Devices Competitiveness and Impact on Public Health Expenditure*, Study prepared for the Directorate Enterprise of the European Commission, 2005.

Piga G. - Zanza M., «An Exploratory Analysis of Public Procurement Practices in Europe», *Quaderni Consip*, no. 1, 2004.

RIZZO I., «Public Procurement in the EU», in MARRELLI M. - PIGNATARO G. (eds.), *Public Decision-making and Asymmetry of Information*, Kluwer Academic Publishers, Norwell, Mass., 2001, pages 147-64.

— —, «I contratti nella pubblica amministrazione: considerazioni metodologiche per una verifica empirica», *Economia Pubblica*, no. 1-2, 1994, pages 7-16.

— —, «Government Purchasing: Some Policy Implications», *Il Politico*, no. 1, 1992, pages 109-26.

ROSE-ACKERMAN S., *Corruption and Government: Causes, Consequences, and Reform*, Cambridge University Press, Cambridge, Mass., 1999.

WHITE H., «A Heteroskedasticity-Consistent Covariance Matrix Estimator and a Direct Test for Heteroskedasticity», *Econometrica*, no. 48, 1980, pages 817-38.

WILLIAMSON O.E., *The Economic Institutions of Capitalism*, The Free Press, New York, 1985.

WOOLDRIDGE J.M., *Introductory Econometrics: a Modern Approach*, Thomson South-Western, Mason (Ohio), Second Edition, 2003.

IV - TRANSPARENCY IN PROCUREMENT

Reputation-Based Governance of Public Works

Lucio Picci

Università degli Studi di Bologna

I propose a governance model of public works that relies on an Internet-based "reputation system". Reputation-based governance of public works is an application of a broader reputation-based governance model, and it inherits its general implications. In particular, it allows for the routine production of statistics that are useful for monitoring purposes, and it provides a coherent framework to limit rent-seeking and corruption. [JEL Classification: H430, H830, C800, H540]

1. - Introduction

Between 1995 and 2000, 43.3% of the construction projects carried out by the private sector in Northern California were awarded through private negotiations, and the rest using some form of bidding. In the same period, public administrations in Northern California used private negotiations only in 1% of the cases. Even when the private sector used bidding, a remarkable difference occurred: public administrations almost always chose open bidding, while the private sector more often opted for bidding upon the invitation of participants[1].

---

[1] See BAJARI P.L. *et al.* (2003). The source of the data that they consider consisting of about 25600 projects, is the Construction Market Data Group.

Such a striking difference is easily explained: while the private sector is free to choose the award system of choice, public procurement is typically constrained by a panoply of rules whose main purpose is to avoid abuses by public officials or, more to the point, corruption (see Kelman, 2002; Rose-Ackerman, 1999, pp. 59-68). The public sector, with few exceptions, is forced to choose (open) bidding. In the United States, for example, the Federal Acquisition Rules strongly limit the use of awarding methods not characterized by "full and open competition"[2]. Full and open competition has much to commend it, because it places the buyer in the best position to exploit the competitive forces of the market in order to obtain the best deal. Limiting competition, by using invited bidding, where the buyer identifies the participating firms or, even more so, private negotiations, would seem to be illogical, because it would weed out of the selection process firms that are potentially more efficient then the chosen ones.

The construction data example here provided, however, by showing that the private sector only rarely uses auctions to solve its procurement needs, suggests that open bidding has its downsides. The benefits of competition may be less important when the object of procurement is complex, so that it is impossible to fully specify within a contract all the possible contingencies. In those cases, contractual flexibility allows both the buyer, and the seller, to better deal with unforeseen occurrences. Moreover, and most importantly, when the good to be delivered is not a commodity, the buyer benefits from the seller's reputation, signaling his ability to deliver high quality goods, and committing him to do so.

Current legislature on public procurement, certainly motivated by commendable reasons, constraints bureaucrats and distorts their choices of procurement methods. Such a distortion has a series of negative consequences, whose seriousness is directly related to the degree of complexity of the procurement

---

[2] U.S. Government, 2005; see also WILSON J.Q. (1989, pages 120-122), citing KELMAN S. (1990), and describing the situation before the reform of the 1990's, on which I'll return.

needs. First, in situations where the outcome of their work presents a substantial degree of uncertainty, firms facing a completaly predetermined contract may ask a higher price as a way to insure themselves against the risk of costs overruns. Secondly, the products delivered may be worse. A fixed contract may force the firm to take actions that could have been optimal *ex-ante*, before production started, but that would be optimally revised once the production process reveals information previously unknown. True, changes within an open bid setup are possible, as with the so-called "change orders" in the US construction industry. However, changes require a renegotiation of the original stipulations, they are costly to obtain and often are the source of acrimony between the parties involved.

In most private negotiations, reputation considerarions play a prominent role, the more important, the greater the difference between the object of procurement with respect to the idealtypical commodity. In open bidding, the reputation of the participating firms matters at best indirectly (for example, through their ability to find the necessary financial guarantees, whenever these are a preconditions for participating to an open bid). Excluding bidders from a selection procedure because they have a bad performance record, even when possible, typically happens infrequently.

Such a lack of concern with respect to reputation considerations has a series of negative effects. It provides the firm with weaker incentives to behave virtuously, because opportunistic behaviours are less likely to be punished by a vindictive administration. Moreover, it weakens market discipline, because contract awards may be given to firms that produce low quality products, but that have successfully specialized in the writing of impeccable tender proposals. On the administration's side, besides provoking an over-regulation of procurement, it puts an emphasys on the drawing of overdetailed "technical specifications" — see the "cookie specs" example offered in Kelman (2002), referring to how the U.S. military had gone to great lenghts to specify the cookies that it deemed fit for its troops. The emphasys on the minute description of the good and services to be procured has organizational implications on the administration, whose focus on the writing of specs is at the expense of the resources, and skills, that are needed for the management of the contract following its adjudication.

In this paper I propose a novel "reputation-based governance" of public works that not only represents a radical departure from traditional reputation-free procurement, but that also significantly innovates with respect to the experience of the United States where, as I will discuss, in the 1990s reputation considerations were introduced within open bidding procedures. Reputation-based governance is based on a full-fledged Internet-based reputation system, akin to other information systems that have already been experimented in different contexts, and it represents a comprehensive approach to governance problems, having a series of important system-wide consequences. Among these, reputation-based governance has an impact on the production of statistical information related to public works, and it represents a coherent framework to fight rent-seeking activities and corruption[3].

The paper is structured as follows. The next section defines an Internet-based reputation system. Section 3 and 4 describe and discuss the proposed method of governance of public works. Section 5 briefly illustrates the U.S. public procurement reform of the 1990s, in order to compare it with the present proposal. Section 6 and 7 treat two important implications of reputation-based governance. The conclusions follow.

2. - Internet-Based Reputation Systems

Word of mouth has always been an essential instrument for spreading information (and often rumors) about the quality and reputation of a supplier, or the trustworthyness of a prospective buyer. We tend to go to restaurants that our friends suggested,

---

[3] The interested reader can find more informations on the general concept of reputation-based governance, and on its implications, in PICCI L. (2006).

and we'd rather entertain business relations with people that have a reputation for being honest. Since such an attitude is fairly generalized, economic actors benefit from having a good reputation, and this provides a strong incentive for virtuous behavior[4].

With respect to this simple story, the Internet innovates in two ways. First, it allows exchanges to be completely impersonal. Unlike in a town where shops have their clientele, in a globalized electronic market the probability that a seller meets twice the same buyer is low. Where contracts are either incomplete, or hard to enforce, such an inherent impersonality would seem to preclude the possibility of repeated exchanges and the emergence of trust. In a world where everyone has a short term incentive to cheat, everyone expects cheating and, as a result, there occur very few business interactions. In extreme cases, the market is simply not viable.

However, the Internet is a powerful tool to spread traditional "word of mouth" to unprecedented levels, so that, even if repeated interactions are rare, prospective buyers and sellers can learn about their business partners from other people who already interacted with them. At least in principle, this allows for the development of the beneficial effects of reputation at a much larger scale than in a traditional context. Recently there has been interest towards "Internet-based reputation systems" (IBRS) that, as Dellarocas (2003) notes, amount to the "digitalization of word of mouth". An Internet-based reputation system is defined by a set of characteristics, that I describe while reporting how they map into what probably is their best known example, the eBay auction electronic market[5].

---

[4] The concept of reputation (and of trust) can be considered using two alternative sets of game theoretic tools. Reputation can be seen as emerging according to the Folk Theorem: in an infinitely repeated game, players may prefer the long-run benefit of not cheating, to the short-run advantage of cheating. Also, reputation can be considered within a bayesian game context, where the quality of a player is not immediately evident to others. See CABRAL L. (2005), for details and for a formal definition of concepts.

[5] eBay is also the most widely studied example of a reputation system. REISNICK P. *et al.* (2002) cite 14 empirical studies on eBay. See also CABRAL L. - HORTAÇSU A. (2006).

First, an IBRS system provides an information infrastructure that allows for a set of transactions to take place. In eBay, sellers can post information on their products. Prospective buyers access the information and place their bids on the products that they desire. The system records the bids and manages the needed interactions between sellers and buyers. A noteworthy characteristic of eBay is that the transactions that it allows are not backed up by formal contractual guarantees, so that in principle there is ample space for cheating, in the form of not paying for a delivered good, of paying late, of delivering merchandise that does not correspond to the published specifications, etc.. Second, an IBRS allows the interested parties to record their assessment of the transaction in a highly structured manner. On eBay, both sellers and buyers can voluntarily rate each other, with marks that can be "positive", "negative", or "neutral", while other existing IBRS's allow for greater granularity of ratings. Third, some function(s) of the opinions expressed are made public: On eBay, the sum of negative, positive and neutral ratings received by each buyer/seller during the past six months. Such a filtering of information is also provided by the "feedback mediator" and the resulting publicly available data is descriptive of the reputation of each agent.

Last, an incentive system is in place prizing a good reputation and punishing a bad one. On eBay, people are wary of conducting business with agents who performed badly in the past. The desired outcome of such a system is one where players have an incentive to behave well in order to build and to maintain a good reputation. When such an outcome is obtained, we expect people to be well behaved: the most effective punishments are the ones that are feared, and that as such are rarely needed and, hence, observed[6].

To summarize, the availability of the Internet offers the potential to drastically renovate the time honored institution of word of mouth. First, it brings it to a huge scale: reported opinions spread vastly and instantaneously. Secondly, it democratizes it,

---

[6] This is the observed outcome On eBay, where less than 1% of the reported comments are negative. See DELLAROCAS C. (2003).

because the assessments are accessible to everyone, and not just to the people who are well placed within an organization or an informal social network. Thirdly, Internet-based reputation systems are not simply the result of social interaction as they manifest themselves, but they can be suitably engineered. Ongoing research is trying to better understand how various characteristics of reputation-systems — their general rules, the way feedback mediators are designed, the required costs to participate or to change one's identity, etc. — influence the equilibrium outcome.

Reputation systems also have shortcomings. The information that they collect is decontextualized. Unlike in a traditional setting, it is not possible to extrapolate information from the non-verbal aspects of communication: for example, if a prospective business partner is maligned by someone who's dressed like Napoleon, such an opinion may as well be discounted. On the other hand, all non-verbal information is lost on the Internet. The availability and truthfulness of reported opinions also represents a thorny issue. Ratings are a public good and, as such, we'd expect their underprovision. Also, there could be manipulation of personal assessments, following strategic behaviors and, possibly, collusive practices, for example in situations where actors exchange good ratings, either in-kind or for money. In the context of the proposed application, I address some of these issues below.

3. - Reputation-Based Governance of Public Works

I here discuss how the concept of IBRS can be used to shape a comprehensive governance model of public works. The purpose of public works is to add to the stock of infrastructure available to an economy, or to provide for its maintenance. Most infrastructure are public, but we are witnessing a shift towards their private provision of infrastructure. Moreover, private financing and management of pieces of infrastruture have become more popular, the English Channel Tunnel being a representative example of such a trend. While such a shift an interesting (and well studied) topic of research, it is on *public* provision of public works that I focus.

At the basis of the proposed governance model there is a taxonomy of possible projects. For example, and limiting our attention to the construction of new pieces of infrastructure, public works can be "roads", "bridges", "buildings", etc. Within each type of good, there are further sub-classes: Buildings may be schools, police headquarters, and so forth. All projects are included in a database, that can be accessed (via a Web-based application) by public administrators, by firms, and by the public. Upon approval, the public administration inserts each project into the database. Preliminary information about a project would include a general description according to the codified taxonomy (type of good, location, expected cost, etc.), technical drawings, and a set of data pertaining to any documentation that may accompany the early stages of the project (such as an environmental impact and a cost-benefit analysis). As the project evolves, more information is provided, eventually to include details on costs and information on the final outcome, comprising, for instance, pictures of the completed works. Each project is associated with the administration and with the contracting firms that are responsible for its execution. In particular, the responsabilities of the contracting firms are recorded, and the information system keeps track of all the projects that each administration and each firm have done. Summary views of the past record of individual administrations and firms should be easily accessible.

To summarize, reputation-based governance of public works rests on the availability of an information system that allows for a careful definition of the types of goods and of their characteristics, and that, through a set of suitable procedures, permits the storing and the publication, via the Web, of data on projects, on administrations and on firms.

Projects outcomes are asssessed by a set of relevant actors, who are allowed to express their opinions on given characteristics of the finished works. Public administrators in charge of a project express their opinion on the quality of the work carried out by the contracting firms. Firms assess how the public administration managed a given project, and the public judges the public works that affect them. For example, a school would be assessed by the local community where it is built, by its personnell, and possibly by its students. A local road would be judged by the people who live in its proximity, while a freeway could be assessed by residents of a vaster area. Such opinions, that we call "voice activities", would be highly structured, and would refer to a small set of well defined characteristics. For example, the public could judge "aesthetic qualities", "usefulness" and "accessibility" of public works. Such assessments would be posted through a Web application, where, after identification, the relevant actors are presented, with a menu of possibile actions.

These digitalized information would allow for the provision of a series of automatically generated summary statistics. Such method of producing statistics in itself represents a novelty with respect to current practices, a topic on which I will return. When all the relevant information on public works are contained in a digital repository, computing summary statistics of interest does not require any *ad hoc* data gathering and processing, because it can be done in an "integrated" fashion by producing a «view» of the available data. The statistics produced in this fashion would include a comprehensive set of summary information on the public works: their general characteristics, the unit costs of projects of the same type (for example, of a km of road of a given category) and their completion time. They would moreover express the overall assessment by the public. Also, the availability of information on many projects would allow for the computation of rankings of individual projects on several dimensions. Summary statistics would be available also for various subsets of the data, providing views by geographic unit, by type of administration, and by contracting firm. The assessments on the quality of completed public works would reverberate to administrations, administrators and firms. The reputation of all these actors would be a function of the assessments that their past projects received.

The system could supply information at two levels. First of all, it would provide highly usable and easy-to-read summaries, using only very simple descriptive statistical concepts. A further level would include more detailed information and would use more sophisticated tools of analysis. The interested person, depending on her time and needs, in order to examine a single project could choose a quick tour, or could opt for a more in-depth analysis. One particular designing issue has to do with the «feedback mediator». Some existing systems limit the visibility of past assessments to the more recent ones: on eBay, only the last six months of past transactions are visible, while in the United States, a case study that I'll discuss in Section 5, it is the contracts that are less than 3 years old that are made to matter. In general, the design of the feedback mediator is a critical aspect of reputation-based governance, and as such it should be carefully crafted, possibly allowing for a trial-and-error approach.

Reputation-based governance of public works would establish a number of incentives and of disincentives. Through the feedback mediator, the general public could access various rankings of completed public works, of the administrations who carried them out, of the administrators involved, and of the contracting firms. By itself, this would put a premium on honest and efficient behaviour, considering that shuch information would influence electoral choices. Also, public administrators would be pressured not to be looked down by their peers. To the extent that reputation matters within the source selection process, firms would also be obviously interested in having good ratings. Moreover, if a firm is active in both the public and in the private sector, a good reputation in the former would be expendable in the latter. Such effects could then be made more cogent by deliberate publicity activities, such as the publishing in newspapers of the "ten best (worst) projects" of the year. The media also would play a role in providing incentives, since journalists could access a very powerful tool to obtain information on public works, to be used to expose both worst and best practices.

Moreover, and most importantly, reputation considerations could be employed within source selection procedures, as it is done today in the United States (see Section 5). Note however that reputation-based governance of public works, thanks to its strong incentives, would make more attractive an allocation mechanism based on off-the-shelf purchases, instead than on competitive biddings, an evolution of procurement systems already hinted at in Rose-Ackerman (2004).

4. - Discussion

Voice activities carried out by the general public raise the problem of who should be allowed to participate. In principle, private citizens and organized private entities could be entitled to assess projects' outcomes. Private citizens could register on a Web site, and then voice their opinions on all works carried out in their proximity. On the other hand, everyone could be entitled to express an opinion on a piece of a major network infrastructures. Participation to voice activities by citizens organizations presents some problems. First, it is not immediately clear how the assessments of organized entities should be weighted — possibly according to the size of their membership, but this would establish an incentive to artificially inflate them. Also, compared to individuals, organizations would be more prone to engage in colluding behaviors.

Collusion and the presence of political scheming, in fact, is a general concern for the working of the voice system. Political parties could encourage their activists to express positive opinions on projects that they sponsor, and to smear projects within the jurisdiction of political adversaries. They could encourage the formation of *ad hoc* organizations for this purpose, possibly leveraging on fake membership by party activists. Enterprises, also, could encourage the formation of organizations to support their projects and to discredit their competitors.

Several answers to these objections are possible. First, the capability of creating some form of consensus on a given public work would somehow reflect its worth. In a context where barriers for entering the voice system are very low, whoever is able to organize consensus on a given project, no matter how that is done, is implicitly showing that, at least to some extent, that consensus is warranted. More importantly, a set of cautionary measures could be taken to limit scheming and collusion. For example, citizens' organizations could be required to post their budget sheets and to declare the origin of any contributions that they receive. Their members could be required to register within the system, and to declare any link that they may have with firms or administrations.

An altogether different route would be to allow only individual participation to voice activities. The proposed information system is also a tool to reduce transaction costs of various kinds, and to the extent that organizations are instruments to counter transaction costs, they would be less needed than before. True, the proposed system would also lower the costs of carrying out watchdog activities, and this would instead put an incentive favoring the formation of citizens' organizations. Again, the fine tuning of the system would require flexibility and experimentation.

I have already mentioned the possibility of collusion among public administrators and firms. The public also could collude both with administrations and with firms. Public works are localized goods and sometimes are supplied as part of a patronage relation between politicians and their clients or, more crudely, they are a manifestation of "pork barrel". Up to a point, people benefit from local public works regardless of their quality. For example, an expensive and poorly built school may be a failure from the point of view of a "social planner", but it may still be preferable, both to the parents of the students and to the home owners who benefit from any increase in real estate valuations, than a good school located in a different neighborhood. For these reasons, administrations, firms and local constituencies could team up to support policies that provide themselves a common benefit, regardless of its social cost.

The possibility of collusion among inefficient and possibly dishonest administrations, firms, and local constituencies who, in exchange for political support to their patrons, cynically appreciate any "pork" that they may get, should be an obvious motive of concern. However, countermeasures can be adopted. First, the information systems would routinely produce statistics on standardized costs. They should be computed and read with care, because the costs of comparable tracts of roads, for example, are influenced, among other factors, by the local cost of labor and by the nature of the terrain. However, the more information accrue into the system, the higher is the sophistication that can be achieved. For example, standadized costs could be computed adopting a conditional expectation model, where several variables affecting production costs are controlled for (for an application, see Golden and Picci, 2005).

The availability of standardized costs could allow for a smart targeting of auditing activities by a dedicated agency. A rule could determine that the probability for an administration of being audited depends both on the cost of the project, relative to what standardized costs would dictate, and on the ratings that it received. Such a "probabilistic auditing rule" would temperate the incentives that local actors may have to team up in order to facilitate the grabbing for themselves of a disproportionate amount of resources. Other characteristics of reputation-based governance would play favorably in this respect. The information systems allows for the computation of very detailed geographic statistics showing the effects of distributive decisions. In such a highly transparent context, it would be relatively difficult to sustain pork barrel expenditures, that to some extent are grounded in secrecy both of the outcomes, whenever detailed and timely geographic information on the allocation of resources are scarce, and of the political process, given that resources are often distributed by parliamentary committees, where log-rolling practices favor the creation of vast majorities[7].

Last, local projects could be audited from the outside. Besides formal auditing by a central authority, possibly following a probabilistic auditing rule, the public also could be involved in the assessments of public works that are located in different communities.

---

[7] This is the case in the United States, where pork barrel is often wrapped in *omnibus legislation* that attracts support from both sides of the aisle. See Golden M. - Picci L. (2006*b*) for more details and for references to the literature.

171

5. - Contractor Performance in the United States

In the 1990's the United States embarked in a sweeping reform of federal public procurement, a part of the then Vice-President Al Gore "reinventing government" intiative. The most relevant changes occurred under the guidance of Steven Kelman, Professor at the Kennedy School of Government who, from 1993 until 1997, served as the Administrator of the Office of Federal Procurement Policy (OFPP). That reform mostly affected what Steven Kelman refers to as «the first two legs of contracting management», namely, business strategy management and source selection, and «largely ignored the third leg», or contract administration (Kelman, 2002). The purpose of the brief account that follows is to allow for a comparison of that experience with the present proposal.

While the collection and use of past performance information had been around for a long time in the United States, such use has been strongly increased by a series of decisions, started by the OFPP Policy Letter No. 92-5 (30 December 1992), requiring all agencies to prepare past performance evaluations for new contracts and to use past performance information as an evaluation factor in awarding contracts. The whole process of reform was marked by two pieces of legislation, the Federal Acquisition Streamlining Act (FASA) in 1994 and the Federal Acquisition Reform Act in 1995. The changes that have occurred during the 90's have brought about a situation where reputation considerations have entered the computation of the relative merits of an offer, and contribute to the final decision, together with quality and price, for all contracts exceeding US$ 100,000.

The Federal Acquisition Streamlining Act (FASA), dated October 13, 1994, «codified the requirements to consider past performance in making awards. It required the Administrator to provide guidance for using past performance. Federal Acquisition Circular 90-26 (dated April 4, 1995) implemented the OFPP and FASA requirements into the FAR» (Office for Government-wide Policy, 1997). Currently, the Federal Acquisition Rules treats with reputation issues in Part 9.104, Part 15.608 and Part 42.1501. In particular, the 1998 rewrite of Part 15 of FAR, dealing with source selection procedures for large buys, requires past performance to be one of two mandatory evaluation factors, where cost/price is the other, for all competitively negotiated acquisitions exceeding established thresholds. The extent and quality of an offeror's past performance is assessed by the source selection authority, using reviews of past projects carried out by a given firm, eventually complemented by other indicators of past performance that may also originate from the private sector.

Of paramount importance are the opinions expressed by public administrators on the quality of work carried out by their contractors. Such opinions are kept on file for three years and form the bulk of evidence on the reputation of firms. Of key relevance, considering also the legal implications that a negative assessment may have, is the procedure that dictates how a public administration is to judge a contractor. The assessment is on four separate dimensions:

— Quality of performance — as defined in contract standards.

— Cost performance — how close to estimates.

— Schedule performance — timeliness of completion of interim and final milestones.

— Business relations — history of professional behavior and overall business-like concern for the interests of the customer, including timely completion of all the administrative requirements and customer satisfaction.

(Office of Federal Procurement Policy, 2000)

Evaluations on this four dimensions are in terms of numeric scores from 0 to 5. Within a codified process, the firm has ample space for voicing its rebuttals to the administration. The relevant official documentation places much emphasys on the right that the firm has to know beforehand how its performance is to be evaluated, and on the continuous communication between the administration and the firm. The shortening of the traditional arm's lenght distance between the administration and the contractor was in fact one of the goals of the reform, that aimed to transform a relation that was often acrimonious, into one among "partners".

173

Such result has been sought for in part by emphasyzing the responsabilities of the contracting official, and correspondingly by giving her more freedom of movement, as is evident, for example, from the concomitant introduction of credit cards for all purchases below the US$ 2,500 mark (Kelman, 2002).

A relevant role in assuring that evaluations are not a mere formality is played by the existence of the Federal Torts Claims Act, protecting the evaluating official "from personal liability for common law torts. In those instances, if an agency official were sued, upon certification by the Attorney General, the official would be dismissed from the lawsuit and the United States would be substituted as the defendant" (Office of Federal Procurement Policy, 2000). Another important characteristic of the evaluations is that they are not made public, being accessible only to those public officials who, for the purpose of source selection, need to assess a firm's reputation.

The relatively long experience with the system shows that firms take their reputation scores very seriously, knowing that a bad reputation would damage their future prospects of being awarded new contracts. This constitutes basic evidence that the system works, in the sense that reputation considerations represent relevant incentives. However, past experience has also raised concerns on the possibility of strategically manipulating the system. For a list of critical issues, see Petrillo (2005).

There are obvious similarities between the U.S. experience and the present model of reputation-based governance of public works. Both provide an institutional framework for the reputation of the contracting firm to arise and to be used within the source selection process. Also, the U.S. experience makes ample use of the Internet. Several administrations have developed their Internet-based information systems to record firms' assessments, and the most popular of them, the Contractor Performance System run by the National Institute of Health (*http://cps.od.nih.gov*), is adopted by several administrations. This system, together with the ones that are run by the National Aeronautics and Space Administration and by the Department of Defense, have teamed up within the "Past Performance Information Retrieval System" (PPIRS) program to exchange reputation information. The resulting integrated system has been available since 2002. Such an emerging integrated information system, in fact, represents a portion of the IBRS that would serve as the technical infrastructure for the proposed model of reputation-based governance.

However, the differences between the U.S. experience and full-fledged reputation-based governance of public works are as important as their similarities. First, in the U.S. only the opinions of the administration with respect to the contractor's job are recorded. Firms are not allowed to produce their assessments on the administrations that they interact with and, most importantly, the people who are affected by the projects are not allowed to voice their opinions[8]. Also, the opinions expressed by the administration on the contracting firms are kept private. In this sense, public procurement in the United States, after the reform of the 1990's, represents an interesting, but only partial, adoption of a reputation-based governance model.

With respect to its full adoption, the partial adoption of the model determines a difference that is not just of degree, but also of kind. Only a full-fledged reputation-based governance model would have a series of important implications, two of which I discuss next.

6. - A Shift in the Production of Statistical Information

The broad implications of reputation-based governance are discussed in Picci (2006c). Here I focus on two consequencies that are particularly relevant, the first one having to do with methods of producing statistical information. Traditionally, the production of statistics starts with the gathering of data, often through questionnaires, that are then processed as desired. Survey-based data present shortcomings of various types, such as lack of response and, possibly, attrition. Running surveys is an expensive and lengthy

---

[8] In the official documentation lip service is payed to the need to listen to final users' opinions (see, among others, OFFICE OF FEDERAL PROCUREMENT POLICY, 2000). However, final users are taken to be the users within the administration, and not the public at large.

process, so that there is a considerable delay between the reference time of the statistical information and the date of its availability.

Within reputation-based governance, most relevant information on public works would be digitally recorded. Useful statistics could be generated simply by means of "views" of data that are already available within the overall information system. There would be a fixed cost to create statistical information for the first time, but the marginal cost for further production would then be negligible. Also, official statistics would reflect real-time data.

To better grasp some the main implications of this new situation, I introduce a simple taxonomy of statistical information. I define *ad hoc* those statistics that, in order to be produced, need statistical information to be gathered and processed. I call *integrated* those statistics produced as a view of the digital information that are present within a computerized information system. An example of the latter is provided by the statistics on accesses to a Web site, that are routinely produced by a dedicated software without the need of any outside interventions, apart from the initial effort to install and configure the program. At present, most statistics are of the *ad hoc* type. Reputation-based governance, on the other hand, allows for the production of integrated statistics.

Another important dimension in which statistics differ is their *degree of institutionalization*, that I define as the prospect for their continuing provision. *Ad hoc* statistics representing the core activities of National Statistical Offices, such as the Census Bureau, are highly insititutionalized: We may expect National Accounts to be produced indefinitely in the future. On the other hand, *ad hoc* statistics that are produced for the first time, or one-shot surveys for which future funding and political support is not secure, are weakly institutionalized.

While the degree of institutionalization of *ad hoc* statistics greatly varies, all integrated statistics tend to be highly institutionalized: Once they have been produced for the first time, their future provision only depends on the continuing existence of the information system, and on the maintenence of the software producing the necessary views of the data. In order to discontinue the production of integrated statistics a clear opposition is needed,

176

and not just a lack of support. To put it differently, *ad hoc* statistics requiring funding need an explicit decision to be continued. On the other hand, integrated statistics, once the continued functioning of the underlying information system is guaranteed, need an explicit decision in order to be interrupted.

Reputation-based governance would naturally lead to the production of statistics that are *integrated and highly institutionalized*. Each piece of public infrastructure would be recorded in the information system, together with the flow of payments to the contractor(s). As a project is completed, a comparison between its actual and predicted costs would immediately become public. A simple view of the data would provide aggregate information on these variables divided by type of public good and by geografic or administrative area. The information system would generate a wealth of data on the geographic localization of the recipients of the benefits, information that policy makers could use to inform their decisions, and that electors would consider when making their choices. The comparison between physical and monetary measures of infrastructure would provide very useful geographic information about the presence of rent-seeking activities, a topic that I will consider next.

Overall, the establishment of a full-fledged model of reputation-based governance would be accompanied by the timely provision of a wealth of easily accessible data, determining what may amount to a revolution in the realm of the production of statistical information.

7. - Rents and Corruption

The second important consequence of reputation-based governance rests on its ability to limit rent-seeking activities and corruption. Rent-seeking often plagues public governance, by subtracting valuable resources from productive ends and by tilting private choices towards the pursue of unproductive activities. It often takes the form of corruption, whose damages are widely documented, deriving in part from the immediate drain of public resources and, more importantly, from its distortionary effects on both private and public choices[9]. Among the latter, the preoccupations with corruption triggers reactions from the public administration that have unintended negative effects, such as the over-regulation of public procurement (see Kelman, 2002, for a discussion).

In the debate on corruption there is a broad agreement on what measures could contribute to its cure. These involve increased accountability, to be obtained through a higher degree of transparency, regular monitoring of the activities that could lead to corruption, and a proper set of incentives, such as the perception that dishonesty is punished with a high probability. However, policy suggestions so far have had a piecemeal character, failing to find a common thread effectively allowing for the packaging of the different proposed measures into a single plan. Reputation-based governance represents a unified framework to address the problem, overcoming the limitations of less comprehensive approaches. In particular, as I have argued, it allows for the computation of "integrated" statistics that provide long sought for objective measures that are related to the governance of public works, and that are an indispensable prerequisite for the necessary monitoring activities.

In this respect, the integrated statistics that are computed within a reputation-based governance would considerably improve the current situation. Corruption indexes available today are mostly based on *perceptions* of corruption. This is the case of the Transparency International Corruption Perception Index, the result of the aggregation of several other indexes (see Lambsdorff, 2003). The characters that are the object of measurement may be aspects of corruption proper, or they may represent occurrences that are understood to be correlated with corruption, such as "public integrity" or various measures of the quality of governance. Sometimes, they describe broad aspects of governance, and as such are more tenuously linked with the corruption phenomenon, as in Kaufmann *et* al. (1999).

---

[9] For a recent survey on the current debate on corruption, from an economist's point of view, see SVENSSON J. (2005).

Corruption indexes may be only weakly related to the character object of observation. For example, an intense exposure of the public opinion to corruption scandals may cause a spurious increase of perception-based indexes. Italy's ranking in the 1995 Transparency International Corruption Percetption Index announced more corruption than in Mexico and Colombia, and marginally less than in Thailand, India and The Philippines. Such an unrealistic ranking is presumably explained in part by the spate of attention that serious (grand) corruption episodes had received in Italy in the early 1990's, following the so called "Tangentopoli" judicial inquiries[10]. Perception-based corruption indexes could also influence the perception of corruption, given the popularity that they enjoy and their visibility on the media, raising the possibilities that they influence the very same perceptions on which they are based.

While most corruption indexes are subjective, being based on perceptions of the character that is the object of measurement, recently an *objective* measure of corruption has been proposed. Golden and Picci (2005) compute for the Italian regions a corruption measure that is based on the contrast between two alternative measures of the public capital stock. The first one represents the total amount of moneys allocated over the years to endow Italy of infrastructure, and is computed using the permanent inventory technique[11]. The second is a physical inventory of the infrastructure that have actually been built — km of roads and railroads, number and dimensions of public buildings, etc. The two measures offer a striking contrast, with Southern Italy having received a disproportionally high amount of financing that only partially was put to good use. Such contrast is the base for the computation of a «corruption index»[12].

---

[10] Italy moved up significantly on the TI-CPI ranking over the years. For a qualitatitve assessment of corruption (in public works) in Italy, see Golden M. - Picci L. (2006*a*).

[11] The permanent inventory techniques computes an estimate of the stock of capital by summing current and past flows of investments. Investments on given types of goods that are older of their relevant «service life» are not included in the computation. For details see Golden M. - Picci L. (2005).

[12] Geographic differences in the effectiveness of public investments in generating infrastructure could also be explained by other factors, such as disparities in the efficiency of the construction industry, in costs, or in the efficiency of public administrations. Golden M. - Picci L. (2005) consider these issues explicitly.

All corruption indexes currently available are of the *ad hoc* type, with varying degrees of institutionalization. The Corruption Perception Index, computed under the sponsorship of Transparency International since 1995, presents a rather high degree of institutionalization. On the other hand, indexes that depend on the effort of academic researchers, such as the one in Golden and Picci (2005), have a "one shot" character and are weakly institutionalized. Reputation-based governance of public works would allow for the routine production of statistics on corruption related phenomena that would be *objective, integrated* and *highly institutionalized*, and that would be central in establishing appropriate incentives and in informing auditing activities.

8. - Concluding Comments

Reputation-based governance is prone to further developments and extensions with respect to the description here provided. For example, if candidate public works are recorded in the information system before they are selected, then room is created for participatory forms of decision making. The public could be entitled not just to assess completed works, but also to express opinions on alternative plans, or even to propose novel projects. In this way, reputation-based governance could support far reaching e-democracy practices, where the word «democracy» would be taken to mean both participation and accountability.

The range of action of the monitoring system could be increased. Public works shape the territory where they are constructed, and suitably organized information on infrastructure that are either desired, planned, under construction or, finally, available, would help planning and analytic activities of various types.

The present proposal, with its emphasis on the establishment of automatic procedures for the gathering and processing of data, should be seen within an ongoing process that is gradually changing our appreciation of the quantitative aspects of public administrations and, more generally, of governance. The study of corruption provides a good exemplification of the issue. In the 1990's several organizations made available perception — based corruption and governance indexes. Golden - Picci (2005) provide a measure of corruption that is based not on perceptions, but on hard data. Moving from measuring perceptions, to constructing measures that are based on objective data, is a process that deserves encouragement. However, such a process is difficult to realize, because objective data are difficult to find and are time consuming to process.

The methodology proposed in Golden - Picci (2005) could certainly be carried out, and indeed has been carried out, for countries other than Italy, but at a high cost. The availability of an information system of the type here proposed, however, would allow for an integrated monitoring system that would routinely compute a vast array of useful indexes and measures. This, in turn, would be helpful in addressing a more general problem that besets current studies on public administrations: the difficulty to collect suitable quantitative information.

These considerations help casting the proposed governance model under a different light. The stated issue is about improving governance of public works. However, it is also about the creation of a conceptual and technological model for the systematic organization and collection of quantitative information about the working of a governance system. The two issues, in fact, are closely related.

BIBLIOGRAPHY

BAJARI P.L. - McMILLAN R.S. - TADELIS, S., «Auctions versus Negotiations in Procurament: An Empirical Analysis», *NBER, Working Paper*, no. 9757, 2003.

CABRAL L., *The Economics of Reputation and Trust*, mimeo, 2005.

CABRAL L. - HORTAÇSU A., *The Dynamics of Seller Reputation: Evidence from eBay*, mimeo, 2006.

DELLAROCAS C., «The Digitalization of Word of Mouth: Promise and Challenge of Online Feedback Mechanisms, *Management Science*, vol. 49, no. 10, 2003, pages 1407-24.

GOLDEN M. - PICCI L., «Proposal for a New Measure of Corruption Illustrated Using Italian Data», *Economics and Politics*, vol. 17, no. 1, 2005, pages 37-75.

— — - —, «Corruption and the Management of Public Works in Italy», in ROSE-ACKERMAN S. (ed.), *Handbook of Economic Corruption*, Cheltenham, Edward Elgar Publisher, 2006a.

— — - — —, *Pork Barrel Politics in Postwar Italy, 1953-1994*, mimeo, 2006b.

KAUFMANN D. - KRAAY A. - ZOIDO-LOBATÓN P., «Aggregating Governance Indicators», *Policy Research, Working Paper*, no. 2195, Washington, D.C., The World Bank, 1999.

KELMAN S., «Remaking Federal Procurement», *Public Contracts law Journal*, Summer, 2002.

LAMBSDORFF J.G., «Framework Document 2003, Background Paper to the 2003 Corruption Perceptions Index», Transparency International, mimeo, 2003, [On-line] Available at: *www.transparency.org/cpi/2003/dnld/framework.pdf* [Retrieved April 28, 2006].

OFFICE FOR GOVERNMENT-WIDE POLICY, «White Paper Past Performance», 1997, [On-line] Available at: *www.arnet.gov/Library/OFPP/BestPractices/pbsc/library/ASIwp-past-perform.pdf* [Retrieved April 28, 2006].

OFFICE OF FEDERAL PROCUREMENT POLICY, «Best Practices for Collecting and Using Current and Past Performance Information», 2002. [On-line] Available at: *www.acqnet.gov/Library/OFPP/BestPractices/pbsc/library/OFPPbp-collecting.pdf* [Retrieved April 28, 2006].

PETRILLO J., «Using past Performance to Steer Contract Awards» *Government Computing News*, vol. 24, no. 17, 2005, 5 July. [On-line] Available at: *appserv.gcn.conil24_17/petrillo/3 6248-1.html?topic=petrillo* [Retrieved April 28, 2006].

PICCI L., «Reputation-Based Governance: a Primer», mimeo, 2006. [On-line] Available at: *www.spbo.unibo.it/picci/rebagprimer.pdf* [Retrieved April 28, 2006].

REISNICK P. - ZECKHAUSER R. - SWANSON J. - LOCKWOOD K., «The Value of Reputation on E-Bay: A Controlled Experiment», *Working Paper*, University of Michigan, Ann Arbor, MI, 2002.

ROBINSON J.A. - TORVIK R., «White Elephants», *Journal of Public Economics*, vol. 89, no. 2-3, 2005, pages 197-210.

ROSE-ACKERMAN S., *Corruption and Government: Causes, Consequences, and Reform*, Cambridge, Cambridge University Press, 1999.

— —, «The Challenge of Poor Governance and Corruption.» *Copenhagen Consensus Challenge Paper*, mimeo, 2004.

SVENSSON J., «Eight Questions about Corruption», *Journal of Economic Perspectives*, vol. 19, no. 3, 2005, pages 19-42.

WILSON J.Q., *Bureaucracy: What Government Agencies do and Why they do It*, New York, Basicbooks, 1989.

Why Do Transparent Public Procurement and Corruption Go Hand in Hand?

Raffaella Coppier - **Gustavo Piga**

Università di Macerata   Università di Roma "Tor Vergata"

In this paper we try to construct an hypothesis as to why, as data seem to show, countries that adopt more "transparent procurement", as calculated by the share of tender advertised publicly, are also the ones where corruption is considered more pervasive. We describe an economy where in equilibrium countries more prone to corruption find it optimal to increase transparency more to curb corruption itself. However, as transparency is costly to implement, this will not be enough to bring corruption levels to those of inherently less corrupt societies. We finally suggest alternative ways to reduce corruption in procurement. [JEL Classification: H57]

1. - Introduction

The greater part of modern States uses public procurement in order to obtain the goods and services that it deems are necessary to support its publicy policy actions. But this procurement is not immune to manipulations through collusion and corruption. As Rose-Ackerman (1999) said:

Corruption occurs at the interface of the public and private sectors. Whenever a public official has discretionary power over distribution to the private sector of a benefit or cost, incentives for bribery are created.(...) When the government is a buyer or a contractor, there are several reasons to pay off officials. First, a firm may pay to be included in the list of qualified bidders. Second, it may pay to have officials structure bidding specifications so that the corrupt firm is the only qualified supplier. Third, once a firm has been selected, it may pay to get inflated prices or to skimp on quality.

Corruption means that the person who runs the auction, the auctioneer, twists the auction rules in favor of a bidder in exchange for a bribe. The World Bank estimated the volume of bribes exchanging hands for public sector procurement alone to roughly 200 billion dollars per year (see Kaufman, 2004). The problem, while more acute in developing countries, is by no means irrelevant for more economically advanced ones: Kaufman (2003) reports that "favouritism in procurement award" remains the number one problem for OECD firms once compared with other sources of bad public governance (illegal political financing, legal political financing influencing politics, firm's capture of laws and regulations, ineffective Parliament). In general, corruption is a problem if the auctioneer is an agent of the seller, as is the case if the seller is a government.

There are different kinds of corruption in procurement. Lengwiler and Wolfstetter (2006) survey most of them, their implications for efficiency and redistribution and the possible solutions to avoid it.[1] They point out, among other things, the central feature that plays, for corrupted outcomes, the use of discretion in evaluating tenders based on the MEAT (most economically advantageous offer) criterion. Rankings by quality are now fully accepted in the new EU directive, to gain flexibility and accuracy in awards, at the obvious expense of some added concern in terms of corruption possibilities. Distortion of quality rankings indeed remains a serious possibility that takes advantage of the sometimes poor monitoring capacity of external agents when analyzing the features of contract performance, mostly because of asymmetric information.

---

[1] Interestingly, they view the shift to e-procurement, with its added layers of security, as a strategic tool to reduce the effectiveness of some ways in which corrupt procurement has traditionally taken place.

Transparency is often suggested as a tool to reduce the potential for corruption. In the European Directive, transparency is considered, together with competition, as a "principle". This creates in the mind of many economists a certain degree of confusion in that some kinds of transparency foster instead more collusion (e.g. in the case of reverse on-line auctions in a collusive environment, greater visibility of rivals' offers increases the possibility of sanctioning any cartel defector) or are necessarily costly (for example the unit costs of an open procedure are larger the smaller the amount procured given the fixed nature of some of these, like publication costs and tender committee costs).

Nevertheless it is clear that publishing a tender improves the knowledge of the needs of the purchaser, fosters participation and raises accountability for the procurer, making corruption a more difficult and therefore less likely outcome.

GRAPH 1

CORRUPTION VERSUS TRANSPARENCY

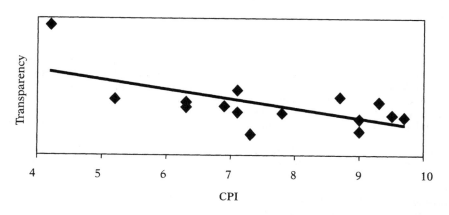

Legend: CPI (Corruption Perception Index) is an index that defines corruption as the abuse of public office for private gain, and measures the degree to which corruption is perceived to exist among a country's public officials and politicians. The scores range from ten (squeaky clean) to zero (highly corrupt). Transparency is measured by the share of total public procurement published in the Official Journal, source: EC, DG Market.

A look at the data seems however to say otherwise. If we rank countries by their inclination to corruption (Corruption Perception Index, CPI) as stated for example by Transparency International[2] we find that the least corrupt countries choose a less transparent way of handling their tenders (lower share of total public procurement published in the Official Journal, source: EC, DG Market) while countries reputed for their higher degree of corrupt behaviour appear more transparent in their procurement.

A more serious empirical analysis would be needed to study the statistical significance and the causality of this result. Here however we concentrate on understanding better the theoretical implications of such an outcome, verifying if it can be replicated in an environment with rational agents and what this tells us in terms of the importance of the role transparency plays in public procurement. The results are reassuring in that we find that the stylized fact mentioned above may have nothing to do with transparency playing a role in enhancing corruption opportunities. However, they also remind us that each country has its own culture and institutions and that transparency might not be enough to eradicate corruption at a cost which is compatible with society's agreement to eradicate it.

---

[2] The index defines corruption as the abuse of public office for private gain, and measures the degree to which corruption is perceived to exist among a country's public officials and politicians. It is a composite index, drawing on 16 surveys from 10 independent institutions, which gathered the opinions of businesspeople and country analysts. Only 159 of the world's countries are included in the survey, due to an absence of reliable data from the remaining countries. The scores range from ten (squeaky clean) to zero (highly corrupt). A score of 5.0 is the number Transparency International considers the borderline figure distinguishing countries that do and do not have a serious corruption problem. More than two-thirds of the 159 nations surveyed scored less than five out of a top score of 10 on the index, which reflects perceptions of business people, academics, and other political observers, both within and outside each country. More than half scored less than three, indicating the perception of a severe corruption problem. The index, first launched in 1995, draws on 16 surveys from 10 independent institutions, including The Economist Intelligence Unit, World Markets Research Centre, and Freedom House. As survey of surveys this index has the advantage that if the errors in the measurements are independent and are identically distributed, then the average used they give TI can reduce the error.

2. - The Model

Consider an economy composed of three types of players: a principal (the State), a population of agents (bureaucrats), and a population of identical firms. Economic agents are risk neutral. The State delegates the good's "y" purchase to a bureaucrat. There is a continuum of bureaucrats and firms, and their number is normalized to 1 for both categories. Bureaucrats earn a fixed salary "w", while firms sell to the State the good "y". We assume that the good's price is given, and let firms compete in quality: the higher the quality offered, the lower the profit for firms and the higher the welfare for the community. The bureaucrats organize an auction for the procurement of a certain good. It is further assumed that an information asymmetry exists, in that the State is unaware of the good's quality. In fact, the quality of the good is observable only after controls by an independent monitor. The State, in order to weed out or reduce corruption 1) *ex-ante* fixes the level of Transparency, "T", of the tender and 2) *ex-post* monitors firms' and bureaucrats' behavior uncorruptable third parties. It is common knowledge that the bureaucrat is corruptible, in the sense that he pursues his own interest, and not necessarily that of the State; in particular, the bureaucrat is open to bribery. In fact only the bureaucrat observes firms' bids' which are submitted in closed envelopes. As a general rule, the firm that offers the highest quality wins the auction. The bureaucrat can, when proclaiming the winner, lie on the bids's true quality in exchange for a bribe "b". Let b^d be the bribe demanded by the bureaucrat. Then, the firm has two options: 1) refuse payment of the bribe, or 2) accept to pay and start negotiating the bribe with the bureaucrat. For simplicity, we assume that the level of quality can take only two values: a high quality level, the highest level of quality — that correspond to the lowest profit level π_l — and a low quality level, the lowest level of quality — that correspond to the highest profit level π_h.

The State fixes the level of transparency "T". We assume that a higher transparency reduces the ability of the bureaucrat to be able to lie on the quality of the offered good. This implies that, there is an inverted relationship between the possibility for the bureaucrat to make a bid of low quality a winning bid and the level of transparency "T". In fact we assume that the bureaucrat supports a cost proportional to the transparency level "T", in order to lie about the quality of good. In our model a higher transparency level will imply the reduction of the surplus that the bureaucrat and the firm can themselves share. The surplus reduction is such that beyond a certain threshold it eliminates the economic convenience of corruption. Furthermore, the State checks on the behavior of firms and bureaucrats. There is an exogenous probability "q" of being detected, given that corruption has taken place. $q \in [0, 1]$ can therefore be thought of as the *ex-post* monitoring level implemented by the State. The bureaucrat in country "i" caught in a corrupt transaction, incurs a cost — for the social stigma associated with being found guilty — equal to "c_i" where $c_i \in [0, 1]$. In our model every country is characterized by its own different "inner honesty", whether due to historical developments, political regime, economic cycle or else. Each country therefore has a different level of costs it associates with finding corrupted actions. In the first part, for simplicity, we assume that bureaucrats all have the same moral cost. In the second part we let bureaucrats differ in this respect, by assuming that bureaucrats of a single country have different moral costs. The firm, if detected, must supply the high quality product — with π_l profit — but is refunded the cost of the bribe, paid to the bureaucrat.[3]

2.1 *The Game: Description and Solution*

Given the model just described, the economic problem can be formalized by the following three-period dynamic game with perfect and complete information (see Graph 2).

---

[3] This assumption can be more easily understood when, rather than corruption, there is extortion by the bureaucrat, even though, in many countries, the relevant provisions or laws, stipulate that the bribe shall in any case, be returned to the entrepreneur, and that combined minor punishment, (penal and/or pecuniary), be inflicted on him/her.

GRAPH 2

GAME TREE

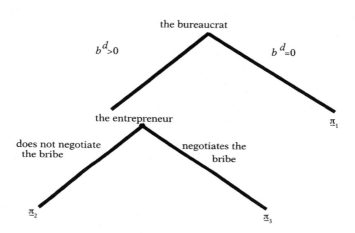

The State
fixes T

the bureaucrat

$b^d{}_{>0}$ $b^d{}_{=0}$

the entrepreneur $\underline{\pi}_1$

does not negotiate   negotiates the
the bribe   bribe

$\underline{\pi}_2$ $\underline{\pi}_3$

(1) In the first stage of the game, the State fixes the level of transparency "T", by minimizing its own loss-function.

(2) In stage two, the bureaucrat, facing a series of entrepreneurs that want to sell the product "y" to the Public Administration, may: *a)* decide not to ask for a bribe ($b^d = 0$) in which case all entrepreneurs will offer the high quality product and one entrepreneur selected by random draw will win the auction — with a π_I profit assumed > 0 — or, *b)* he may negotiate the payment of a bribe ($b^d > 0$) with one entrepreneur.

(2.1) If $b^d = 0$ no bribe is asked for, and the payoff vector for the entrepreneurs and bureaucrats is:

(1) $$\underline{\pi}_1 = (\pi_I , w)$$

The game ends in the equilibrium NC (No Corruption).

(2.2) Otherwise, let $b^d = 0$ be the positive bribe asked for by the bureaucrat. In this case the game continues to stage three.

(3) At stage three the firm decides whether to negotiate the bribe or turn it down.

(3.1) If the firm refuses the bribe, then the entrepreneur must supply the high quality product and the payoff vector is given by:

(2)
$$\underline{\pi_2} = (\pi_l, w)$$

Then, in this case the game ends. There is no penalty for the bureaucrat.

(3.2) Otherwise negotiation occur, and the two parties will find the bribe corresponding to the Nash solution to a bargaining game (b^{NB}) and the game ends. The bureaucrat supports a cost "T", proportional to the level of transparency of the tender, in order to lie about the quality of good. This bribe is the outcome of a negotiation between the bureaucrat and the firm, who will be assumed to share in a given surplus. The payoffs will depend on whether the bureaucrat and the firm are detected, (with probability "q") or not detected, (with probability $(1-q)$). There is a moral cost (c_i) for the detected bureaucrat. The firm, if detected, must sell a high quality product, but is refunded the cost of the bribe, paid to the bureaucrat. If the firm decides to pay the bribe, the expected payoff vector is given by:

(3)
$$\underline{\pi_3} = ((1-q)\pi_h + q\pi_l - (1-q)b,\ w + (1-q)b - qc_i - T)$$

The game ends in the equilibrium C (Corruption).

In what follows, we refer to the firm payoff by a superscript (1), to the bureaucrat payoff by a superscript (2): they represent respectively the first and the second element of the payoff vector $\underline{\pi_i}$, $i = 1, 2, 3$.

We first determine the equilibrium bribe (b^{NB}) (see *Appendix A* for the proof).

Proposition 2.1. Let $q \neq 1$[4]. Then there exists a unique non negative bribe (b^{NB}), as the Nash solution to a bargaining game, given by:

(4)
$$b^{NB} = \mu \left[\Delta\pi + \frac{T}{(1-q)} + \frac{qc_i}{(1-q)} \right]$$

---

[4] If $q = 1$ this stage of the game is never reached.

where:

$$\mu \equiv \frac{\lambda}{\lambda + \eta}$$

is the share of the surplus that goes to the bureaucrat and η and λ are the parameters that can be interpreted as the bargaining strength measures of the firm and the bureaucrat respectively and where $\Delta\pi = \pi_h - \pi_l$.

As a consequence of the model, let us assume that the bureaucrat and the firm share the surplus on an equal basis. This is the standard Nash case, when $\eta = \lambda = 1$ and the bureaucrat and the firm get equal shares. In this case the bribe is:

(5)
$$b^{NB} = \left[\frac{\Delta\pi}{2} + \frac{T}{2(1-q)} + \frac{qc_i}{2(1-q)} \right]$$

In other words, the bribe represents 50 percent of surplus. The payoff vector is given by:

(6)
$$\underline{\pi_3} = \left(\frac{(\pi_h + \pi_l)(1-q)}{2} + q\pi_l - \frac{T}{2} - \frac{qc_i}{2}, w + \frac{\Delta\pi(1-q)}{2} + \frac{T}{2} - \frac{qc_i}{2} \right)$$

Comparative Statics

(1) By analyzing this derivative we observe that:

(7)
$$\frac{\partial b^{NB}}{\partial T} = \frac{1}{2(1-q)} > 0$$

Therefore, increasing the transparency's level increases the bribe's level;

(2) And by analyzing:

(8)
$$\frac{\partial b^{NB}}{\partial q} = \frac{T + c_i}{2(1-q)^2} > 0$$

Therefore increasing monitoring increases the equilibrium bribe, because the greater bribe serves to compensate the greater risk of being discovered.

By solving the static game, we can prove the following proposition:[5]

Proposition 2.2. Let

$$0 \leq \left(\frac{\Delta\pi(1-q)}{q} - \frac{T}{q} \right) = c_i^* \leq 1. \text{ Then,}$$

(a) if $c_i \in [0, c_i^*)$ the payoff vector is

(9)
$$\underline{\pi_3} = \left(\frac{(\pi_h + \pi_l)(1-q)}{2} + q\pi_l - \frac{T}{2} - \frac{qc_i}{2}, w + \frac{\Delta\pi(1-q)}{2} + \frac{T}{2} - \frac{qc_i}{2} \right)$$

(b) if $c_i \in [c_i^*, 1]$ the payoff vector is

(10)
$$\underline{\pi_1} = (\pi_l, w)$$

Then, once a transparency level equal to T is set:

(a) if $c_i \in [0, c_i^*)$, all the bureaucrats will be corrupt at that level of transparency T. If this condition (equilibrium C) applies, the firm finds it convenient to pay a bribe. The surplus is such as to make up for the expected cost of corruption. Thus the surplus to be shared between the firm and the bureaucrat will keep a negotiation going, whose outcome is the bribe corresponding to the Nash solution to a bargaining game. In this equilibrium all bureaucrats will be corrupt at that level of chosen transparency.

(b) if $c_i \in [c_i^*, 1]$, all the bureaucrats will be honest at that level of transparency T. If this condition (equilibrium NC) applies the difference in profits is not enough to make up for the expected cost of corruption. With this in mind, the bureaucrat will not ask the entrepreneur for a bribe and then all the bureaucrats will be honest and quality will be of a high level.

---

[5] See *Appendix B* for the proof.

It follows that, once a transparency level equal to "T" is set, if the moral cost of the i-th country c_i is lower than

$$c_i^* = \left(\frac{\Delta\pi(1-q)}{q} - \frac{T}{q} \right)$$

then all the bureaucrats will be corrupt at that level of chosen transparency.

If the moral cost c_i is greater or equal than c_i^* then all the bureaucrats will be honest. Therefore, because all bureaucrats incur the same moral costs, this leads to a corner-solution: either all bureaucrats will be corrupt or they will be honest, depending on the moral cost of a specific country.

One implication of this very simple model is that, for a given level of predisposition to corruption in country, if the State wants to eradicate corruption it will have to fix a level of transparency so that: $c_i = c_i^*$. Then,

(11) $$T_i^* = (1-q)\Delta\pi - qc_i$$

is the minimum transparency level that country "i" – given its predisposition to corruption c_i – will have to put in place to eliminate corruption in procurement. Notice that with great moral costs (a country "innerly honest") the needed level of transparency in procurement is low and viceversa.

2.2 *Transparency with Heterogeneous Moral Costs*

In the previous section we have shown that if all bureaucrats incur the same moral costs, this leads to a corner-solution: in fact, once a transparency level equal to T is set, if the moral cost is lower than c_i^*, then all the bureaucrats will be corrupt at that level of transparency; if moral cost c_i is greater or equal than c_i^* then all the bureaucrats will be honest. The corruption level depends on the hypothesis made on the distribution of costs.

That moral costs are equal across bureaucrats is a convenient assumption, but not necessarily a realistic one. For this reason we introduce the hypothesis that these costs may vary across the various bureaucrats ($c_{i,j}$ the i-th country j-th bureaucrat), reflecting different ethical, moral and religious individual values or denoting a greater or lesser sense of their own impunity.

The cumulative density of probability, defines the distribution of individual costs for the i-th country $F(c_{i,j})$, where "i" is the country and "j" the specific bureaucrat of country "i". This function represents the proportion of bureaucrats who agree to be corrupted when the transparency level is "T". If, as we will assume, the distribution of bureaucrats' costs is uniform in the interval $[c_{i,\min}, c_{i,\max}]$, (in a different interval for each country), then the cumulative density function will be:

(12)
$$F(c_{i,j}) = \int_{c_{i,\min}}^{c_j} \frac{1}{c_{i,\max} - c_{i,\min}} dc_j = \frac{c_j - c_{i,\min}}{c_{i,\max} - c_{i,\min}}$$

We now solve the model by identifying the optimal level of transparency for country "i". We then focus on a heuristic cross-country analysis. $F(c_{i,j})$ represents the number of bureaucrats in country "i" that will be corrupt, given a certain level of transparency "T". Since

$$c_i^* = \left(\frac{\Delta\pi(1-q)}{q} - \frac{T}{q} \right)$$

substituting in (12) we obtain:

(13)
$$F(c_{i,j}) = \frac{\frac{\Delta\pi(1-q)}{q} - \frac{T}{q} - c_{i,\min}}{c_{i,\max} - c_{i,\min}}$$

Comparative Statics

(1) By analyzing this derivative we observe that:

(14)
$$\frac{\partial F(c_{i,j})}{\partial q} = -\frac{\Delta\pi - T}{(c_{i,\max} - c_{i,\min})q^2} < 0$$

Therefore increasing monitoring reduces the equilibrium level of corruption, because this reduces the potential surplus that the bureaucrat and firm can share, and thus reduce the corruption level. In particular we can demonstrate that the monitoring level that eliminates corruption is:

(15)
$$F(c_{i,j}) = 0 \Rightarrow q = \frac{\Delta\pi - T}{\Delta\pi + c_{i,min}} < 1$$

Then to eradicate corruption a level of monitoring lower than 1 is necessary;

(2) And by analyzing:

(16)
$$\frac{\partial F(c_{i,j})}{\partial T} = -\frac{1}{(c_{i,max} - c_{i,min})q} < 0$$

Therefore, increasing the transparency' level also reduces the corruption level. If State "i" wanted to eradicate corruption it should fix a level of transparency T_i such that:

(17)
$$F(c_{i,j}) = 0 \Rightarrow -\frac{\dfrac{\Delta\pi(1-q)}{q} - \dfrac{T}{q} - c_{i,min}}{c_{i,max} - c_{i,min}} = 0$$

i.e. when:

(18)
$$T_i^* = \Delta\pi(1 - q) - qc_{i,min}$$

This level of transparency is necessary to eliminate corruption in country "i". However the State, in fixing transparency "T", beside its benefits must also take into account of the costs deriving from reaching a certain degree of transparency. Let us assume for simplicity that each State will have similar marginal benefit and marginal cost functions from increasing transparency. The marginal benefit is due to the advantage of obtaining a high quality product instead of a low quality product.

Let us assume the marginal benefit BMA(T) to be constant as the value of procurement increases and equal across countries: BMA = a. Instead we assume that the marginal cost of transparency increases with transparency. With this assumption we want to capture the standard and partly exogenous structure of public procurement, characterized by some tenders with large values making up large shares of total procurement and a large amount of small tenders with small values: as the value of transparent procurement rises by one unit of value we reach smaller and smaller tenders and as the cost of tenders has a fixed component (e.g. tender committees and publication costs) the marginal cost per unit of value of procurement progressively increases. The loss function of the State in the first stage of the game will be given by:

(19) $$L = -aT + bT^2$$

Minimizing with respect to "T" we obtain:

(20) $$\frac{\partial L}{\partial T} = 0 \Rightarrow T° = \frac{a}{2b}$$

GRAPH 3

OPTIMAL TRANSPARENCY LEVEL

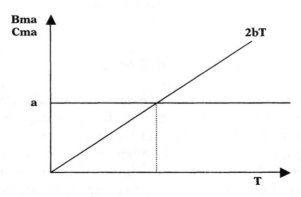

This figure shows the optimal transparency level. The horizontal line is the marginal cost BMA=a, while the positively sloped line is the marginal cost equal to 2bT.

So each country "i" there will be two relevant values of transparency:

- $T_i^* = (1 - q)\Delta\pi - qc_{i,\min}$

is the specific level of minimum transparency needed to eliminate corruption due to the distribution of bureaucrats' costs uniform in the interval;

- $T° = \dfrac{a}{2b}T$

is the optimal level of transparency, assumed equal across countries.

3. - Analysis Cross-Country

In a heuristic fashion, let us consider the implications of this set-up for two countries: country "i", with a low "inner honesty", i.e. with, a distribution of bureaucrats' costs uniform in the interval $[c_{i,\min}, c_{i,\max}]$ and country "k" with higher "inner honesty", i.e. a distribution of bureaucrats' costs uniform in the interval $[c_{k,\min}, c_{k,\max}]$ such that $c_{i,\min} < c_{k,\min}$ and $c_{i,\max}, < c_{k,\max}$. Assume also that the distributions of moral costs are such that:

- $T_i^* = (1 - q)\Delta\pi - qc_{i,\min} > T° = \dfrac{a}{2b}$

- $T_k^* = (1 - q)\Delta\pi - qc_{k,\min} < T° = \dfrac{a}{2b}$

What will emerge is that country "k" with high "inner honesty" will choose a level of transparency of total procurement T_k^*, that will allow the eradication of corruption in procurement. Country "i" will instead not find it convenient to eradicate all corruption

— since $T_i^* > T°$ — and fixing the share of transparent public procurement at $T = T°$ would imply not maximizing total welfare given the costs of transparency. This implies that for country "i" the optimal level of transparency will be $T°$, even if such a level will note eradicate corruption. A share of bureaucrats, those with a level of moral costs lower than,

$$c° = \left(\frac{\Delta\pi(1-q)}{q} - \frac{T°}{q} \right) = \left(\frac{\Delta\pi(1-q)}{q} - \frac{a}{2bq} \right)$$

will continue to be corrupt.

This simple example shows that in equilibrium what emerges is that a country with greater honesty will fix a level of transparency in its procurement lower than a country that will appear more corrupt, confirming the only apparent paradox shown by the data that less corrupt countries choose to make transparent a lower share of their total procurement through open procedures.

4. - Conclusions

The European Union calls transparency a principle of procurement. It must be a principle to be pursued with pragmatism however, as the same EU Directives allow for different degrees of transparency depending on the size of the tender, recognizing implicitly that transparency has a cost for society. If transparency is costly, then we have shown that countries where corruption is more pervasive and less easy to eradicate will stop short of implementing the level of transparency in procurement that would dissolve corruption. It will however find it beneficial to implement larger transparency in procurement compared to countries with a better track-record for corruption intolerance. If we agree that corruption in procurement plays a large role in influencing total corruption in a country, this leaves one with a final question: how to eradicate corruption if transparency is costly? It is not an easy answer that we might want to leave open. We suggest however, following the approach taken by other scholars, that other types of transparency might be imagined. Picci (2005) suggests using IT technologies to publish on user-friendly platforms the results of similar tenders across the country so as to allow public procurement stake-holders (including citizens) to monitor contract characteristics across administrations. This best-practice, benchmarking approach may create a strong constituency in the country, able to further raise the cost of corrupt behaviour and thereby reduce corruption. "Voice" and "Public Governance" will thus acquire new power thanks to the quality of specifically tailored e-based solutions.

A APPENDIX

The Nash Bargaining Bribe

Let $\pi_\Delta = \pi_4 - \pi_3 = \pi_\Delta^{(1)}, \pi_\Delta^{(2)}$ be the vector of the differences in the payoffs between the case of agreement and disagreement about the bribe, between bureaucrat and entrepreneur. In accordance with generalized Nash bargaining theory, the division between two agents will solve:

$$(21) \qquad \max_{b \in \Re^*} \left[\pi_\Delta^{(1)\eta} \right] \left[\pi_\Delta^{(2)\lambda} \right]$$

in formula

$$(22) \qquad \max_{b \in \Re^*} [\Delta\pi(1-q) - (1-q)b]^\eta \, [(1-q)b - qc_i - T]^\lambda$$

that is the maximum of the product between the elements of π_Δ and where $[0, w]$ is the point of disagreement, i.e. the payoffs that the entrepreneur and the bureaucrat respectively would obtain if they did not come to an agreement. The parameters η and λ can be interpreted as measures of bargaining strength. It is now easy to check that the bureaucrat gets a share

$$\mu \equiv \frac{\lambda}{\lambda+\eta}$$

of the surplus , i.e. the bribe is $b=\mu\tau$. More generally μ reflects the distribution of bargaining strength between two agents. Then the bribe b^{NB} is an asymmetric (or generalized) Nash bargaining solution and is given by:

$$(23) \qquad b^{NB} = \mu \left[\Delta\pi + \frac{T}{(1-q)} - \frac{qc_i}{(1-q)} \right]$$

that is the unique equilibrium bribe in the last subgame $\forall q \neq 1$.

Solution to the Static Game

Backward induction method. The static game is solved with the backward induction method, which allows identification at the equilibria. Starting from stage 3, the entrepreneur needs to decide whether to negotiate with the bureaucrat. Both payoffs are then compared, because the bureaucrat asked for a bribe.

(3) At stage three the entrepreneur negotiates the bribe if, and only if

$$\pi_3^{(1)} \geq \pi_2^{(1)} \Rightarrow$$

$$\left(q\pi_l + \frac{\pi_l(1-q)}{2} + \frac{\pi_h(1-q)}{2} - \frac{qc}{2} - \frac{T}{2} \right) \geq \pi_l \Rightarrow$$

(24)
$$c < \left(\frac{(1-q)\Delta\pi}{q} - \frac{T}{q} \right) = c^*$$

(2) Going up the decision-making tree, at stage two the bureaucrat decides whether to ask for a positive bribe.

Let
$$c < \left(\frac{(1-q)\Delta\pi}{q} - \frac{T}{q} \right) = c^*$$

then the bureaucrat knows that if he asks for a positive bribe, the entrepreneur will accept the negotiation, and the final bribe will be b^{NB}. Then at stage two, the bureaucrat asks for a bribe if, and only if

$$\pi_3^{(2)} \geq \pi_1^{(2)} \Rightarrow$$

(25)
$$w + \frac{\Delta\pi(1-q)}{2} - \frac{T}{2} - \frac{qc}{2} > w$$

that is the bureaucrat's payoff. If

$$c < \left(\frac{(1-q)\Delta\pi}{q} - \frac{T}{q} \right) = c^*$$

holds, then *(18)* is always verified. Then, in this case if $c \leq c^*$, then bureaucrat ask for the bribe b^{NB}, that the entrepreneur will accept. The expected payoff vector is given by:

(26)
$$\underline{\pi_3} = \left(\frac{(\pi_h + \pi_l)(1-q)}{2} + q\pi_l - \frac{T}{2} - \frac{qc_i}{2}, w + \frac{\Delta\pi(1-q)}{2} + \frac{T}{2} - \frac{qc_i}{2} \right)$$

The game ends in the equilibrium C (Corruption).

Let

$$c < \left(\frac{(1-q)\Delta\pi}{q} - \frac{T}{q} \right) = c^*$$

then the bureaucrat knows that the entrepreneurs will not accept any possible bribe, so he will be honest and the firm must sell the product at high level quality. The payoff vector for the entrepreneurs and bureaucrats is:

(27)
$$\underline{\pi_1} = (\pi_l, w)$$

The game ends in the equilibrium NC (No Corruption).

(1) At stage one the State fixes the transparency' level T, by minimizing own loss-function.

BIBLIOGRAPHY

BECKER S.G., «Crime and Punishment: An Economic Approach», *Journal of Political Economy*, no. 76, pages 169-217, 1968.

KAUFMANN D., *Rethinking Governance. Empirical Lessons Challenge Orthodoxy*, World Bank Institute, paper prepared for the workshop on Corruption: its Consequences and Cures, Stanford University, January 31st-February 1st, 2003.

— —, «Six Questions on the Cost of Corruption with World Bank Institute Global Governance Director Daniel Kaufmann», in *News-The World Bank*, Washington, D.C. 2005.

LENGWILER Y. - WOLFSTETTER E., «Corruption in Procurement Auction», in DIMITRI N. - PIGA G. - SPAGNOLO G. (eds.), *Handbook of Procurement*, by Cambridge University Press, forthcoming 2006.

ROSE-ACKERMAN S., «The Economics of Corruption», *Journal of Public Economics*, pages 187-203, 1975.

— —, *Corruption, A Study in Political Economy*, Academic Press, 1978

— —, *Corruption and Government*, Cambridge University Press, 1999.

SHLEIFER, A. - VISHNY R., «Corruption», *The Quarterly Journal of Economics*, pages 599-617, 1993.

V - PROCUREMENT DESIGN

Environmental Issues in Public Procurement: How Much Decentralization?

Alessio D'Amato

Università di Roma "Tor Vergata"

Concerns about the environmental effects of procurement decisions are gaining momentum. We investigate how the environmental quality of public purchases changes under two possible institutional settings: a centralized one, where a single regulator is in charge of both production efficiency and environmental quality, and a decentralized one, where two separate bodies operate, namely an environmental agency securing environmental quality and a procurement agency pursuing efficiency. Informational asymmetries that affect such regulatory relationship are taken into account. We conclude that, under certain conditions, non-cooperation tightens the trade off between incentives to efficiency and rent extraction, resulting in a downward distortion in environmental quality. [JEL Classification: D82, L51, Q58].

1. - Introduction

Until recently, environmental quality has not been a relevant issue for public procurement authorities. However, both consumers and public and private decision makers are increasingly concerned with problems related to "sustainable development" — development that meets the needs of the present

The Author wishes to thank Laura Castellucci and Gianni De Fraja for their very valuable suggestions and ideas. The Author is also indebted to Gianmaria Bernareggi, Vincenzo Denicolò, Laurent Franckx, Stefano Gorini, Alberto Iozzi, Claudio Mezzetti, Francesca Stroffolini and Edilio Valentini, the participants in the 2002 GPE Conference, and seminar audience at CEIS-«Tor Vergata», for helpful comments. The usual disclaimer applies.

generation without compromising the chance of future generations to meet their own needs. As a result, much effort is currently being devoted by international institutions and national governments to deal with environmental problems. The field of public purchases is not an exception, so that the prospects of a *Green Public Procurement* are gaining relevance both at a European and at an Italian level[1].

As the European Commission (2004) suggests, the "greening" of public procurement could generate significant benefits for the environment. For example, if all public authorities across the EU demanded "green" electricity, this would save the equivalent of 60 million tonnes of CO_2, which is equivalent to 18% of the EU's greenhouse gas reduction commitment under the Kyoto Protocol. Further, by reducing the environmental impact of purchases, public authorities would implicitly "advertise" sustainability objectives to private consumers and firms. At the same time, they would provide incentives for the development of environmental technologies when they are mostly needed, namely when technologies themselves are in their very early stages.

This paper focuses on a specific issue in green public procurement, namely, the consequences of choosing the environmental quality standards in a decentralized way. Following Laffont and Tirole (1993), we develop a stylized principal/agent framework where a firm is performing a public project on behalf of a Procurement Agency (PA), who is in charge of efficiency in production. As it is standard, we assume that the objective function of the PA includes consumers' and producers' surplus resulting from the output produced. We then introduce an Environmental Regulator (ER), in charge of environmental quality, who is interested in balancing the related social benefits and social costs. We compare the case when the two agencies act in a cooperative way with a situation in which they behave non cooperatively. In the latter case, we are facing what Berhneim and Whinston (1986) call a problem of *Common Agency*[2].

---

[1] For an introduction see EUROPEAN COMMISSION (2004).

[2] DIXIT A. *et* AL. (1997, page 752) provide a clear definition, suitable for the framework of our paper: "Common agency is a multilateral relationship in which

Asymmetries of information are assumed, in that only the firm knows its "technology" and the effort exerted in improving efficiency in production and in the promotion of environmental quality. In such a setting, it is a well known result[3] that the regulated firm gains a rent tied to its informational advantage and that the first best outcome cannot be reached.

Under non cooperative behavior, however, a further distortion arises. Specifically, in our highly stylized framework, the environmental quality standard imposed by the ER to the inefficient firm and the effort the same firm exerts in reducing the related costs are never higher than those obtained in the case when the two regulators cooperate. As a result, under non cooperation we observe a reduction in the power of incentive schemes with respect to cooperation, and a "weaker" environmental policy. This is the main result of our paper, and is a consequence of the fact that the environmental regulator is not interested in the firm's profit performance. A stricter trade off between incentives to efficiency and rent extraction arises, because the non cooperating environmental agency perceives the rent accruing to the efficient firm due to asymmetric information as more costly.

Early contributions to the analysis of environmental quality regulation under asymmetric information are Kwerel (1977), Dasgupta *et* al. (1980) and Spulber (1988). The main insight provided is that «each polluter should be residual claimant of all the costs and benefits associated with its actions» (Lewis, 1996, page 826). This is obtained, for example, in Dasgupta *et* al. (1980) by applying a modified version of the Groves-Clarke-Vickrey public choice mechanism, so that truth telling becomes

---

several principals simultaneously try to influence the actions of an agent". Common agency can be, in turn, distinguished in *delegated* and *intrinsic*. Under *delegated* common agency, the choice of the contractual relationship is delegated to the agent who can choose to contract with one, a part or all the principals; when common agency is *intrinsic*, instead, the agent's choice is more limited: he can only choose to contract or not with all the principals, and cannot exclude one or more principals from contracting. This is our case, in which a regulated firm can only choose between the option of contracting with all the regulators and the one of not producing.

[3] See, among others, the extensive survey by LEWIS T.R. (1996).

a dominant strategy for regulated firms, and the full information optimum can be obtained.

Although theoretically there are ways to force firms to reveal information concerning their technology and costs, privately informed regulated entities can obtain information rents by claiming that the introduction of environmental policy can force them out of business[4]. These unverifiable claims have to be accounted for if the regulatory bodies perceive the activities performed by regulated firms as valuable. The incentive regulation literature suggests different mechanisms to reduce information rents. Such mechanisms typically require, as we will show in section 3, a sacrifice in terms of efficiency in production and/or environmental quality improvements[5].

The earliest paper explicitly accounting for regulation of environmental quality by an independent agency is, to our knowledge, the one by Baron (1985). He assumes that a polluting Public Utility is regulated by a federal Environmental Protection Agency (EPA), that acts as a leader, and a state-level Public Utility Commission (PUC) that acts as a follower in a von Stackelberg game. In this game, the EPA moves first, establishing emissions policy, while the PUC, then, sets a pricing policy for the firm, that is privately informed about its efficiency in pollution reduction[6].

By moving first, the EPA may act strategically. It realizes that information concerning the firm's cost of abatement will be revealed by the pricing arrangement adopted by the PUC. Consequently the EPA makes its policy contingent on price regulation, free riding on the information extracted by the PUC itself. This allows the EPA to choose the abatement standard to be imposed to the firm without accounting for the need to limit information rents. As a consequence, noncooperative regulation results, under certain conditions, in an emissions standard that is stricter than the cooperative second best level.

We put ourselves in the stream of Baron's paper, but we follow

---

[4] In general, it could be desirable from a social welfare point of view that some firms exit the market or relocate. We rule out this case.

[5] See also LAFFONT J.J. (1994).

[6] Baron's setting is built up to describe the institutional framework in the U.S.

a quite different modeling strategy, as we assume that the two agencies share the burden of rent extraction. This could be the case when they act at the same hierarchical level. As we will show, such hypothesis can have a significant impact on the consequences of non cooperation.

The paper is organized as follows: in section 2 we introduce the main features of the model, section 3 derives results in a cooperative setting, while in section 4 the non cooperative case is analyzed. Section 5 discusses results and, finally, section 6 concludes.

2. - The Model

We study the regulation of a firm performing a production activity consisting in an indivisible public project. Firm's output is exogenously given and normalized to 1.

The firm can also engage in activities aimed at reducing the environmental impact of the public project; we call x the corresponding level of environmental quality[7]. We assume the simplest possible cost functions for the two activities: the firm performs the public project bearing a cost equal to

$$C_q (e_q, \beta) = (\beta - e_q)$$

Constant marginal (and average) costs of environmental quality are

$$C_x (e_x, \beta) = (\beta - e_x)$$

Total costs are therefore:

(1) $C (\beta, e_q, e_x, x) = C_q (.) + C_x (.) x = (\beta - e_q) + (\beta - e_x) x$

---

[7] What we call x might be, for example, the polluting potential of a new-built electric power plant, with lower values of x implying higher emissions per unit of energy produced.

211

where: β is a technological parameter that represents the efficiency of the firm in the two activities, with higher values implying higher costs, that is, lower efficiency; e_q and e_x are the levels of effort exerted by the firm in reducing, respectively, the costs of production and environmental quality. These two values may be regarded as a measure of all the possible actions the firm (or its managers) may undertake in order to improve the efficiency in performing its two tasks.

The firm is controlled by two (risk neutral) regulators: a first one, that we call Procurement Agency (PA), controls efficiency in production, while a second one, that we call Environmental Regulator (ER), is in charge of environmental problems.

The PA is concerned with both the firm's and consumers' welfare deriving from the production activity. As it is standard, we follow the accounting convention that the PA reimburses costs related to the production activity, C_q, to the firm. Furthermore, in order to guarantee that the public project is performed, the PA provides the firm with a net positive transfer t_q. The needed resources are raised via distortionary taxation, and this causes a deadweight cost, that we assume strictly positive. Analytically, the PA offers a take-it-or-leave-it contract, specifying (C_q, t_q), to the firm, to maximize the following objective function:

$$(2) \qquad W_q = S - (1 + \lambda)(C_q + t_q) + U,$$

where:

λ (assumed > 0) denotes the shadow cost of public funds,

S is the social surplus tied to the production activity, given and supposed sufficiently large as to guarantee that there is no threshold level for the parameter β above which the regulator finds it convenient to shut down the firm.

U is the profit level of the regulated firm, that will be defined shortly.

The Environmental Regulator (ER) acts to balance social welfare deriving from environmental quality with its social costs. We assume that ER does not take into account all the consequences of its actions on the regulated firm's profits.

Specifically, we think it is realistic to assume that the ER gives less weight than the PA in his objective function to such profits. We take the extreme case in which this weight is 0. ER has the power to impose an environmental quality standard, x, reimburses costs related to that standard and makes a net transfer, t_x, to the firm. As in the case of the PA, there is a deadweight loss tied to the need to raise the necessary public funds via distortionary taxation. ER, therefore, offers a take-it-or-leave-it contract, specifying (C_x, x, t_x), to the firm, in order to maximize the following objective function[8]:

(3) $$W_x = V(x) - (1 + \lambda)(C_x x + t_x),$$

where $V(x)$ is a function representing social benefits tied to environmental quality, with $V'(x) > 0$ and $V''(x) < 0$, implying decreasing marginal benefits.

Given total cost reimbursement and net transfers, the firm's profit function may be written as follows:

(4) $$U = t_q + t_x - \psi(e_q) - \psi(e_x)$$

The term $\psi(e_q) + \psi(e_x)$ is the sum of (monetary measures of) the disutility the firm has to bear in order to reduce costs in both its activities[9]. The disutility of each effort level is increasing at an increasing rate, that is $\psi' > 0$, $\psi'' > 0$. Furthermore, to guarantee the concavity of all objective functions, we assume

$$-\psi''(.) V''(x) > (1 + \lambda), \text{ and } \psi'''(.) \geq 0^{[10]}.$$

The two regulators can cooperate, in which case they behave as a merged entity, or act independently. In both cases, we assume they have all the bargaining power. The firm can either accept or

---

[8] As it is reasonable, we assume that the ER never sets its policy variables in such a way to cause the firm to close down. The reason behind this hypothesis is to exclude the uninteresting case in which no public project is actually performed.

[9] The additive separability of U in effort levels rules out possible distortions related to what MARTIMORT D. - STOLE L. (2003) call *indirect contractual externalities*. These distortions are already well investigated in the common agency literature (see, for example, STOLE L., 1991).

[10] Assuming $\psi'''(.) \geq 0$ also allows us to rule out stochastic mechanisms.

refuse both the contracts offered by the regulators in the non cooperative case[11], while, when the two regulators act jointly, the firm can only choose to accept or refuse the single contract offered. Once accepted, we assume the contract(s) to be perfectly enforceable. Each of the two regulators, acting cooperatively or not, can observe total realized costs, can identify the part of costs that is due to the activity it is in charge of and can observe environmental quality. On the other hand, the two regulators do not know the true value of β and cannot observe the effort levels exerted by the firm. We are, therefore, in a principal/agent framework, where the firm is an agent performing two activities on behalf of one principal (in the cooperative case) or two principals (in the case the two regulators do not cooperate).

The efficiency parameter β may take two values: $\bar{\beta}$ (inefficient type) and $\underline{\beta}$ (efficient type) with $\bar{\beta} > \underline{\beta}$ and $\Delta\beta = \bar{\beta} - \underline{\beta} > 0$. The two regulators have identical a priori beliefs about the distribution of β, that is $\beta = \bar{\beta}$ with probability π and $\beta = \underline{\beta}$ with probability $1 - \pi$.

We will start analyzing the cooperative case. We expect the presence of asymmetric information to lead to the standard distortions tied to the moral hazard/adverse selection problem, that is lower than first best effort levels required from the inefficient type firm. We will then use the results obtained as a benchmark to evaluate "new" distortions introduced by non cooperative behavior under asymmetric information.

3. - Cooperative Case

Thank to the Revelation Principle[12], we can limit our analysis, without loss of generality, to *direct revelation mechanisms*[13]. The

---

[11] In other words, the firm cannot choose to contract with only one of the two principals. We are therefore in the *intrinsic common agency* case; see footnote 2.

[12] See LAFFONT J.J. - MARTIMORT D. (2002).

[13] Indeed, we also limit to *deterministic* mechanisms. LAFFONT J.J. - TIROLE J. (1993, *Appendix* A1.1) show that, under certain conditions, offering a lottery over a given set of contracts is suboptimal in the single regulator case. Their proof extends straightforwardly to our cooperative case, given our assumptions (see, in particular, footnote 10).

cooperating regulators offer a menu of contracts specifying cost levels, a single transfer (we call it t) and environmental quality for each firm's type; the contracts offered are, therefore:

$$\{C_q(\bar{\beta}), C_x(\bar{\beta}), t(\bar{\beta}), x(\bar{\beta})\} \text{ for type } \bar{\beta} \text{ and}$$

$$\{C_q(\underline{\beta}), C_x(\underline{\beta}), t(\underline{\beta}), x(\underline{\beta})\} \text{ for type } \underline{\beta}$$

For expositional ease let $\bar{C}_q = C_q(\bar{\beta})$, $\bar{C}_x = C_x(\bar{\beta})$, $\bar{t} = t(\bar{\beta})$, $\bar{x} = x(\bar{\beta})$ etc. Using $e_q = \beta - C_q$ and $e_x = \beta - C_x$, we call $U(\beta) = t(\beta) - \psi(\beta - C_q(\beta)) - \psi(\beta - C_x(\beta))$ the profits of type β firm when it chooses the contract designed for its type, so that $\bar{U} = \bar{t} - \psi(\bar{\beta} - \bar{C}_q) - \psi(\bar{\beta} - \bar{C}_x)$ are profits of the $\bar{\beta}$ firm when it acts according to the contract designed for its type, while $\underline{U} = \underline{t} - \psi(\underline{\beta} - \underline{C}_q) - \psi(\underline{\beta} - \underline{C}_x)$ are the corresponding profits of the $\underline{\beta}$ type firm.

The timing of the game is as follows. Once nature has determined the firm's type or, equivalently, the firm has drawn its type β from the distribution described by the two probabilities π and $1 - \pi$, the regulator resulting from cooperation offers a menu of contracts specifying cost reimbursements, environmental quality and a transfer for each firm's type. Then the firm chooses to accept or refuse to contract with the regulator. If it refuses, the game ends and the firm gets its reservation profits (normalized to 0). If it accepts, it sends a message to the regulator itself concerning β, for example choosing from the offered menu of contracts the one designed for its type. Finally, the contract is executed.

In order for the firm to be provided the appropriate incentives, we must ensure that each firm (weakly) prefers the contract designed for its type to the one designed for the other type. The contracts proposed to both types must satisfy the so called Incentive Compatibility Constraints.

Incentive compatibility implies that the profit gained by the efficient type by choosing "its" contract must be at least as high as those that would be obtained choosing the one designed for the inefficient type and vice versa. Given the relationship between costs and effort levels, we can express this requirement in the following way:

215

(5) $\underline{t} - \psi(\underline{\beta} - \underline{C}_q) - \psi(\underline{\beta} - \underline{C}_x) \geq \overline{t} - \psi(\underline{\beta} - \overline{C}_q) - \psi(\underline{\beta} - \overline{C}_x)$

(we will call this constraint $\underline{IC}$ from now on), and

(6) $\overline{t} - \psi(\overline{\beta} - \overline{C}_q) - \psi(\overline{\beta} - \overline{C}_x) \geq \underline{t} - \psi(\overline{\beta} - \underline{C}_q) - \psi(\overline{\beta} - \underline{C}_x)$

(we will call this constraint $\overline{IC}$ from now on).

Two other constraints must be accounted for. Namely, the regulator must provide the firm at least with its reservation profit level in each possible state, in order to guarantee that the activities the firm has to perform will effectively take place.

The resulting Individual Rationality Constraints imply:

$$\underline{t} - \psi(\underline{\beta} - \underline{C}_q) - \psi(\underline{\beta} - \underline{C}_x) \geq 0$$

(we will call this constraint $\underline{IR}$ from now on), and

$$\overline{t} - \psi(\overline{\beta} - \overline{C}_q) - \psi(\overline{\beta} - \overline{C}_x) \geq 0$$

(we will call this constraint $\overline{IR}$ from now on).

We can rewrite $\underline{IC}$ as:

(7) $$\underline{U} \geq \overline{U} + \phi(\overline{e}_q) + \phi(\overline{e}_x)$$

where $\phi(e) = \psi(e) - \psi(e - \Delta\beta)$, $\Delta\beta = \overline{\beta} - \underline{\beta}$ and $\overline{e}_i = \overline{\beta} - \overline{C}_i$ ($i = x, q$).

The function $\phi(.)$ plays a very important role. It is, in fact, the rent that the efficient firm gains because of its informational advantage. Given the properties of $\psi(.)$, the rent is increasing in the level of effort of the inefficient type. This is a key property, and is the source of the trade off between the socially costly efficient firm's rent and the efficiency in the effort level contracted by the regulator with the inefficient firm.

To simplify further the analysis, in solving the maximization problem of the regulator, we will use the following Lemma:

LEMMA 1 $\underline{IC}$ and $\overline{IR}$ imply $\underline{IR}$.
Proof. The proof follows the steps in Laffont and Tirole (1993,

section 1.16, p. 58). From condition *(5)* we have: $\underline{U} \geq \overline{t} - \psi\,(\beta - \overline{C}_q)$ $- \psi\,(\beta - \overline{C}_x)$; using $\overline{IR}$ we can show that inequality $\underline{U} \geq \psi\,(\overline{\beta} - \overline{C}_q) +$ $\psi\,(\overline{\beta} - \overline{C}_x) - \psi\,(\beta - \overline{C}_q) - \psi\,(\beta - \overline{C}_x)$ holds, and because $\psi\,(.)$ is increasing we have: $\underline{U} \geq 0$.

The two cooperating regulators aim at maximizing the expected value of the sum of *(2)* and *(3)*, that is:

(8)
$$E\,(W_{co}) = S + \pi\,[V\,(\overline{x}) - (1 + \lambda)\,[\overline{C}_q + \overline{C}_x\overline{x} + \overline{t}]] +$$

$$+ (1 - \pi)\,[V\,(\underline{x}) - (1 + \lambda)\,[\underline{C}_q + \underline{C}_x\underline{x} + \underline{t}]] + [\pi\overline{U} + (1 - \pi)\,\underline{U}]$$

We will solve the corresponding maximization problem leaving the $\overline{IC}$ constraint out of the analysis, verifying then that the solutions satisfy such condition.

Using the definition of firm's profits, the problem of maximizing *(8)* may be rewritten as:

(9) $\displaystyle\max_{\substack{\{\overline{C}_q,\overline{C}_x,\overline{U},\overline{x} \\ \underline{C}_q,\underline{C}_x,\underline{U},\underline{x}\}}} E(W_{co}) = S + \pi[V(\overline{x}) - (1 + \lambda)[\overline{C}_q + \overline{C}_x\overline{x} + \psi(\overline{\beta} - \overline{C}_q) + \psi(\overline{\beta} - \overline{C}_x)]] +$

$$+(1 - \pi)[V(\underline{x}) - (1 + \lambda)[\underline{C}_q + \underline{C}_x\underline{x} + \psi(\underline{\beta} - \underline{C}_q) + \psi(\underline{\beta} - \underline{C}_x)]] - \lambda[\pi\overline{U} + (1 - \pi)\underline{U}]$$

subject to $\overline{IR}$:

$$\overline{U} \geq 0$$

and $\underline{IC}$ constraints:

$$\underline{U} \geq \overline{U} + \phi\,(\overline{\beta} - \overline{C}_q) + \phi\,(\overline{\beta} - \overline{C}_x)$$

The objective function *(9)* is strictly decreasing in $\overline{U}$ and $\underline{U}$, so that, from $\overline{IR}$ and $\underline{IC}$, we get the following conditions for $\overline{t}$ and $\underline{t}$:

$$\overline{U} = 0 \Rightarrow \overline{t} = \psi\,(\overline{\beta} - \overline{C}_q) + \psi\,(\overline{\beta} - \overline{C}_x)$$

$$\underline{U} = \phi\,(\overline{\beta} - \overline{C}_q) + \phi\,(\overline{\beta} - \overline{C}_x) \Rightarrow \underline{t} = \psi\,(\underline{\beta} - \underline{C}_q) + \psi\,(\underline{\beta} - \underline{C}_x) +$$

$$+ \phi\,(\overline{\beta} - \overline{C}_q) + \phi\,(\overline{\beta} - \overline{C}_x)$$

No rent is left to the inefficient type, while, as seen above, the rent accruing to the efficient type is increasing in the effort level of the inefficient one.

Substituting these two conditions in the objective function (9), it becomes:

$$(10) \quad S + \pi \left[V(\bar{x}) - (1+\lambda) \left[\bar{C}_q + \bar{C}_x \bar{x} + \psi(\bar{\beta} - \bar{C}_q) + \psi(\bar{\beta} - \bar{C}_x) \right] \right]$$

$$+ (1-\pi) \left[V(\underline{x}) - (1+\lambda) \left[\underline{C}_q + \underline{C}_x \underline{x} + \psi(\underline{\beta} - \underline{C}_q) + \psi(\underline{\beta} - \underline{C}_x) \right] \right] +$$

$$- \lambda(1-\pi) \left[\phi(\bar{\beta} - \bar{C}_q) + \phi(\bar{\beta} - \bar{C}_x) \right]$$

The first order conditions for this problem are:

$$(11) \qquad \psi'(\bar{e}_q) = 1 - \frac{\lambda}{1+\lambda} \frac{1-\pi}{\pi} \phi'(\bar{e}_q)$$

$$(12) \qquad \psi'(\underline{e}_q) = 1$$

$$(13) \qquad \psi'(\bar{e}_x) = \bar{x} - \frac{\lambda}{1+\lambda} \frac{1-\pi}{\pi} \phi'(\bar{e}_x)$$

$$(14) \qquad \psi'(\underline{e}_x) = \underline{x}$$

$$(15) \qquad V'(\bar{x}) = (1+\lambda)\bar{C}_x = (1+\lambda)(\bar{\beta} - \bar{e}_x)$$

$$(16) \qquad V'(\underline{x}) = (1+\lambda)\underline{C}_x = (1+\lambda)(\underline{\beta} - \underline{e}_x)$$

The last two conditions imply that optimal environmental quality is, for each type, at the level that equalizes the related marginal social gains with marginal social costs. The optimal efforts are at their first best levels for the efficient type, as conditions *(12)* and *(14)* imply that marginal costs and marginal benefits related to each kind of effort are equal. On the other hand, optimal efforts are distorted downward w.r.t. first best for the inefficient type[14]. This is a standard result in moral hazard/adverse

---

[14] The result is straightforward concerning e_q; see *Appendix* A for the proof concerning e_x.

selection models, and is due to the fact that the regulator has to leave a higher amount of (socially costly) rent to type β if it imposes higher effort levels to type $\bar{\beta}$. The latter will be required by the regulator to exert effort levels as high as to equate expected marginal social gains (given by marginal cost savings *minus* the related marginal disutility) to the loss deriving from the expected marginal rent left to the efficient type.

Our next step is to check that the solution to this problem satisfies $\overline{IC}$.

We can rewrite the $\overline{IC}$ constraint as:

$$\bar{U} \geq \underline{U} - \phi\,(\bar{\beta} - \underline{C}_q) - \phi\,(\bar{\beta} - \underline{C}_x)$$

that, substituting for $\underline{U}$ and $\bar{U}$, becomes:

$$0 \geq \phi\,(\bar{\beta} - \bar{C}_q) + \phi\,(\bar{\beta} - \bar{C}_x) - \phi\,(\bar{\beta} - \underline{C}_q) - \phi\,(\bar{\beta} - \underline{C}_x)$$

As conditions *(11)* and *(12)* tell us that $\underline{e}_q > \bar{e}_q$, we have:

$$(\bar{\beta} - \bar{e}_q) > (\underline{\beta} - \underline{e}_q) \Rightarrow \bar{C}_q > \underline{C}_q$$

Appendix A shows, furthermore, that

$$\bar{C}_x \geq \underline{C}_x$$

so that, given $\phi'\,(.) > 0$, $\overline{IC}$ is satisfied.

4. - Non Cooperative Case

We now relax the assumption of cooperation among regulators, but retain the assumption that the regulated firm provides a single report concerning its efficiency. This hypothesis allows us to rule out the chance for the firm to lie to one principal and tell the truth to the other; the firm can only tell the truth or lie to both regulators[15]. Furthermore the two regulators, acting at

---

[15] In a more general setting, we would expect the firm to be able to provide two different reports to the two regulators. The main implication of our assumption

the same hierarchical level, are assumed to share the burden of rent extraction. In this way we depart from Baron (1985), where the Environmental Regulator free rides on the information extracted by the Public Utilities Regulator.

As in the cooperative case, we limit our analysis to *direct revelation* mechanisms. Each principal, therefore, selects a direct mechanism (i.e. a contract), specifying the dimensions of regulation he is in charge of as a function of the firm's type.

The timing of the game is as follows. Once nature has determined the firm's type or, equivalently, the firm has drawn its type β from the distribution described by the two probabilities π and $1 - \pi$, each regulator offers a menu of two contracts, one for each firm's type, specifying the regulatory variables he is in charge of. The firm can choose to contract with both the regulators or refuse it. In this second case the game ends, and the firm gets its reservation level of profits. If the firm accepts, it sends a message to the regulators themselves concerning its β, for example choosing from the offered menus of contracts the couple of mechanisms (one coming from the PA and one from the ER) designed for its type. Finally, the perfectly enforceable contracts are executed.

We must issue one important warning before proceeding to analyse the non cooperative regulatory outcome. Specifically, when the two regulators do not cooperate we cannot appeal to the standard revelation principle, since it does not hold in general in a common agency setting. In such a framework, the agent contracts with each principal with the knowledge of the mechanism(s) that the other principal(s) have offered[16]. Thus the contract each principal offers may depend not only on the firm's type but also on the mechanism(s) offered by other principal(s) and so on in an "infinite regress"; Epstein and Peters (1999) solve theoretically this problem demonstrating the existence of a universal message space for which the revelation principle is valid

---

is that we can solve our model just imposing what MARTIMORT D. - STOLE L. (2001) call *global incentive compatibility* constraints.

[16] See EPSTEIN L.G. - PETERS M. (1999) and MARTIMORT D. - STOLE L. (2002).

in a multi principal context. Specifically, in the framework developed there, the agent's type space is augmented to include the mechanisms offered by all the principals. This "universal message space" is, however, difficult to use in practice. The set of mechanisms and types involved is complex because the agent's type should describe, for the revelation principle to hold, all the mechanisms offered by the principals and how they are connected.

In our setting, the contracts offered by the two regulators are linked only through the transfer payment each of them provides. As we will show, the optimal effort levels chosen by each regulator are defined by first order conditions that do not depend on any variable controlled by the other one. Nevertheless, a caveat concerning the generality of results still holds[17].

Our next step is to solve the regulatory problems of the PA and the ER[18].

The menus of contracts offered will be given by the Nash equilibria of the one shot game where each regulator chooses the contractual variables it is in charge of, taking as given the mechanism chosen by the other regulator. Provided that the firm cannot send different signals concerning its type to the two regulators, the conditions that have to be satisfied in order for incentive compatibility to hold are the same as in the cooperative case, with $t(\beta) = t_q(\beta) + t_x(\beta)$, that is:

$$\underline{t}_q + \underline{t}_x - \psi(\underline{\beta} - \underline{C}_q) - \psi(\underline{\beta} - \underline{C}_x) \geq \overline{t}_q + \overline{t}_x - \psi(\underline{\beta} - \overline{C}_q) - \psi(\underline{\beta} - \overline{C}_x)$$

$$\overline{t}_q + \overline{t}_x - \psi(\overline{\beta} - \overline{C}_q) - \psi(\overline{\beta} - \overline{C}_x) \geq \underline{t}_q + \underline{t}_x - \psi(\overline{\beta} - \underline{C}_q) - \psi(\overline{\beta} - \underline{C}_x)$$

We will therefore solve both the PA the and ER problems

---

[17] The difficulties in applying the Revelation Principle when there is more than one principal create the need to check if there is any indirect mechanism to which the regulators could profitably deviate. For other papers limiting attention to direct revelation mechanisms in a common agency framework see, for example, BOND E.W. - GRESIK T.A. (1996) MEZZETTI C. (1997) and MARTIMORT D. - STOLE L. (2001).
[18] Provided that we limit to direct revelation mechanisms, and that the firm sends the same signal to both regulators, we can focus our attention on deterministic contracts without loss of generality. As in the cooperative case, the proof follows closely LAFFONT J.J. - TIROLE J. (1993) (*Appendix* A.1.1), and is available from the author on request.

following the same steps as in the cooperative case: we will impose
incentive compatibility for the efficient type in both regulators'
maximization problems, and then we will verify that the solutions
satisfy the incentive compatibility constraint for the inefficient
type as well. Furthermore, provided that Lemma 1 holds
unchanged in the noncooperative case, we can impose Individual
Rationality for the inefficient type and eliminate from the two
regulators' problems the one for the efficient type because
redundant.

4.1 *The Problem of the Procurement Agency*

The PA offers a menu of contracts specifying, for each type,
a transfer and a cost level related to the production activity, that
is $(\bar{t}_q, \bar{C}_q)$ for type $\bar{\beta}$ and $(\underline{t}_q, \underline{C}_q)$ for type $\underline{\beta}$, to maximize the
expected value of *(2)*, given the *a priori* beliefs about the
distribution of the firm's possible types:

(17) $\quad E(W_q) = S - (1 + \lambda)\,[\pi\,(\bar{C}_q + \bar{t}_q) + (1 - \pi)\,(\underline{C}_q + \underline{t}_q)] + \pi\bar{U} + (1 - \pi)\,\underline{U}$

subject to $\overline{IR}$ and $\underline{IC}$.

Using the definition of firm's profits, the PA objective function
may be rewritten as:

(18) $\quad E(W_q) = S - (1 + \lambda)\,[\pi\,(\bar{C}_q + \psi\,(\bar{\beta} - \bar{C}_q) + \psi\,(\bar{\beta} - \bar{C}_x) - \bar{t}_x) +$

$\qquad + (1 - \pi)\,(\underline{C}_q + \psi\,(\underline{\beta} - \underline{C}_q) + \psi\,(\underline{\beta} - \underline{C}_x) - \underline{t}_x)] - \lambda\,(\pi\bar{U} + (1 - \pi)\,\underline{U})$

The PA objective function is strictly decreasing in the value
of profits for both types; it is therefore at its maximum when:

$$\bar{U} = 0 \Rightarrow \bar{t}_q = \psi\,(\bar{\beta} - \bar{C}_q) + \psi\,(\bar{\beta} - \bar{C}_x) - \bar{t}_x$$

$$\underline{U} = \phi\,(\bar{\beta} - \bar{C}_q) + \phi\,(\bar{\beta} - \bar{C}_x) \Rightarrow \underline{t}_q = \psi\,(\underline{\beta} - \underline{C}_q) + \psi\,(\underline{\beta} - \underline{C}_x) +$$

$$+ \phi\,(\bar{\beta} - \bar{C}_q) + \phi\,(\bar{\beta} - \bar{C}_x) - \underline{t}_x$$

Substituting in *(18)*, the FOCs w.r.t. $\underline{C}_q$ and $\bar{C}_q$ require that:

(19)
$$\psi'(\bar{e}_q) = 1 - \frac{\lambda}{1+\lambda}\frac{1-\pi}{\pi}\phi'(\bar{e}_q)$$

(20)
$$\psi'(\underline{e}_q) = 1$$

First order conditions *(19)* and *(20)* are identical to those in the cooperative case, leading therefore to the same results in terms of effort levels.

4.2 *The Problem of the Environmental Regulator*

The environmental regulator (ER) offers a menu of contracts to the regulated firm: $(\bar{C}_x, \bar{x}, \bar{t}_x)$ for the inefficient type and $(\underline{C}_x, \underline{x}, \underline{t}_x)$ for the efficient type. These contracts specify a value for transfer, environmental quality and the related cost level for each firm type, to maximize the expected value of objective function *(3)*, given *a priori* beliefs about the distribution of the firm's efficiency parameter. The problem the ER solves is, therefore:

(21)
$$\max_{\bar{C}_x,\underline{C}_x,\bar{x},\underline{x},\bar{t}_x,\underline{t}_x} \pi[V(\bar{x}) - (1+\lambda)(\bar{C}_x\bar{x} + \bar{t}_x)] +$$
$$+(1-\pi)[V(\underline{x}) - (1+\lambda)(\underline{C}_x\underline{x} + \underline{t}_x)]$$

subject to $\overline{IR}$ and $\underline{IC}$. Being the ER's problem strictly decreasing in $\bar{t}_x$ and $\underline{t}_x$, from the constraints we get:

$$\bar{t}_x = \psi(\bar{\beta} - \bar{C}_q) + \psi(\bar{\beta} - \bar{C}_x) - \bar{t}_q$$

$$\underline{t}_x = \psi(\underline{\beta} - \underline{C}_q) + \psi(\underline{\beta} - \underline{C}_x) + \phi(\bar{\beta} - \bar{C}_q) + \phi(\bar{\beta} - \bar{C}_x) - \underline{t}_q$$

Substituting in *(21)*, ER's problem becomes:

(22) $\displaystyle\max_{\overline{C}_x, \underline{C}_x, \overline{x}, \underline{x}} \pi[V(\overline{x}) - (1+\lambda)[\overline{C}_x\overline{x} + \psi(\overline{\beta} - \overline{C}_q) + \psi(\overline{\beta} - \overline{C}_x) - \overline{t}_q] +$

$$+(1-\pi)[V(\underline{x}) - (1+\lambda)[\underline{C}_x\underline{x} + \psi(\underline{\beta} - \underline{C}_q) + \psi(\underline{\beta} - \underline{C}_x) - \underline{t}_q)] +$$

$$-(1-\pi)(1+\lambda)[\phi(\overline{\beta} - \overline{C}_q) + \phi(\overline{\beta} - \overline{C}_x)]$$

The FOCs for problem (22) are:

(23) $$\psi'(\overline{e}_x) = \overline{x} - \frac{1-\pi}{\pi}\phi'(\overline{e}_x)$$

(24) $$\psi'(\underline{e}_x) = \underline{x}$$

(25) $$V'(\overline{x}) = (1+\lambda)(\overline{\beta} - \overline{e}_x)$$

(26) $$V'(\underline{x}) = (1+\lambda)(\underline{\beta} - \underline{e}_x)$$

Conditions $(23\text{-}26)$ have important implications. Note that, while (24), (25) and (26) are the same as in the cooperative case, condition (23) is different (compare it with (13)), and is the key result of the paper.

Specifically, if we call $\overline{e}_x^{co}$ the level of $\overline{e}_x$ obtained in the cooperative case and $\overline{e}_x^{nc}$ the corresponding level under non cooperation, it is shown in Appendix B that:

$$\overline{e}_x^{nc} \leq \overline{e}_x^{co}$$

This leads us to Proposition 1.

PROPOSITION 1. If we restrict our attention to direct revelation mechanisms, non cooperative behavior under asymmetric information generates, compared to the cooperative case, a distortion in the effort exerted by the inefficient firm in reducing costs related to environmental quality. Specifically, the optimal $\overline{e}_x$ under non cooperation is never higher than the one obtained in the cooperative case.

Before discussing this result, we need to check that the

incentive compatibility constraint for the inefficient type is satisfied by the solutions to the PA and ER problems.

Following the same steps as in the cooperative case, we can rewrite the incentive compatibility constraint $\overline{IC}$ as:

$$0 \geq \phi\,(\overline{\beta} - \overline{C}_q) + \phi\,(\overline{\beta} - \overline{C}_x) - \phi\,(\overline{\beta} - \underline{C}_q) - \phi\,(\overline{\beta} - \underline{C}_x)$$

From *(19)* and *(20)* and from $\overline{\beta} > \underline{\beta}$ it is straightforward to conclude that:

$$(\overline{\beta} - \overline{e}_q) > (\underline{\beta} - \underline{e}_q) \Rightarrow \overline{C}_q > \underline{C}_q$$

Furthermore, we show in Appendix B that also under non cooperation the following result holds:

$$\overline{C}_x \geq \underline{C}_x$$

As a consequence $\overline{IC}$ is satisfied by the non cooperative solution.

A final remark concerns the existence of multiple equilibria under non cooperation; specifically any set of transfers satisfying $\overline{t}_q + \overline{t}_x = \psi\,(\overline{e}_q) + \psi\,(\overline{e}_x)$ for the inefficient type and $\underline{t}_q + \underline{t}_x = \psi\,(\underline{e}_q) + \psi(\underline{e}_x) + \phi\,(\overline{e}_q) + \phi\,(\overline{e}_x)$ for the efficient type can characterize an equilibrium in the non cooperative setting[19].

5. - Discussion of Results

The first implication of Proposition 1 is that non cooperative behavior among regulators brings about a decrease in the power of incentives: the effort exerted by the inefficient firm in reducing the costs of environmental quality is (weakly) lower than the one obtained under cooperation. Another important consequence of non cooperation in our setting is summed up in the following Proposition:

---

[19] The two regulators share the total transfer in a way that recalls a "Divide the Dollars" game. MYERSON R.B. (1991) shows that such a game has a multiplicity of equilibria, and that one way of selecting among them could be to appeal to the concept of focal equilibrium. In our regulatory setting, the role of a focal arbitrator could be played, for example, by a "central government".

PROPOSITION 2. The environmental quality standard imposed by the ER under non cooperation is never higher than the one that would result under cooperation.

The proof of this result can be derived by taking the total differential of *(25)* and solving with respect to $d\bar{x}/d\bar{e}_x$:

$$V''(x)\frac{d\bar{x}}{d\bar{e}_x} = -(1+\lambda) \Rightarrow \frac{d\bar{x}}{d\bar{e}_x} = -\frac{(1+\lambda)}{V''(\bar{x})} > 0$$

because $V''(\bar{x})$ is assumed to be negative.

As a consequence, in a setting where ER and PA share the burden of rent extraction and the ER does not account for the firm's profits, environmental policy turns out to be weaker under non cooperative regulation.

The intuition behind propositions 1 and 2 is fairly simple, and can be evaluated analytically comparing *(10)* with *(22)*: while in the first the efficient firm's expected rent has a negative weight $-\lambda$, in the non cooperating ER's objective function the negative weight is $-(1+\lambda)$. The two regulators, cooperating and acting as a unique regulator, face the standard trade off between efficiency and rent extraction. On the other hand, under separate regulation, the ER perceives the rent left to the efficient firm as more costly with respect to a cooperative setting; under non cooperation, then, the level of $\bar{e}_x$ is chosen in a way that is biased towards rent extraction when compared with the standard second best case.

Finally, an interesting implication of Proposition 1 arises concerning the regulated firm's profits: provided that $\bar{e}_x^{nc} \le \bar{e}_x^{co}$, separate regulation does not affect the inefficient firm's profits but lowers those for the efficient firm. The regulated firm is, therefore, never better worse off under non cooperation.

6. - Conclusion

We have analyzed, using a principal/agent framework, the consequences of choosing the environmental quality standards for public procurement in a decentralized way. We have, in particular, extended the standard *moral hazard/adverse selection* setting to the case when efficiency in production and environmental quality are subject to the control of two different agencies who share the burden of the firm's information rent extraction.

The conclusions of our paper are the following: on one hand we find that if the two agencies cooperate then "standard" distortions arise, confirming the established literature. On the other hand, and most importantly, our paper shows that non cooperative behavior implies both a lower environmental quality standard and higher related average costs for the inefficient firm, with respect to those resulting under cooperation.

Our framework could be extended in several ways. It would be possible to investigate more general cost functions for production and environmental quality, for example allowing the efficiency of the firm to differ among the two activities it performs. We could also generalize our simple setting introducing complementarity or substitutability among efforts in the regulated firm's objective function. Finally, it could be worthwhile to endogenize the choice of the two regulators between cooperation and non cooperation, as well as the one between sharing the burden of rent extraction and free riding on the information extracted by the other regulator.

In this Appendix we follow closely Laffont and Tirole (1993, ch. 2, page 136) to prove that, in the cooperative case:

1. the inefficient type's average cost of environmental quality is never lower than that of the efficient type, that is:

$$\bar{C}_x \ge \underline{C}_x$$

so that incentive compatibility holds for the inefficient firm;

2. the effort required from the inefficient firm in reducing the average cost of environmental quality is never higher than the one that would be required from the same type under first best (call it $\bar{e}_x^*$), that is:

$$\bar{e}_x \le \bar{e}_x^*$$

1.: $\bar{C}_x \ge \underline{C}_x$

Proof. We call x^* the optimal value of x defined by *(13)* (for the inefficient type), by the corresponding first best condition or by *(14)* (for the efficient type), as well as by the following first order condition:

$$V'(x^*) = (1 + \lambda) C_x$$

$\underline{C}_x$ and $\bar{C}_x$ maximize:

$$W(C_x,\beta,\xi) = V(x^*) - (1+\lambda)[(C_x x^* + \psi(\beta - C_x)] - \xi\lambda\frac{1-\pi}{\pi}\phi(\beta - C_x)$$

for ($\beta = \underline{\beta}$, $\xi = 0$) and for ($\beta = \bar{\beta}$, $\xi = 1$) respectively.

Revealed preference implies that:

$$W(\underline{C}_x, \underline{\beta}, 0) \ge W(\bar{C}_x, \underline{\beta}, 0)$$

$$W(\bar{C}_x, \bar{\beta}, 1) \ge W(\underline{C}_x, \bar{\beta}, 1)$$

Adding up these two inequalities and accounting for the definition of the ϕ (.) function we get:

$$\left[(1 + \lambda) + \lambda \frac{1 - \pi}{\pi}\right][\phi(\bar{\beta} - \underline{C}_x) - \phi(\bar{\beta} - \bar{C}_x)] \geq 0$$

Provided that ϕ (.) is increasing in its arguments, we get $\bar{\beta} - \underline{C}_x \geq \bar{\beta} - \bar{C}_x$, that is, $\underline{C}_x \leq \bar{C}_x$.

2.: $\bar{e}_x \leq \bar{e}_x^*$

Let $\bar{e}_x$ and $\bar{e}_x^*$ be the optimal values of $\bar{e}_x$ under asymmetric ahd full information, respectively, and let $\bar{x}$ and $\bar{x}^*$ denote the corresponding levels for environmental quality.

Revealed preference implies that:

$$W(\bar{e}_x^*, \bar{\beta}, 0) \geq W(\bar{e}_x, \bar{\beta}, 0)$$

$$W(\bar{e}_x, \bar{\beta}, 1) \geq W(\bar{e}_x^*, \bar{\beta}, 1)$$

Summing up these two inequalities we get:

$$\lambda \frac{1 - \pi}{\pi}[\phi(\bar{e}_x^*) - \phi(\bar{e}_x)] \geq 0 \rightarrow \bar{e}_x^* \geq \bar{e}_x$$

We are going to prove the following result:

$$\bar{e}_x^{co} \geq \bar{e}_x^{nc}$$

where $\bar{e}_x^{co}$ is optimal effort level required, in the cooperative case, from the inefficient type firm in reducing the costs of environmental quality while $\bar{e}_x^{nc}$ is the corresponding optimal effort level in the non cooperative case.

Proof. We call $\bar{x}$ the optimal value of x defined by *(13)* and *(23)* (for the cooperative and the non cooperative case, respectively) and by the condition:

$$V'(\bar{x}) = (1 + \lambda)(\bar{\beta} - \bar{e}_x)$$

$\bar{e}_x^{co}$ and $\bar{e}_x^{nc}$ maximize:

$$W(\bar{e}_x, \bar{\beta}, \xi) = V(\bar{x}) - (1+\lambda)[(\bar{\beta} - \bar{e}_x)\bar{x} + \psi(\bar{e}_x)] - (\xi + \lambda)\frac{1-\pi}{\pi}\phi(\bar{e}_x)$$

for $\xi = 0$ and $\xi = 1$ respectively.

Revealed preference implies, therefore, that:

$$W(\bar{e}_x^{co}, \bar{\beta}, 0) \geq W(\bar{e}_x^{nc}, \bar{\beta}, 0)$$

$$W(\bar{e}_x^{nc}, \bar{\beta}, 1) \geq W(\bar{e}_x^{co}, \bar{\beta}, 1)$$

Adding up the two inequalities we get:

$$\frac{1-\pi}{\pi}[\phi(\bar{e}_x^{co}) - \phi(\bar{e}_x^{nc})] \geq 0 \rightarrow \bar{e}_x^{co} \geq \bar{e}_x^{nc}$$

Finally, for incentive compatibility to hold under non cooperation, we need to prove that:

$$\bar{C}_x \geq \underline{C}_x$$

holds in the non cooperative case as well.

Call $\bar{C}_x^{co}$ and $\underline{C}_x^{co}$ the cost levels for the two types under cooperation and $\bar{C}_x^{nc}$ and $\underline{C}_x^{nc}$ those corresponding to the noncooperative case. From appendix A we know that $\bar{C}_x^{co} \geq \underline{C}_x^{co}$ and from first order conditions *(14)* and *(24)* in the text (and the related FOCs with respect to environmental quality) we know that $\underline{C}_x^{co} = \underline{C}_x^{nc}$. Therefore $\bar{C}_x^{co} \geq \underline{C}_x^{nc}$.

Finally, given that $\bar{e}_x^{co} \geq \bar{e}_x^{nc}$, and, therefore, $\bar{C}_x^{nc} \geq \bar{C}_x^{co}$, we can conclude that:

$$\bar{C}_x^{nc} \geq \underline{C}_x^{nc}.$$

BIBLIOGRAPHY

BARON D., «Non-cooperative Regulation of a Non-localized Externality», *RAND, Journal of Economics*, no. 16, 1985, pages 553-68.

BERNHEIM D. - WHINSTON M., «Common Agency», *Econometrica*, no. 54, 1986, pages 923-43.

BOND E.W. - GRESIK T.A., «Regulation of Multinational Firms with Two Active Governments: a Common Agency Approach», *Journal of Public Economics*, no. 59, 1996, pages 33-54.

DASGUPTA P.S. - HAMMOND P.J. - MASKIN E.S., «On Imperfect Information and Optimal Pollution Control», *Review of Economic Studies*, no. 47, 1980, pages 857-60.

DIXIT A. - GROSSMAN G.E. - HELPMAN E., «Common Agency and Coordination: General Theory and Application to Government Policy Making», *Journal of Political Economy*, no. 105, 1997, pages 752-69.

EPSTEIN L.G. - PETERS M., «A Revelation Principle for Competing Mechanisms», *Journal of Economic Theory*, no. 88, 1999, pages 119-60.

EUROPEAN COMMISSION, *Buying Green! A Handbook on Environmental Public Procurement*, Office for Official Publications of the European Communities, Luxembourg, 2004.

KWEREL E., «To Tell the Truth: Imperfect Information and Optimal Pollution Control», *Review of Economic Studies*, no. 44, 1977, pages 595-601.

LAFFONT J.J., «Regulation of Pollution with Asymmetric Information», in DOSI C. - TOMASI T. (eds.), *NonPoint Source Pollution Regulation: Issues and Analysis*, Kluwer Academic Publishers, 1994, pages 39-66.

LAFFONT J.J. - TIROLE J., *A Theory of Incentives in Procurement and Regulation*, MIT Press, Cambridge (MA), 1993.

LAFFONT J.J. - MARTIMORT D., *The Theory of Incentives: The Principal-Agent Model*, Princeton University Press, Oxford, 2002.

LEWIS T.R., «Protecting the Environment when Costs and Benefits are Privately Known», *RAND, Journal of Economics*, no. 27, 1996, pages 819-47.

MARTIMORT D. - STOLE L., «Common Agency Equilibria with Discrete Mechanisms and Discrete Types», *CESifo, Working Paper Series*, no. 572, 2001.

— — - — —, «The Revelation and Delegation Principles in Common Agency Games», *Econometrica*, no. 70, 2002, pages 1659-73.

— — - — —, «Contractual Externalities and Common Agency Equilibria», *Advances in Theoretical Economics*, no. 3, Article 4, 2003.

MEZZETTI C., «Common Agency with Horizontally Differentiated Principals», *RAND Journal of Economics*, no. 28, 1997, pages 323-45.

MYERSON R.B., *Game Theory - Analysis of Conflict*, Harvard University Press, Harvard, 1991.

SPULBER D.F., «Optimal Environmental Regulation under Asymmetric Information», *Journal of Public Economics*, no. 35, 1988, pages 163-81.

STOLE L., «Mechanism Design under Common Agency», *mimeo, GSB*, Chicago University, 1991.

Optimal Information Releasing in Multidimensional Public Procurement

Nicola Doni

Università di Firenze

In this paper we analyse a multidimensional auction where quality scores are private information of the Public Administration (PA). We introduce a multistage procedure: in the first stage every participant submits a technical proposal, without knowing what the buyer evaluation is. In the second stage every bidder proposes a price. We investigate the best strategic use of the PA's information comparing three different policies: a) secrecy b) private revelation c) public revelation. We show that only the second one is able to achieve allocative efficiency. At the same time, generally, this strategy is associated with a lower PA's expected utility. [JEL Classification: H57, D44, D82].

1. - Introduction

The classical literature on multidimensional auctions (Che, 1993; Branco, 1997; Asker *et* al., 2004) assumes that competing bidders decide autonomously on the quality and price of their bids, and that awarding of the contract takes place in a completely automatic way, without the auctioneer making any discretional judgement. At the same time, it is hypothesised the simultaneous submission of complete bids, without investigating what the result

This research was supported by Italian Ministry of University under PRIN project "Public services and infrastructures: regulatory, financial and institutional problems". The Author wishes to thank P.A. Mori, D. Menicucci and two anonymous referees for their helpful suggestions. Needless to say, the usual disclaimer applies.

may be of multistage procedures, in which the qualitative aspects are evaluated before firms have to present their economic requests for the realisation of the contract.

This article wishes to analyse in particular the context of public auctions. The most recent European regulations on public procurement have introduced several new types of procedures, in which the proposal relative to various aspects of the contractual bid may be formulated in different moments. Competitive dialogue and electronic auctions can assume the characteristics of multistage auctions, and the directive 2004/18/EC explicitly requires that in the call for tenders be specified «the information which will be made available to the tenderers in the course of the electronic auction and, where appropriate, when it will be made available to them»[1].

In a multistage auction the policy chosen by the public administration (PA) with regard to revealing its qualitative judgements is very relevant. In fact, it directly affects firms' bidding strategies and consequently it influences the effective outcome of the procedure. In this work we shall compare three different revelation strategies which, we consider, represent three cases permitted by the legislation in force. In the first case, the PA maintains absolute secrecy regarding its valuation of the qualitative aspects of the bids. In the second case, the PA reveals to every bidder only the value assigned to its qualitative bid. In the third case, we shall assume that the PA publicly reports the ranking with the scores assigned to the qualitative aspects of the various participants.

To model this problem, we shall assume that the social well-being associated with each contractual proposal depends exclusively on the quality of the bid and on the price requested for its realisation. In line with the standard literature[2], we shall hypothesise that the production costs can be represented by means of random independent variables known privately by each

---

[1] See art. 54.3.c, 2004/18/EC.

[2] Actually, BRANCO F. (1997) assumes costs affiliation and for this reason his conclusion is that the optimal procedure requires quality renegotiation after contract awarding.

individual firm. The originality of our model consists, however, in the assumption that the quality of the bids is not decided by competing bidders, but depends exclusively on the discretional judgement of the PA. We shall assume that this valuation is its own private information, and that it is totally uncorrelated to firms' production costs. This latter hypothesis is definitely rather strong: in reality, it is easier to find situations in which the quality of the bids depends both on the characteristics of the commodity, which are reflected on the cost, and also on the tastes of the buyer, which are totally discretional. This model, however, is capable of representing those situations in which among the awarding criteria aspects appear such as the aesthetic value of the commodity or the reliability of the firm[3]. In both cases, these elements are unconnected with the costs for producing the commodity, and it is difficult for the firms to know *ex-ante* the PA's judgement in their regard. Our model also makes it possible to analyse the case in which the quality of a contractual proposal is known to the firm that formulates it, but not to competing bidders. Also in this situation, in fact, we are obliged to wonder how opportune it may be to reveal publicly the quality of all the technical proposals presented in the auction.

The model that we are proposing is as simplified as possible, and hopefully constitutes a starting point for further investigations. We describe the PA as a purchaser (P) who wishes to buy a commodity by means of an auction in which only two sellers are taking part. We hypothesise that the utility that the P derives from the exchange is equal to the difference between the quality of the bid and the price asked by the seller. The quality depends exclusively on the tastes of the P, and is therefore his private information. The prices, instead, are proposed by the sellers. Their

---

[3] A model that hypothesises that the "quality" of competing bidders is an exogenous variable totally uncorrelated to its costs is that of GANUZA J.J. (1996), in which it is supposed that competing bidders differ precisely in their degree of reliability. BRAYNOV S. *et* AL. (2003) hypothesise that bidders have a differing reliability, but they assume that this variable affects not only the utility of the auctioneer, but also the firm's costs. In BRANCO F. (1994) and McAFEE R.P. *et* AL. (1989), instead, it is hypothesised that the PA prefers to contract with national firms rather than foreign ones, and that the costs of these firms are symmetric.

bidding strategy thus regards only the latter element, and we shall see that each seller will decide upon the price requested depending on her own production cost, which is her own private information, and on the information available to her regarding the judgement that the P has made of her quality and of that of the rival bidder. Thus, the policy chosen by the P as far as releasing his private information is concerned directly influences the sellers' price strategy. The P's objective is to choose the policy of revealing the information that will permit him to maximise his expected utility.

Even if the sellers can choose only one element of the bid, i.e. the price, the auction can be considered multidimensional in that it is awarded by means of a criterion that considers several elements at the same time, i.e. the quality of the bid and the price asked. We assume that the awarding rule coincides with the utility function of the P and that the procedure is of the first score (FS) type[4]. According to this, the winner is the seller that achieves the highest overall score and is paid on the basis of the price requested in her bid.

The costs of the different sellers are represented by means of independent and symmetric random variables (r.v.). For this reason, this element mirrors the characteristics of an independent private value (IPV) model. We shall see that if the P chooses not to release any information or if he reveals to each seller only her level of quality, then the model maintains the characteristics of a multidimensional auction with private, independent and symmetric valuations. If, instead, the P chooses to reveal publicly the quality assigned to the two different bids, then the model will have to consider the possibility that the valuations of the two rival bidders are private and independent, but asymmetrically distributed.

The analysis is aimed at comparing the different strategies from two different points of view: that of allocative efficiency and that of the maximisation of the P's expected utility. From the first point of view, it is demonstrated that the auction mechanism is efficient from an allocative point of view only when the P uses

---

[4] The definitions of first score and second score rules can be found in CHE Y.K. (1993).

the strategy of privately revealing his information. At the same time, however, this strategy is found in general to be *sub*-optimal, compared to the other objective. In fact, some sufficient conditions are identified so that the P's utility expected with this strategy is lower than the expected utility associated with the strategy of publicly revealing the information. Lastly, it is showed that, in the presence of significant potential differences in the qualitative judgements, the strategy of secrecy is found to be better than that of public revelation.

Therefore, as in Ganuza (2004), a trade-off between allocative efficiency and rent extraction stands out. In order to increase his own expected utility, P has to give up allocative efficiency of the mechanism. It is also interesting to note that the P's optimal strategy is generally not the "intermediate" one of privately revealing his information, but one of the two extreme solutions: i.e. public revelation or complete secrecy.

The article is organised as follows: the next section provides a synthetic illustration of the literature correlated to this argument. Section 3 introduces the model and the strategies available to the auctioneer. Section 4 demonstrates the bidding strategies of the sellers associated with each different policy of the P with regard to the information releasing. Section 5 compares the results obtained by the P in terms of expected utility, in an attempt to identify the optimal strategy. Section 6 synthesises the principal conclusions and indicates the most interesting developments of the research dealt with in this work. All proofs can be found in the mathematical appendix.

2. - Related Literature

As already pointed out, this article is closely linked to all the works that deal withmultidimensional auctions. In this group we understand not only the models which assume that competing firms can autonomously determine more than one of the elements making up the bid (Che, 1993; Branco, 1997; Asker *et* al., 2004), but also all those auction models in which the awarding criterion takes into account not only the price asked, but also other attributes of the bid, or of the bidder, which influence the utility of the auctioneer in some way (Ganuza, 1996; Branco, 1994; McAfee *et* al., 1989, Celentani *et* al., 2002). The originality of this work lies in the introduction of the possibility of structuring the auction in two stages, by predicting that the qualitative aspects are evaluated before the competing bidders have to formulate their economic requests. This allows us to study what the auctioneer's optimal strategy is with regard to the revealing of his information that, in general, is not known to bidders, i.e. his discretional judgement regarding the bids presented.

This is the reason why this article is similar to the literature that studies auctions with an endogenous structure of the information available to bidders. Milgrom *et* al. (1982) consider the case in which the auctioneer has private information regarding several characteristics of the object of the auction which have an effect on bidders' valuation. Under the hypothesis of affiliated valuations, these authors demonstrate that the best strategy for the auctioneer is that of revealing to all participants all the information that he possesses (linkage principle).

The main difference between our model and that of Milgrom *et* al. (1982) is that in their case bidders' valuations are symmetrically correlated to the information revealed by the auctioneer, so that either all of them increase or all of them decrease. Instead, in our model the auctioneer has information that can have an asymmetric influence, in that it may happen that the valuation of the quality of a bid is high, while that of a competing bid is low.

Two recent articles study a model that is similar to ours. The first, by Ganuza (2004), hypothesises that the auctioneer of a second-price auction has private information regarding the characteristics of the object. Their revelation can be more or less precise, and has an effect on bidders' valuations. In absence of information releasing, bidders are all completely homogeneous, while, with an increase in the accuracy of the information revealed, bidders become more heterogeneous. The result obtained by the author is that the auctioneer's optimal strategy is that of revealing information that is less accurate than it would be efficient at an overall level. This conclusion derives directly from the fact that more precise information increases the valuation that the most efficient bidder attributes to the object, and thus the price that she will bid; but at the same time, it also increases her informative rent, making her more heterogeneous compared to the others.

The second model is by Esö et al. (2005). The main difference between it and that of Ganuza (2004) consists of the hypothesis that the auctioneer can decide contemporaneously both the degree of accuracy of the information revealed and also the allocation mechanism. In this context, the authors conclude that the auctioneer would do well to reveal all the information at his disposal, making bidders pay a price to acquire these data.

Our model has a structure that is found to be midway between these two models. As in Esö et al. (2005), but differently from Ganuza (2004), it is assumed that competing bidders are always heterogeneous, independently of the policy selected by the auctioneer regarding the revealing of his information. In fact, one of the factors that differentiates each bidder is her costs, which is her own private information. We differ, however, from Esö et al. (2005) in that, as occurs in Ganuza (2004), we analyse which the optimal policy is regarding the information releasing, given a certain mechanism: that is, a multidimensional auction with FS awarding rule. This hypothesis seems to us to be more appropriate, in that it is more adequate in representing the context of public procurement, where it is difficult to imagine that the PA could make firms pay in order to obtain information.

There is also an element that differentiates our article from all the works mentioned up until now. In these models, in fact, the revealing of the auctioneer's information can make bidders more heterogeneous, but their beliefs on the valuation of the opponents remain symmetric. In our case, instead, the revealing of information regarding the quality of the bid may leave competing bidders symmetric, but it can also make them asymmetric in beliefs. This happens in the case in which the auctioneer decides to reveal publicly the quality associated with each bid and it happens that the quality of the two rival bidders is revealed to be not identical. Since the information on the quality of the opponent bidder changes the beliefs regarding her valuation of the contract, in this case the beliefs become asymmetric. Lastly, in our model, it is hypothesised that the auctioneer cannot decide the level of accuracy of the information that he reveals, but can only choose whether or not to reveal it[5].

Because of this peculiarity, another relevant trend of the literature for this article is that on asymmetric auctions. For the purposes of our model, the conclusions reached by Maskin et al. (2000) are very relevant. According to them, in the presence of a specific kind of asymmetry in bidders' valuations, a first-price auction generates greater expected profit than a second-price auction. We shall see that Kaplan et al. (2003) utilise this result to compare auction mechanisms with participants with symmetric beliefs and mechanisms in which the beliefs of the participants are asymmetric. Their article identifies the conditions that, from the auctioneer's point of view, make the presence of an asymmetry preferable. Their result is directly applicable to our model, and enables us to establish the cases in which it is convenient for the PA to publicly reveal the quality of both firms.

Instead, Kaplan et al. (2000) and Landsberger et al. (2001) are auction models that can describe situations in which the auctioneer knows bidders' valuations or, at least, their ranking. The similarity with the context that we have analysed derives from the fact that in these models it is verified that the auctioneer's strategy regarding the information releasing can make initially symmetric competing bidders asymmetric. However, the difference derives from the fact that, in our model, it is assumed that the PA does not know the valuation that bidders assign to the contract, but only one of its components, i.e. the quality of their bid.

---

[5] Another article that deals with the problem of the optimum revealing of information is BERGEMANN D. et AL. (2001). In their model, however, it is assumed that the auctioneer's policy can be asymmetric in the sense that it makes it possible to reveal to one rival bidder more information than was revealed to the others. This type of behaviour does not satisfy the requisites that must be respected by the PA, as we shall attempt to clarify here as follows.

3. - The Model and P's Strategies

We consider a case in which a purchaser (P) wants to buy a commodity, or a service, by means of an auction in which only two rival sellers, A and B, participate. All the players are assumed to be risk-neutral. Utility U, which the P derives from the exchange, is equal to the difference between the quality of the winning bid and the price requested by it:

$$U = q - p$$

The quality of the bid, which can be correlated to characteristics of the commodity, or of the supplier, depends exclusively on the P's preferences, and it is his own private information. It is formally assumed that the quality of the two rival bidders is the result of two random binary variables that are symmetric and independent:

$$q_i \in \{q_L, q_H\}, \text{ with } Prob(q_i = q_L) = \alpha, \forall i = A, B,$$
$$\text{and where } q_H - q_L = \Delta$$

Instead, the price is decided by the rival bidders in such a way as to maximise their expected profit. The profit in the case of victory is given by the price minus the production costs, which is private information and, it is assumed, is the result of independent, symmetric r.v. distributed over a compact support in accordance with a continuous and increasing c.d.f., $F_c(c)$:

$$c_i \in [\underline{c}, \bar{c}], \forall i = A, B^6$$

The bidding strategy of the sellers is influenced, however, also by the information available to them regarding the quality assigned by the P to their bid and to that of the opponent seller. It can thus be established from now on that the price bidding

---

[6] All the figures presented in the paper assume that $\bar{c} - \underline{c} > \Delta$, but the theoretical results reached in this model are valid also in the reverse case.

function depends not only on the costs, but also on the type of message[7] f sent by the P regarding his private information. As the two rival bidders are symmetric, their bidding strategy will also be so:

$$p_i = p(c_i;f_i), \ \forall i = A, B$$

The auction is awarded according to a multidimensional rule in which the score assigned to each bid s_i coincides with the utility that the P derives from it:

$$s_i = q_i - p_i, \ \forall i = A, B$$

while the payment mechanism is FS type. Therefore, the pay-off of each seller is:

$$\pi_i = \begin{cases} p_i - c_i, \forall i > s_j \\ 0, \dots \dots \forall i > s_j \end{cases} \qquad \forall i, j = A, B; \ i \neq j.$$

The timing of the model is the following: chance decides on the quality of each firm, and the P comes to know of this privately. Having observed the quality of the two sellers, the P can send a message to each of the two sellers. The type of admittable messages will be clarified subsequently. The sellers receive the message regarding their own quality and that of their adversary; they privately observe their production costs, and decide on the price required for fulfilling the contract. The seller that receives the higher score wins the auction and is paid in an amount equal to the price requested. Her pay-off will be equal to the difference between this price and her costs, while the P's pay-off will be equal to the score reached by the winning bid.

It is evident that this is a sequential game in which the strategy chosen by the sellers, which must move in a second time,

---

[7] A definition of the concept of "message" and the description of the messages that the P could send will be given further on.

is a function of the strategy implemented by the P, who is a leader à la Stackelberg. We shall therefore resolve the problem by means of the backward induction method, according to which we shall first investigate which is the sellers' best strategy, depending on the choice made by the P. We shall examine which strategy will be best for the P only in a second moment.

We now formally define which strategies are at the P's disposal. In the first place, we note that in this model the set of the states of the world that can be realised by chance includes four elements:

$$\Omega = \{LL, LH, HL, HH\},$$

where the first letter denotes the quality level associated with seller A, and the second, that associated with seller B.

The P can send to each seller a different message, where by "message" is meant some information regarding the quality of the two different bids. The peculiarity is that, in addition to saying whether the quality level of a generic seller is high or low, he can also choose not to declare his opinion on what this level is (white message). This means that the set of the potential messages that can be sent is more numerous than the set of the states of the world. Formally:

$$Z = \{UU, UL, UH, LU, LL, LH, HU, HL, HH\},$$

where U stands for unspecified. The strategies available to the P can be defined as pairs of functions, each of which links the message to be sent to seller A and the one to be sent to seller B with every possible state of the world:

$$S = (f_A, f_B), \text{ where } f_i: \Omega \rightarrow Z, \forall i = A, B.$$

However, the P is not free to send the messages that he wishes nor to determine his strategy in the moment that he prefers. Here as follows, we shall define several restrictions on his choices.

Assumption 1: The P cannot tell a lie to either of the two sellers.

It is hypothesised, that is, that the quality of the bids is initially unknown to the sellers, but can be verified *ex-post*[8]. For this reason, the P cannot try to influence the strategies of the sellers by means of untruthful messages. Formally, this means that:

$$f_i(XY) \in \{UU, UY, XU, XY\}, \forall X,Y, = L, H; \forall i = A, B$$

Assumption 2: The P cannot reveal his information in an impartial way.

This means that the P cannot discriminate against the sellers releasing information of a differing refinement. Therefore, if he specifies the quality of a bid to firm i, he cannot leave the quality of the other bid unspecified to firm j. Formally:

$$f_i(XY) = K_i W_i \Leftrightarrow f_i(XY) = W_j K_j$$

$$\forall K_i, K_j = X,Y; \forall W_i, W_j = U,X,Y; \forall X,Y = L,K; \forall i_j = A,B; i \neq j$$

Assumption 3: The P must "weakly" respect privacy.

It is hypothesised, that is, that the P cannot reveal information regarding the bid of a seller if it has not also been made known to that seller himself. Formally:

$$f_A(XY) = W_A K_A \Rightarrow f_B(XY) = W_B K_B \text{ e } f_B(XY) = K_B W_B \Rightarrow f_A(XY) = K_A W_A$$

$$\forall K_i = X,Y; \forall W_i = U,X,Y; \forall i = A,B; \forall X,Y = L,H$$

The aggregate of these assumptions enables us to restrict the set of messages available to the P. In fact, we can demonstrate the following lemmas.

Lemma 1: Whatever the state of the world, the P has only

---

[8] In reality, the verifiability is plausible in the case of the quality assigned during the awarding phase, while it is more difficult for elements that depend on the PA's preferences to be verifiable *ex-post*. For this reason it would be useful to investigate whether the PA can have an incentive to lie, hoping that in this case however it will have to award the contract in a way that is coherent with the contents of its message. See CELENTANI M. *et* AL. (2002) for an example of a multidimensional auction in which the public official during the awarding can lie, in exchange for a percentage, regarding the real quality of the bids.

three messages available to send to each seller, characterised as follows:

$$f_A(XY) \in \{UU,\ XU,\ XY\}\ \text{e}\ f_B(XY) \in \{UU,\ UY,\ XY\},\ \forall X,Y, = L,H$$

Lemma 2: A symmetry must exist between the messages sent to the two sellers. Formally:

$$1)\ f_A(XY) = UU \Leftrightarrow f_B(XY) = UU,$$

$$2)\ f_A(XY) = XU \Leftrightarrow f_B(XY) = UY,$$

$$3)\ f_A(XY) = XY \Leftrightarrow f_B(XY) = XY,\ \forall X,Y, = L,H$$

Thus, whatever the initial state of the world that he observes may be, the P can send to each seller only three types of messages, each one characterised by a different philosophy: with the first, he reveals nothing to either of the two sellers, maintaining an attitude of total reserve. With the second type of message, he reveals to each seller only the quality of its bid, implementing a less closed attitude, but with a respect for privacy. With the third type, he reveals all the information to both sellers, assuming a totally open attitude.

To complete the restrictions that we are imposing on the strategies available to the P, we introduce a fourth and final assumption.

Assumption 4: The type of message chosen by the PA must be independent of the state of the world that he has observed.

This hypothesis requires that P's policy with regard to information releasing be independent of the state of the world that is verified. In reality, in fact, it happens that the P must already establish in the call for tenders what information it will reveal during the course of the procedure, and in that moment it is not yet acquainted with either the identity of the rival bidders or with their proposals. The strategy must, therefore, be independent of the quality level of the bids.

Thus, our assumptions have identified only three possible strategies, characterised here as follows:

Definition: In the sequential game, the P has only three strategies at his disposal:

$$S^1 = (f_A^1, f_B^1), \text{ where } f_i^1 (XY) = UU, \forall X,Y = L,H; \forall i = A,B$$

$$S^2 = (f_A^2, f_B^2), \text{ where } f_A^2 (XY) = XU \text{ e } f_B^2 (XY) = UY, \forall X,Y = L,H$$

$$S^3 = (f_A^3, f_B^3), \text{ where } f_i^3 (XY) = XY, \forall X,Y = L,H; \forall i = A,B$$

In the first strategy, the P sends to each seller an unspecified message regarding the valuations of the two bids, so that neither seller knows which of the four possible results has been chosen by chance. With the second strategy, instead, he succeeds in restricting to just two cases the uncertainty of the rival bidders regarding the outcomes of the "choices" of Nature: in fact, each seller will know with certainty the quality of her own bid, but will remain uncertain regarding the quality of the rival bidder's bid. Lastly, in the third strategy all the information available to the P is revealed publicly, so that both bidders will know with certainty the result that has initially been realised. Therefore, the P's choice regarding his information releasing consists in selecting a specific sub-game that sellers have to play.

In the following section we will show which price strategy is optimal for the two sellers depending on the different strategy chosen by the P, in such a way that the strategies at the P's disposal can be compared as regards their relative convenience.

4. - Sellers' Bidding Strategies

In this section, we shall examine which bid strategy is optimal for the two sellers depending on the strategy implemented by the P. At the end, it will thus be possible to compare the different policies available to the P for revealing the information from the point of view of their relative convenience.

In general, we can follow the method of Asker *et* al. (2004) and define the valuation that each rival bidder assigns to the contract with the maximum score that she could bid obtaining a non negative profit:

$$v_i = q_i - c_i, \ \forall i = A,B$$

To affirm that each seller bids a price in function of her costs is equal to saying that each rival bidder bids a score in function of her valuation. In fact, by supposing that the price is not lower than the costs, it means that:

$$p(c) = c + x, \text{ with } x \geq 0; \text{ notice that this implies:}$$

$$s(q,c) = q - p(c) = q - c - x = v - x = s(v)$$

The price bid, however, does not depend only on the cost of the seller, but also on her information regarding the quality of the bid itself and of the rival bidder. With the first information, in fact, it is possible to make the knowledge of one's own valuation of the contract more precise; with the second, it is possible to have a greater knowledge of the distribution from which the valuation of the competitor is "extracted". We shall see how the sellers' bidding function is modified in accordance with the information at their disposal.

Case 1: Secrecy of the information

In this case, each rival bidder has to formulate her own price bid without knowing what the quality of the bids presented is. Graphically speaking, the game in which she finds herself having to choose can be represented by the diagram in Graph 1.

The fact that the four possible outcomes of the first choice of the Nature are enclosed in the same oval indicates that the generic bidder i does not know at which node she is, compared to the quality of the bids, when she must formulate her own request. This means that this type of game fits the situation in which the qualitative bid and the economic bid must be presented simultaneously. In this case, in fact, the sellers cannot receive any information on the quality of their proposals before formulating the economic tender.

GRAPH 1

GAME 1: SECRECY OF THE INFORMATION

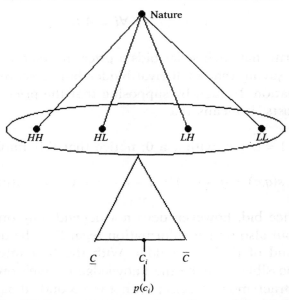

The lack of information regarding the quality of the two bids and the symmetry of the beliefs on the costs means that, in this game, the two sellers have symmetric valuations, in the sense that they share the same beliefs on the valuation of the adversary. The two rival bidders, however, do not know their own valuation of the contract and so cannot decide deliberately on the score to bid. They can choose only what price to bid on the basis of their observed costs and of the beliefs on the costs of the rival bidder. The price strategy is found to be equivalent to that of a standard first price sealed bid auction model in an IPV environment, where the only private information is that relative to the production costs:

$$p^1(c_i) = c_i + \frac{\int_{c_i}^{\bar{c}} (1 - F_c(s))ds}{1 - F_c(c_i)}, \forall i = A, B$$

The P ranks the bids received according to the scorig function s, where each rival bidder is found to have bid, even if unknowingly, the initially observed quality. This means that the implicit overall bid strategy can be defined as follows:

$$s^1(q_i,c_i) = q_i - p^1(c_i) = q_i - c_i - \frac{\int_{c_i}^{\bar{c}} (1 - F_c(s))ds}{1 - F_c(c_i)}, \forall i = A, B$$

It can be noted that the scores assigned to each rival bidder are not a univocally determined function of her valuation, i.e. of the difference between her quality and her costs. In fact, the same valuation can be the result of two different cost levels, and in this case the score received will be different, the valuations being equal. This means that the firm with the higher valuation does not necessarily win. This observation is briefly synthesised here as follows:

Observation 1: If the P uses strategy 1, then the auction mechanism is not necessarily efficient, since it can assign the contract to the rival bidder who has a lower valuation.

GRAPH 2

FIRMS' BIDDING STRATEGIES IN GAME 1

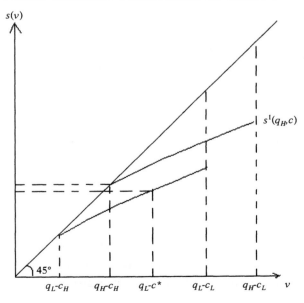

249

Graph 2, which illustrates the scores reached by the sellers' bids in function of their cost and their quality, enables us to show this result graphically. In fact, it can be noted that a generic firm with a valuation equal to $(q_L - c^*)$ obtains a lower score than that of a potential rival bidder having a lower valuation, equal to $(q_H - c_H)$.

The fact that the allocative mechanism is not efficient is very important, since it means that in this context the Revenue Equivalence Theorem (RET) is not valid. In fact, in this game, it can be established that the expected value of the maximum price bid in an auction coincides with the expected cost of the seller with a lesser productive efficiency. But this does not imply that the expected value of the higher score is equal to the valuation of the seller that is less efficient on the whole.

GRAPH 3

GAME 2: PRIVATE REVELATION OF THE INFORMATION

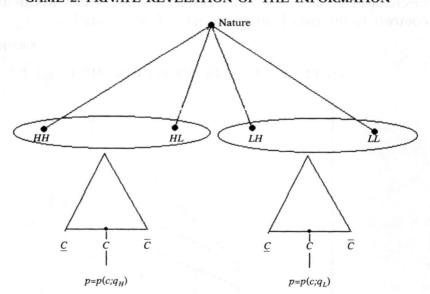

Case 2: Private revelation of the information
In this case, the two sellers have to formulate their bid while knowing what their quality is, but remaining ignorant regarding

the real quality of the opponent's bid. They find themselves therefore having to play a games that can be described by means of the tree described in Graph 3.

It can be noted that the two rival bidders remain symmetric, in the sense that they still have symmetric beliefs on the valuation of the competitor, except that now they are represented by a different random variable.

$$v_i \in [q_L - \bar{c}, q_H - \underline{c}] \; \forall i = A,B$$

(1)
$$F_{v_i}^2(v) = \mathrm{Prob}(v \leq q - c) = \mathrm{Prob}(c \geq q - v) =$$

$$\alpha \, \mathrm{Prob}(c \geq q_L - v) + (1 - \alpha) \, \mathrm{Prob}(c \geq q_H - v)$$

hence[9]:

$$F_{v_i}^2(v) = \alpha(1 - F_c(q_L - v)) + (1 - \alpha)(1 - F_c(q_H - v))$$

In this case, each bidder, aware of the quality of her own bid, can choose the score to bid in function of the valuation that she assigns to the contract. As all the conditions of an IPV auction model have been respected, it can be deduced that her bidding function is:

$$s^2(v_i) = v_i - \frac{\int_{\underline{v}}^{v_i} F_v(s)\,ds}{F_v(v_i)}, \forall i = A,B$$

hence, knowing that $v_i = q_i - c_i$, and substituting the distribution $F_{v_i}^2$ as showed in *(1)*, we obtain:

(2) $$s^2(q_i,c_i) = q_i - c_i - \frac{\int_{q_L - \bar{c}}^{q_i - c_i} \alpha[(1 - F_c(q_L - Z)] + (1 - \alpha)[1 - F_c(q_H - Z)]dz}{\alpha[(1 - F_c(q_L - q_i + c_i)] + (1 - \alpha)[1 - F_c(q_H - q_i + c_i)]}$$

$$\forall i = A,B$$

---

[9] It must be noted that this r.v. also represents the beliefs of the P on the valuation of the two rival bidders before he can observe the quality of their bids. Since the P will have to identify his strategy before receiving this information, this will be the probability distribution that he will use to calculate his expected utility.

We can demonstrate that the following properties hold:

Property A: $s^2(q_L,c) = s^1(q_L,c) \ \forall c \in [\overline{c} - \Delta, \overline{c}]$;

Property B: $s^2(q_L,c) \geq s^1(q_L,c) \ \forall c \in [\overline{c}, \overline{c} - \Delta]$;

Property C: $s^2(q_H,c) \leq s^1(q_H,c) \ \forall c \in [\underline{c}, \overline{c}]$;

Property D: $v(q_H,c_i) = v(q_L,c_j) \Leftrightarrow c_i = c_j + \Delta \Rightarrow s^2(q_H,c_i) = s^2(q_L,c_j), \ \forall c_i, \ c_j \ \forall c \in [\underline{c}, \overline{c} - \Delta]$

GRAPH 4

FIRMS' BIDDING STRATEGIES IN GAME 2

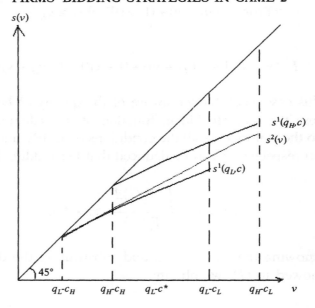

Property D is very important because it tells us that the sellers choose a score level in function of their overall valuation, no matter what the level of the costs and the quality of their bid are. Therefore, from a strategic point of view, nothing would be changed if they did not know the specific values of c and q.

We can thus illustrate in Graph 4 the trend of the score function in this second context by comparing it with the one obtained in the first case. It should be noted that this time the bidding function is monotonically increasing with respect to firm's valuation. Therefore, with this kind of information flow, the auction guarantees an efficient allocation. This fact enables us to infer that the expected score, which is equal to the P's expected utility, will be equal to the expected value of the valuation of the less efficient seller.

Observation 2: if the P adopts the strategy S^2, then the FS mechanism is efficient, since the seller with the higher valuation will win with certainty.

The increase in the surplus created by the mechanism does not, however, imply an increase in the expected utility of the P. In fact, it is plausible to think that having increased the private information of the rival bidders has increased their informational rent. It will thus be necessary to investigate as to who takes possession of the greater surplus created by this type of strategy on the part of the P.

Case 3: Public revelation of the information

In the latter case, the P reveals all the information available to him, and for this reason the sellers have a precise knowledge of the node in which they will find themselves when they have to choose the price, and thus the score, to bid. The situation is represented by Graph 5.

GRAPH 5

GAME 3: PUBLIC REVELATION OF INFORMATION

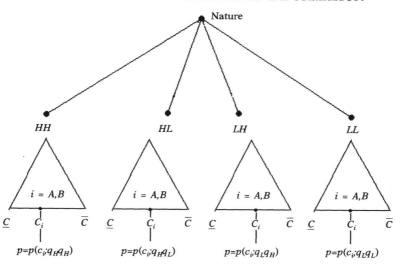

253

As well explained by Kaplan *et* al. (2003), while having an auction *ex ante* with symmetric rival bidders, the fact of the public revelation of this information makes their beliefs, regarding competitor's valuation, potentially asymmetric[10]. It can also be noted that the beliefs are independent of the valuation, since no type of correlation exists between the valuations of the two firms. It is easy to qualify this type of potential asymmetry as the first one described by Maskin *et* al. (2000). In fact, the probability function maintains the same form, except that it is shifted sideways.

Formally, the seller's beliefs regarding the competitor's valuation depend on the quality of the opponent bidder, and are represented by the two following distributions:

$$v_{Li} \in [q_L - \bar{c}, q_L - \underline{c}], \text{ where } F^3_{v_L}(v) = F_c(q_L - v), \forall i = A, B$$

$$v_{Hi} \in [q_H - \bar{c}, q_H - \underline{c}], \text{ where } F^3_{v_H}(v) = F^3_{v_L}(v - \Delta) = F_c(q_H - v), \forall i = A, B$$

In the case that the realization of the choice of the Nature is *HL* or *LH*, the two rival bidders have to bid in the presence of an asymmetric auction. We know from the work by Maskin E. *et* al. (2000) that, in general, the "weak" ("strong") bidder bids more (less) aggressively than if she had to face a symmetric rival bidder. Furthermore, the valuations being equal, the weak bidder bid more than the strong one. Thus, thanks to these results, we can be certain that the following properties hold:

Property E: $s^3(q_H, c; q_L) \leq s^3(q_H, c; q_H)$, $\forall c \in [\underline{c}, \bar{c}]$;

Property F: $s^3(q_L, c; q_H) \geq s^3(q_L, c; q_L)$, $\forall c \in [\underline{c}, \bar{c}]$;

Property G: $s^3(q_L, c_j; q_H) \geq s^3(q_H, c_i; q_L)$, $\forall c_i, c_j \in [\underline{c}, \bar{c}]$; $|c_i = c_j + \Delta$.

Proof: see Maskin *et* al. (2000), proposition 3.5 *ii-iv*, pages 424.

---

[10] The public revelation of information known to the auctioneer does not always make the beliefs of the rival bidders asymmetric. As noted by KAPLAN T.R. *et* AL. (2003), this does not occur in the model of MILGROM P. *et* AL. (1982), and we can add that this effect is also lacking in GANUZA J.J. (2004) and in ESÖ P. *et*. AL. (2005).

Should the P reveals that the quality of the two bids coincides, there will be no asymmetry, and the sellers will formulate their bids in function of their own costs according to the same rule adopted in the first case. The score function in the presence of symmetric qualities then coincides with the one identified in the first game, except that now each seller is aware of the score that she will obtain. The following Graph reports the score functions that characterise this third game.

It should be noted that the auction can produce an inefficient result also in this case. As always happens in the case of a first price auction in the presence of asymmetric bidders, it can occur that the seller with the higher valuation can lose. This is due to property G, according to which a strong bidder tends to shade her bid much more compared to a weak one.

GRAPH 6

FIRMS' BIDDING STRATEGIES IN GAME 3

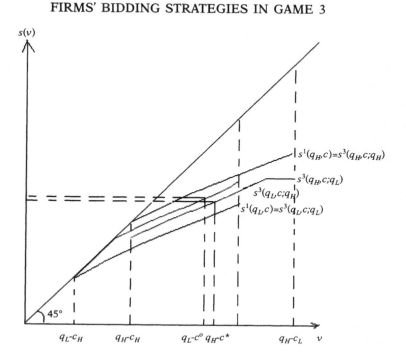

Observation 3: if the P adopts S^3, then the FS auction mechanism does not necessarily choose the most efficient seller.

This result can be demonstrated by the preceding figure. It is easily seen that the score obtained by the seller with the q_L-c° valuation is higher than the one obtained by the more efficient seller, q_H-c^*.

5. - Results: Comparison of the Outcomes Linked to Different P's Strategies

In the first place it must be highlighted that the second case which we examined has the same characteristics of the symmetric game described by Kaplan *et* al. (2003). Each player in fact has to decide the score to bid without knowing whether the opponent is of high or low quality. In their model it is assumed that each rival bidder does not know her own quality level, but on the other hand she knows her own valuation in its entirety. In our case 2, the firms know the quality of their own bids, but in reality this information would be irrelevant for them once their own valuation of the contract were known to them. As has already been showed in fact, by illustrating property D, their bidding strategy is to reach a score s as a function of v, whatever the associated costs and qualities may be.

At the same time, the third case illustrated has the same characteristics as the asymmetric game analysed by the same authors, since also in our model each seller knows both her own valuation and also the distribution from which the opponent's valuation has been extracted. Their result can thus be utilised to demonstrate that the following result is valid in our model:

Proposition 1: the P's expected utility is higher with strategy S^3 than with strategy S^2 if and only if the potential asymmetry of the rival bidders is such that the first score (FS) auction dominates the second score auction (SS).

Proof: see Kaplan *et* al. (2003), proposition 1 and its proof, page 13.

Here we give a brief sketch of their reasoning, adapting it to our context. In both case 2 and case 3, if the auction were SS, each rival bidder would have as her (weakly) dominant strategy that of bidding a score equal to her own valuation. Since, furthermore, the distribution of the players' valuations is the same in both cases, the P's expected utility would be equal in both cases to the valuation of the less efficient seller. Also, in case 2, in view of the monotonicity of the bidding function, RET is valid. Therefore, the P's expected utility would have been equivalent also in the case of an FS auction. Thus, an FS auction in case 2 attains the same result as an SS auction in case 3. But, if in case 3 the FS auction generates an increased (decreased) utility compared to the SS type, this means that in the presence of an FS auction, strategy S^3 entails a pay-off higher (lower) than the one associated to strategy S^2.

As we have already said, however, the asymmetry of the distributions from which the rival bidders' valuations were extracted in case 3 is of the "distribution shift" type. For this reason, the result obtained by Maskin *et* al. (2000) can be applied:

Proposition 2: if it is valid that:

i)
$$F_{v_L}'' \geq 0;$$

ii)
$$\frac{d}{dv} \frac{F_{v_L}'(v)}{F_{v_L}(v)} < 0;$$

iii)
$$-v F_{v_L}'(v) + 1 + F_{v_L}(v) \geq 0, \forall v \in \left[q_L - \bar{c}, q_H - \bar{c} \right]$$

then in the presence of asymmetric distributions, characterized as F_{v_L}, F_{v_H}, the FS auction generates expected revenues greater than the SS auction.

Proof: see Maskin *et* al. (2000), Proposition 4.3.

Therefore, given several conditions of regularity on the probability distributions that characterise the costs of the sellers, it means that the FP auction as higher expected pay-off than the SP one and thus, by applying propostion 1, the strategy of publicly revealing the information is better than that of a private revelation.

The comparison between strategies S^1 and S^3 is more complex.

They lead to equivalent results in the case that the initial state of the world has produced two symmetric sellers. Instead, in the case of asymmetric sellers, S^3 makes it possible to increase the aggressivity of the weak rival's bid, but at the same time induces the strong firm to make slacker bids. By Graph 6 we can infer how S^3 brings down both the maximum and the minimum highest score and for this reason we can suspect that in this case the expected utility of the P will be lower. Nevertheless, calculation of the P's expected utility in function of sellers' bidding strategy is generally found to be more complex.

It is just possible to point out which of the two strategies is preferable for the P when the potential difference in quality between the two sellers is very great:

Proposition 3: if

$$\frac{d}{dv} \frac{F'_{v_L}(v)}{F_{v_L}(v)} < 0$$

and

$$\Delta \geq \bar{c} - \underline{c} + \frac{1}{F'_{v_L}(\bar{v}_L)},$$

then the strategy S^1 entails a higher expected utility for the P than the strategy S^3.

The latter proposition enables us to understand that the strategy of publicly revealing his information is less convenient for the P, compared to the strategy of secrecy, when the advantage potentially assigned to the preferred rival bidder is so great that it makes any sort of form of effective competition impracticable.

6. - Conclusions

In this work we have analysed what the PA's optimal strategy is when this expresses discretional judgements on the quality of the bids submitted in an auction, and it is possible to structure the procedure in two sequential stages. We have compared three different PA's strategies regarding the releasing of its private information: secrecy, private revelation, and public revelation. The second strategy is found to be the only efficient one from an overall point of view. It is optimal when the PA's objective is to maximise the surplus of the exchange or when the competition in the auction is so high that it independently neutralises the trade-off between allocative efficiency and rent extraction. It must be noted that this sort of strategy for utilising information is provided for by the new guidelines in the case of electronic auctions. Since with this strategy RET holds, we can infer that it renders irrelevant the choice regarding the closing procedure of the auction, since the profit expected by the auctioneer is the same, whether the auction is English style or first-price. Clearly, this conclusion is not true if there are reasons for considering that the firms' costs are not independent of each other.

If the aim of the PA is to maximise its utility, the strategy of publicly revealing its information is, in general, superior to the strategy of private revelation. This conclusion is very important, since it allows us to affirm that, when the rival bidders know the PA's discretional value regarding their offers, then the auctioneer's best strategy is that of revealing this information publicly. Such a result can be applied to the procedure of competitive dialogue, in which it is plausible to believe that, during the dialogue phase, the PA is led to explicitly express its valuation on the technical solutions submitted by the different firms. In this case, it could be opportune to make public the scores assigned to the technical solutions presented before requesting the final economic bid.

Lastly, we have seen that the strategy of secrecy is better than that of public revelation when the potential difference in the quality of the bids is very great. This result enables us to affirm that, when the weight of the PA's discretional valuations is very relevant, a public releasing of this information is not appropriate. In this case, the best procedure remains that of the simultaneous presentation of technical and economic bids, as generally happens. Thus, a greater flow of information on the PA's preferences can be efficacious only when the PA commits itself to limiting the relevance of its discretional judgements of the bids.

The problem faced has been described with a very simplified model. For this reason, a first extension of the research can consist precisely of making the results more general. For example, it could be assumed that there are n rival bidders, or that the PA's information on the quality of their bids is represented by a continuous r.v. In the second place, the set of strategies available to the PA could be enlarged in order to verify whether this subject has incentives or not for respecting the rules that we established initially. We could thus investigate as to whether the PA can have an interest in lying in several circumstances, sending untruthful messages, or if it can obtain advantages through a discriminatory behaviour, in which it reveals to one party more information than it does to the other. Furthermore, we could analyse what the best strategy would be for the PA if it could decide which messages to send, depending on the state of the world realised.

Lastly, it is necessary to reveal that, however relevant, the problem confronted does not capture the trade-off present in most multidimensional auctions. In reality, in fact, the quality of a bid, while being conditioned by the discretional judgement of the PA, is not however independent of the level of the firm's costs. A much more plausible model should assume that both the quality of the bid and the firm's costs are growing functions of firm's effort in preparing the contractual proposal. Formally:

$$q = q(e,w), \text{ with } q' > 0$$

In this case, the PA's strategy regarding the information releasing on the quality of the bids can influence not only the price strategy, but also the strategy relative to how much effort to exert. In fact, the choice of the effort has an effect on the quality of one's own bid, which, if it is communicated publicly, modifies the beliefs of competing bidders regarding their own valuation. For this reason, the choice of the effort must take into account not only the direct effect on one's own valuation of the contract, but also on the indirect one which is produced through a change in competitors' bidding strategy.

Lemma 1: Whatever the state of the world, P can send to each seller only three messages, that are synthesised in the following way:

$$f_A(XY) \in \{UU, XU, XY\} \text{ e } f_B(XY) \in \{UU, UY, XY\}, \forall X,Y, = L,H$$

Proof: for each possible state of the world XY, we define the set of all possible messages:

$$Z = \{UU, UX, UY, XU, YU, XY, XX, YY, YX\}$$

since the message cannot contain false information, as stated in assumption 1, we obtain:

$$f_i(XY) \in \{UU, UY, XU, XY\}, \forall X,Y, = L,H; \forall i = A,B$$

moreover, given the assumptions 2 and 3, $f_A(XY)$ cannot be UY; in fact, suppose that this kind of message is sent by the P:

$$f_A(XY) = UY \Rightarrow f_B(XY) = W_B Y, \text{ from assumption 3}$$

$$f_B(XY) = W_B Y \Rightarrow f_A(XY) = K_A W_A, \text{ from assumption 2}$$

where $K_A \neq U$, that is in contradiction with the starting point.

Appealing to symmetry, we can be sure that $f_B(XY)$ cannot be equal to XU. Therefore P can send only three kind of messages to each seller:

$$f_A(XY) \in \{UU, XU, XY\}, \text{ e } f_B(XY) \in \{UU, UY, XY\}, \forall X,Y, = L,H$$

Lemma 2: A symmetry must exist between the messages sent to the two sellers. Formally:

1) $$f_A(XY) = UU \Leftrightarrow f_B (XY) = UU$$

2) $$f_A(XY) = XU \Leftrightarrow f_B (XY) = UY$$

3) $$f_A(XY) = XY \Leftrightarrow f_B (XY) = XY, \forall X,Y, = L,H$$

Proof: 1) By absurd, let $f_i(XY) = UU$ and $f_j(XY) \neq UU$. Then $f_j(XY)$ can be K_jW_j, or UK_j. At first we assume that $f_j(XY) = K_jW_j$; from assumption 2 we get:

$$f_j(XY) = K_jW_j \Rightarrow f_i(XY) = W_iK_i, \forall i,j = A,B; \forall K_i,K_j = X,Y; \forall W_i,W_j = U,X,Y; \forall X,Y = L,H$$

since $Ki \neq U$ we obtain a contradiction with the starting point. Then we analyse the secon type of message and we note that:

$$f_j(XY) = UK_j \Rightarrow f_i(XY) = K_iW_i, \forall i,j = A,B; \forall K_i,K_j = X,Y; \forall W_i,W_j = U,X,Y; \forall X,Y = L,H$$

so, also in this case we achieve a contradiction with the starting point, as $K_i \neq U$. The generality of the proof entails that both the implications in 1) are valid.

2) we start showing that $f_A(XY) = XU \Rightarrow f_B (XY) = UY$; notice that:

$$f_A(XY) = XU \Rightarrow f_B(XY) = W_iK_i$$

since $X \neq U$ and assumption 2. But, from assumption 1:

$$f_B(XY) \notin \{UX, XX, YX, YY\}$$

in fact, all these messages are false;
moreover, from assumption 2:

$$f_B(XY) \neq XY$$

in fact, $f_B(XY) = K_BY \Rightarrow f_A(XY) = XK_A$, but, as $K_A \neq U$, this conclusion would be in contradiction with the starting point. Hence:

$$f_A(XY) = XU \Rightarrow f_B(XY) = UY$$

For a similar argument, $f_A(XY) = XU \Leftarrow f_B(XY) = UY$, and the formal proof is unnecessary.

3) generally, from assumption 2 we know that:

$$f_i(XY) = XY \Rightarrow f_j(XY) = K_j K_g, \ \forall K_j, K_g = X, Y$$

then, being K different from U, it must be true that:

$$f_i(XY) \in \{XX, \ YY, \ YX, \ XY\}$$

it is easy to note that the first three messages are in contradiction with assumption 1 because they are false. So, it remains only one possibility:

$$f_i(XY) = XY.$$

Thank to the generality of the proof, the conclusion is valid for the implication regarding each seller.

Property A: $s^2(q_L, c) = s^1(q_L, c) \ \forall c \in [\bar{c} - \Delta, \ \bar{c}]$;

Proof: in the integral of (2) we can do a change of variable: $t = q_L - z$. So, rearranging, (2) we get :

$$s^2(q_j) = q_j - c - \frac{\int_{q_L - q_j + c}^{\bar{c}} \alpha[1 - F_c(t)] + (1 - \alpha)[1 - F_c(t + \Delta)]dz}{\alpha[1 - F_c(q_L - q_j + c)] + (1 - \alpha)[1 - F_c(q_H - q_j + c)]}, \ \forall j = L, H;$$

then, if $q = q_L$:

$$s^2(q_L, c) = q_L - c - \frac{\int_c^{\bar{c}} \alpha[1 - F_c(t)] + (1 - \alpha)[1 - F_c(t + \Delta)]dt}{\alpha[1 - F_c(c)] + (1 - \alpha)[1 - F_c(c + \Delta)]}$$

now, notice that:

$$c \geq \bar{c} - \Delta \Rightarrow F_c(c+\Delta) = 1;$$

therefore we obtain:

$$c \geq \bar{c} - \Delta \Rightarrow s^2 = q_L - c - \frac{\int_c^{\bar{c}} \alpha[1 - F_c(t)]dt}{\alpha[1 - F_c(c)]} = s^1(q_L, c).\|$$

Property B: available upon request to the author.
Property C: available upon request to the author.
Property D: $v(q_H, c_i) = v(q_L, c_j) \Leftrightarrow c_i = c_j + \Delta \Rightarrow s^2(q_H, c_i) = s^2(q_L, c_j)$, $\forall c_i, c_j \in [\underline{c}, \bar{c} - \Delta]$.
Proof: by (2) we know that, for a generic c_j:

$$s^2(q_L, c_j) = q_L - c_j - \frac{\int_{c_j}^{\bar{c}} \alpha[1 - F_c(t)] + (1 - \alpha)[1 - F_c(t + \Delta)]dt}{\alpha[1 - F_c(c_j)] + (1 - \alpha)[1 - F_c(c_j + \Delta)]}$$

while, for $c_i = c_j + \Delta$:

$$s^2(q_H, c_i) = q_H - c_i - \frac{\int_{c_i - \Delta}^{\bar{c}} \alpha[1 - F_c(t)] + (1 - \alpha)[1 - F_c(t + \Delta)]dt}{\alpha[1 - F_c(c_i - \Delta)] + (1 - \alpha)[1 - F_c(c_i)]}$$

substituting to c_i the equation $c_j + \Delta$, we obtain:

$$s^2(q_H, c_i) = q_H - c_j - \Delta + \frac{\int_{c_j}^{\bar{c}} \alpha[1 - F_c(s)] + (1 - \alpha)[1 - F_c(t + \Delta)]dt}{\alpha[1 - F_c(c_j)] + (1 - \alpha)[1 - F_c(c_j + \Delta)]} = s^2(q_L, c_j).\|$$

Proposition 3: if $\frac{d}{dv}\frac{F'_{v_L}(v)}{F_{v_L}(v)} < 0$ and $\Delta \geq \bar{c} - \underline{c} + \frac{1}{F'_{v_L}(v_L)}$, then the strategy S^1 entails a higher expected utility for the P than the strategy S^3.
Proof: in order to compare the pay-off associated to S^1 and S^3

264

it is sufficient to analyse sellers' strategies in the case they are asymmetric. At first, we want to show what is sellers' best strategy when P adopts S^3 and Δ assume a value according to the condition reported in proposition 3. Thank to the paper of Maskin E. *et* al. (2000) we know that when the "distance" between the strong and the weak bidder is large enough, the latter bids equal to her own valuation. As far as the former is concerned, she proposes a score equal to the maximum valuation of the weak bidder, whatever her own valuation v. We want to show what are the values of Δ that entail this kind of equilibrium. Assume that the weak bidder offers a score equal to her own valuation; then strong bidder's best response is:

$$\max_{\underline{v}_L \le s \le \bar{v}_L} (v_H - s)F_{v_L}(s);$$

the derivative of this equation is:

$$(A.1) \qquad (v_H - s)F'_{v_L}(s) - F_{v_L}(s);$$

if this derivative is always positive, then we obtain a corner solution, that is, $s^* = \bar{v}_L$; notice that if the strong bidder plays this strategy, it is indeed optimal for the weak bidder to bid her own valuation. Then we look for a condition that makes (A.1) surely positive:

$$(A.2) \qquad (v_H - s)F'_{v_L}(s) > 0 \Rightarrow v_H > s + \frac{F_{v_L}(s)}{F'_{v_L}(s)};$$

it is easy to show that:

$$\frac{d}{dv}\frac{F'_{v_L}(v)}{F_{v_L}(v)} < 0 \Rightarrow \frac{d}{dv}\frac{F_{v_L}(v)}{F'_{v_L}(v)} > 0,$$

then the right-hand side of (A.2) is increasing. Hence, in order to state that the derivative in (A.1) is always positive, it is sufficient to verify that the inequality in (*A.2*) is true for the minimum value of v_H and the maximum one of s:

$$\underline{v}_H > \bar{v}_L + \frac{F_{v_L}(\bar{v}_L)}{F'_{v_L}(\bar{v}_L)}$$

knowing that $F_{v_L}(\bar{v}_L) = 1$ and substituting to $\underline{v}_H$ and $\bar{v}_L$ their values in term of q and c we obtain:

$$q_H - \bar{c} > q_L - \underline{c} + \frac{1}{F'_{v_L}(\bar{v}_L)}$$

rearranging terms we get:

$$\Delta \geq \bar{c} - \underline{c} + \frac{1}{F'_{v_L}(\bar{v}_L)}$$

Therefore the conditions of proposition 3 are sufficient to make it sure that the strong bidder wins the auction offering a score equal to weak bidder's maximum potential valuation. Then, when P plays strategy S^3 his expected utility is equal to $\bar{v}_L < \underline{v}_H$. On the contrary, when P adopts S^1 every seller bids a score not lower than her valuation. This means that the strong bidder surely offers more than $\underline{v}_H$ and so the P's expected utility cannot be lower than that threshold. The conclusion is that, in the presence of the conditions reported in proposition 3, P's expected utility is larger with strategy S^1 than with S^3.

BIBLIOGRAPHY

ASKER J. - CANTILLON E., «Properties of Scoring Auctions», *CEPR, Discussion Paper*, no. 4734, 2004.

BERGEMANN D. - PESENDORFER M., «Information Structures in Optimal Auctions», Cowles Foundation, *Discussion Paper*, no. 1323, 2002.

BRANCO F., «Favoring Domestic Firms in Procurement Contract», *Journal of International Economics*, vol. 37, 1994, pages 65-80.

— —, «The Design of Multidimensional Auctions», *RAND, Journal of Economics*, vol. 28, 1997, pages 63-81.

BRAYNOV S. - SANDHOLM T., *Auctions with Untrustworthy Bidders*, mimeo, 2003.

CELENTANI M. - GANUZA J.J., «Corruption and Competition in Procurement», *European Economic Review*, vol. 46, 2002, pages 1273-1303.

CHE Y.K., «Design Competition through Multidimensional Auction», *Rand Journal of Economics*, vol. 24, 1993, pages 668-680.

ESÖ P. - SZENTES B., «Optimal Information Disclosure in Auctions and the Handicap Auction», Northwestern University, *Discussion Papers*, no. 1361, 2005.

GANUZA J.J., «Optimal Procurement Mechanism with Observable Quality», Universidad Carlos III de Madrid, *Working Paper*, no. 96-08, 1996.

— —, «Ignorance Promotes Competition: an Auction Model with Endogenous Private Valuations», *RAND, Journal of Economics*, vol. 35, 2004, pages 583-598.

KAPLAN T.R. - ZAMIR S., «The Strategic Use of Seller Information in Private-Value Auctions», Hebrew University, *Center For Rationality, Working Paper*, no. 221, 2000.

— —, *An Observation about Revenue Effects of Belief Asymmetry in Private-Value Auctions*, mimeo, Hebrew University, 2003.

LANDSBERGER M. - RUBINSTEIN J. - WOLFSTETTER E. - ZAMIR S., «First Price Auction when the Ranking of Valuations is Common Knowledge», *Review of Economic Design*, vol. 6, 2001, pages 461-480.

MASKIN E. - RILEY J., «Asymmetric Auctions», *Review of Economic Studies*, vol. 67, 2000, pages 413-438.

MCAFEE R.P. - MCMILLAN J., «Government Procurement and International Trade», *Journal of International Economics*, vol. 26, 1989, pages 291-308.

MILGROM P. - WEBER R., «A Theory of Auctions and Competitive Bidding», *Econometrica*, vol. 50, 1982, pages 1089-1122.